SOUL RECIPROCITY

SoulReciprocity
Quest to SOUL-FULL Relationships

by

HEATHER BEVERLY

Foreword by

Mathew Knowles

Atlanta, GA

Soul Reciprocity: Quest to Soul-Full Relationships
Copyright © 2024

All rights reserved.

No part of this book may be reproduced or transmitted in any form or by any means, electronic or mechanical, including photocopying, recording or by any information storage and retrieval system, without written permission from the publisher, except for the inclusion of brief quotations in a review.

This book is intended to provide general information and advice on the topics discussed. It is not a substitute for professional medical, psychological, or therapeutic advice, diagnosis, or treatment. The author is not a licensed mental health professional. Readers are encouraged to consult with a qualified healthcare provider for advice regarding any specific health concerns or conditions.

Some names have been changed to protect people's privacy.

Address inquiries to the publisher:
Soul Reciprocity, LLC
3605 Sandy Plains Rd., Suite 406
Marietta, GA 30066

Learn more about the author at: www.soulreciprocity.com

ISBN: 979-8-9895537-0-9 (paperback)
ISBN: 979-8-9895537-1-6 (ebook)

Library of Congress Control Number: 2024925935

Cover Art Design by CJ Norwood, Norwood Creative, LLC
Cover Photography by Wardell Malloy
Logo Design by CJ Norwood & Launi King
Developmental Editor: Annette Purkiss Johnson, Allwrite Publishing
Proofreader: Iliana Schmidt, Allwrite Publishing
Interior Design & Layout: Kimberley Seals and Annette Purkiss Johnson

Printed in the United States of America

DEDICATION

To my Soul Tribe – my Soul Work warriors who've protected, cheered, and marched with me on the front lines through every joy and trial on my quest to Soul Reciprocity

To Cornell, my king, my inspiration and soul's refuge, my "WHY"

To my Mother, the foundation of my soul's identity

To FD and Brandon, proof that family is bound by soul connections, filling spaces once thought impossible

To my cherished Girl Tribe, who anchor, uplift and nourish my soul

To Doreen, Annette, Kayla, and CJ – with gratitude for understanding my Soul Needs and breathing life into my vision

TABLE OF CONTENTS

Foreword, xi
Preface, xiii
Introduction, xvii

SECTION 1: THE UNDERSTANDING. 1
                     "Lessons from the Soul"

1. THE BASICS PART I: Relationships 3
    Circumstantial Perspective 5
    Experiential Perspective 5
    Soul Perspective. 6
2. THE BASICS PART II: The Soul 9
    What Is and Why the Soul? 10
    Philosophical Views 11
    Religious Views. 12
    Non-Religious Views. 14
    Soul Reciprocity View 18
    Importance of the Soul Perspective 19
3. THE BASICS PART III: Reciprocity 22
    Why Reciprocity 22
    Sacrifice. 24
    Reciprocal Expectations 25
    Lessons Learned 29
4. SOUL + RECIPROCITY = Soul-Full Relationships 34
    What Is Soul Reciprocity? 35
    What Soul Reciprocity is Not 37
    Experiencing Soul-Full Connections 39
    Is Your Relationship Soul-Full? 40
SECTION 1 SUMMARY: Soul Reflections. 45

SECTION 2: THE PREPARATION 49
                     "Lessons from Bees"

5. THE BEES: Understanding Your Role 51
    The Bee in You 52
    Kinds of Honeybees 53
    Human Complexities 58
    Wannabees 58
    Busy as a Bee - Soul Work. 63
6. THE MEADOW: Discovering Your Soul Identity 67
    Soul Identity: Discovering Who You Really Are 68
    The Crossroads 69
    Making Changes 71
    Rediscovering Authenticity 74
    The Key: Self-Examination 76
    Getting Feedback 77
    The Right Questions. 79
    The Right Steps – Soul Work 79
    The Right Setting 81
    Next Steps. 84
7. THE NECTAR AND POLLEN: Identifying Soul Needs 85
NECTAR: Identifying Your Soul Needs. 86
    Basic (Universal) Soul Needs. 88
    Diverse (Unique) Needs 95
    The Path to Purpose 103
    The Bottom Line. 105
POLLEN: Identifying Others' Soul Needs. 106
    Model of Soul Needs 111
    Next Steps. 112
8. THE HONEY: Producing Reciprocity 113
    Types of Reciprocity. 115
    Shortcuts 116
    Shortfalls 118
    Next Steps. 124
9. THE BEE TRIBE: Finding Your Soul Tribe 125
    Types of Friends 126
    Identifying Your Soul Tribe 127
    The Revelation 129
    Next Steps. 133
SECTION 2 SUMMARY: Soul Reflections. 135

SECTION 3: THE APPLICATION 141
"Lessons from Life"

10. LOVE AND ROMANCE: The Bee Dance 143
- The Picture 144
- Understanding the Dance 148
- Failing Relationships 151
- Successful Relationships 154
- Questions 156

11. FRIENDS: How Many of Us Have Them? 159
- "Friends" Who Aren't Friends 161
- Friend You Overlooked 165
- Perfect Peace: The Soul Tribe 166
- Failing Friendships 167
- Successful Friendships 168
- Questions 170

12. FAMILY: The First Tribe 173
- The Foundation 174
- My Familial Soul Tribe 176
- Family Tribe Members 178
- Failing Relationships 186
- Successful Relationships 187
- Questions 189

13. BUSINESS: The Trade of Reciprocity 192
- In Spirit 195
- In Theory 199
- Failing Work Relationships 201
- Successful Work Relationships 202
- Questions 204

14. GENESIS: Time to Fly! 207
- Soul Reciprocity in Relationships 208
- Bee Analogy: A Blueprint for Human Behavior 210
- Honoring Soul Needs to Achieve Success 211
- Nourishing Soul Needs: The Key to Flying 212
- The Journey to Soul Reciprocity 213
- Flying Together 214

SECTION 3 SUMMARY: Soul Reflections 215

APPENDIX 212
A. Relationships Questionnaire. 214
B. Soul Questionnaire 218
C. Reciprocity Questionnaire 220
D. Soul Reciprocity Questionnaire 222
E. Soul Identity Questionnaire 224
F. Soul Needs Identifier Survey 229
G. Reciprocity Test 234
H. Soul Tribe Identifier Survey. 238

Bibliography. 242

FOREWORD

My entire career, what's helped me produce some of the greatest acts the world has ever seen is my steadfast ability to recognize greatness in people. What's different? What's fresh? What's unique? What is being approached or presented in a way that hasn't been done before? My ability to recognize greatness is a mix of the pragmatic, the measurable, the tangible along with the unexplainable, the indescribable, and what many may label as the intangible or esoteric.

It's this same methodology that ultimately brought me to working with Heather Beverly. Ironically, though, I find her to also be the perfect mix of the exact formula I've just described above.

My professional relationship with Heather is also borne from the discernment I've gained from my own inner work. From that work, I unequivocally understand myself, as well as the qualities I need in the people who play key roles in my life. I am able to recognize the types of Soul Connections (personal and professional) that Heather speaks of in this book. And because of that ability, we have an attorney-client relationship with Soul Reciprocity.

Heather Beverly—the professional—is amongst the highest caliber of people I've ever worked with throughout my 40-year career, which spans across Corporate America, the entertainment industry, academia, and global public speaking. As an attorney, she's reached a level of success and recognition where she's leaned on, relied upon, and known for her pragmatism and effectiveness. She is more than just my attorney, as she sits beside me and at the table in most of my business endeavors. I trust her wholeheartedly to advise, strategize and execute.

Heather Beverly—the human being—possesses powerful potential, possibilities, and ideas that exist beyond the veil of what's visible on the surface. Just as in business, she is consistent and reliable in her personal life. She is multi-faceted, wearing many hats but still prioritizing the people and things that matter to her most. And among the things that matter to her the most are fulfilling connections with others in all aspects of her life.

In the book, the concepts and ideas about Soul Reciprocity that Heather shares, at first, seem challenging to actualize or even conceptualize. Yet, if you take just a small leap of faith and apply the principles you're about to learn, your results—and your entire life—will be all the evidence you need.

This isn't an act of blind faith either.

As mentioned, you're learning from someone I consider to be the best of the best in her field, someone who thrives in each area of her life – both personally and professionally. Through Heather's own accounts, she transparently explains that thriving doesn't mean that life is always perfect. It doesn't mean that there aren't hiccups, challenges or obstacles. By shifting your perspective and doing the Soul Work she suggests, you can go through life with a certain "knowing" about where and with whom you belong despite the challenges. And it's that knowing which brings to you the deeper understanding, the higher standard of living, the trust in your own essence, the belief in who you truly and unapologetically are, and the right people and fulfillment you need.

The concepts you'll learn in this book will teach you to trust the subtle signs, symbols, and metaphors that life uses to communicate with you for deeper meaning. It's not about whether or not these signs exist in your life, it's just about whether you know how to identify and trust them.

I believe that something brought you to this book. I believe you're reading these words for a reason. I believe whatever brought you to this very moment exists in the unexplainable, the intangible, and the esoteric. I also believe Heather Beverly's "Soul Reciprocity" will teach you to trust in what you already know to be true. And it's that very trust that will bring you to the next phase of life that you already know you're ready to live.

Whether I knew it or not at the time, many of the concepts and ideas Heather shares in this book are the same ones I've used and applied in my own life and career. They worked for me. They'll work for you, too.

So let today, let this very moment be the catalyst for the rest of your life, a life of love, abundance, joy, and fulfillment surrounded by a tribe of people that see, know, and love you for who you truly are.

Most importantly, let the words you're about to read lead to an inner knowing that will guide you through the rest of your journey.

~Mathew Knowles

Speaker, Music Executive, Entrepreneur, Author, Professor, Film & TV Executive

PREFACE

I'm not a doctor, a psychiatrist, psychologist, or a therapist. I have no formal training in self-development. I'm not a theologian or philosopher.

I'm a woman who has lived a life like all of you – with wins, losses, amazing decisions and horrible ones. I've walked this life's journey looking for and seeking my place in the world, wanting acceptance from others and connectedness. I've been both confident and totally insecure. I've seen myself as both beautiful and ugly, skinny and fat– sometimes at exactly the same time. At different points in my life (sometimes in the same day), I've felt powerful and weak; smart and dumb; worthless and enough. I've sought balance and truth while learning lessons that I never asked to be taught. Through it all, I have been open and willing to grow. I've always striven to be a better version of me. I've been observant of the successes and failures of others. I've been willing to admit my faults and mistakes, forgive myself, learn and grow from them.

Luckily, this walk hasn't been alone. No matter how lonely I have felt at times, the reality is, I have never been alone. There have always been multiple people who have been present in my life, whether on the front lines or lying in wait in the trenches. Even when I believed everyone was going about their lives and too busy to realize my struggles, the truth is, they were always there. Even if they were waiting for me to see them.

I've been extraordinarily blessed with what I call my "Soul Tribe": a collective of souls sent by God to guide me through my life. This includes my mother, stepfather, grandmother, grandfather, aunts, "aunties," uncles, a sister-circle, girl-gang, "sister-wives," female advisors and others who have been teachers, soulful examples (of what to do and not to do), constructive critics, cheerleaders, protectors, and motivators who have all filled me with wisdom. Like a colony of bees, my Soul Tribe has nurtured my Soul and pollinated my life.

Together, my Soul Tribe members have supported me along my path and given me encouragement and strength throughout. The lessons I've learned from my Soul Tribe along with resources I've sought out myself have ordered my most recent steps and led me to this current place of clarity. This book comes from the cumulative lessons from my Soul Tribe and pays homage to each and every one of them.

I also give credit to those from whom I've learned some life lessons the hard way: the absent father, the failed relationships, the ex-husband, those who betrayed me or who betrayed those I love, and those who hurt or disappointed me in some way. Just like the lessons I learned from years of playing competitive tennis, even though it is called the game of "love" and I enjoyed a lot of wins, there are still the double faults, the unforced errors, and heartbreaking losses. But we learn and grow through situations that aren't perfect and don't work out how we planned. We sometimes learn the most about ourselves from painful experiences. Learning who you are is the first step to finding Soul Reciprocity, so even those who have let us down provide invaluable lessons from which we heal and grow. From those who disappoint us, we learn the things that are hurtful to us, we discover our limitations, we redefine where our "lines in the sand" lie. Maybe most importantly, we learn what we don't want in our lives from those who have caused us the most pain.

Soul Reciprocity is not just a book title, it was a concept born from life-altering revelations in my life. "Revelations" are the truths we learn after having gone through a process of discovery. We all have them through the course of our lives. Lessons learned, epiphanies, and "aha" moments are forms of revelations. I discovered that Soul Reciprocity was something missing from places in my life that it shouldn't have been. Yet, it existed in places I hadn't fully realized. Those revelations didn't just hit me one day, they evolved slowly and as a result of a 5-year-or-so "journey to self" that I undertook in order to figure out what I was missing in my life and why. That journey took me through a process of doing "Soul Work" in order to learn my "Soul Identity" and "Soul Needs." Through it all, I uncovered a pathway that led me to my Soul Tribe and to understanding what fulfilling relationships with significant others, family, friends, and colleagues is supposed to look and feel like. And I wrote this book to arm others with tools to assist them in taking their relationships to another level.

I'm so grateful that you chose to read this book. There are a million options out there to choose from when you are navigating the world of self-help, motivation, and relationship advice. Experts with multiple levels of degrees in sociology, psychology or social work have written about how to improve yourself, your family and so forth. Religious and spiritual leaders have created programs and systems. Authors and journalists have written award-winning books. As I said at the beginning, I realize that I am none of these people. I am just a woman who has had some life-changing experiences in personal relationships that caused me to take a close look at them (and myself), make a change, fight to get back to who I really am, and discover what I need and what I deserve in my life and from those in it. My journey is not even close to being done. However, I am so grateful for having found this current level of clarity and peace in my soul, and now you can soul-fully benefit.

~Heather Beverly

INTRODUCTION

This book is written and organized to explain and explore "Soul Reciprocity," a place of balance that is reached when we (1) do Soul Work to achieve a deep understanding of ourselves, (2) discover our Soul Identity, or who we are at our core and what we are capable of giving, and (3) understand our Soul Needs, or what we truly need from others for optimally fulfilling relationships with the people who are closest to us (significant others, family, friends, co-workers). The ultimate goal is to form and experience Soul-Full relationships, which become our Soul Tribe.

Symbolisms

I have a keen interest in the interpretations and symbolism found in traditions, spirituality, and nature. Through my studies of various cultures and religions, I appreciate how we use symbols—like the Earth, stars, and mythology—to guide our lives. While I don't strictly adhere to symbolic meanings, I find them grounding and inspiring.

In the journey of Soul Reciprocity, the bee serves as a powerful and fitting symbol. Bees are not only diligent workers, but they are also the embodiment of harmony, cooperation, and balance within a larger ecosystem. They represent the interconnectedness of life and the mutual relationships we all share, whether in nature or in our personal lives.

Bees also have symbolism in many cultures and religions. In the Egyptian hieroglyphic language, the bee was the symbol of royal nomenclature, a reflection of hierarchical organization as well as of industry, creative activity, and wealth. In ancient times, bees were symbols of collective work, fertility, and generosity. Celts and Saxons believed bees bring messages from the Divine and prosperity. The Greek philosopher Pythagoras believed that the soul of the wise and ingenious passed into the bodies of bees. (BuzzAbout-Bees.net n.d.)

Bees work tirelessly to gather nectar and create honey—nature's sweet reward. In the same way, Soul Reciprocity teaches us to gather meaningful experiences, connections, and exchanges, transforming them into something more—nourishing ourselves and others at a deeper, soul level. The bee doesn't hoard the fruits of its labor for itself but shares its honey, feeding its entire hive and promoting the health of the larger world. Similarly, when we engage in true Soul Reciprocity, we take what we've gained—insight, love, compassion—and use it to nurture others in ways that go beyond surface-level exchanges.

Just as bees are crucial for the ecosystem to flourish, Soul Reciprocity is essential for the growth and well-being of our relationships. It transcends transactional exchanges and invites us to create lasting, nourishing bonds, grounded in empathy, awareness, and mutual care. Through this book, you will explore how to cultivate and produce reciprocity in your relationships, like the bee gathering nectar to produce honey, enriching both your life and the lives of those around you.

Integrated into the logo, the lotus, in particular, holds profound significance across multiple traditions. Growing from mud, it symbolizes resilience, rising above struggles to bloom. Buddhists view it as a metaphor for overcoming life's obstacles, while Ancient Egyptians associate it with fertility, rebirth, and purity. Women often liken themselves to lotuses, embodying strength and beauty amidst life's challenges. The blue lotus, one of the rarest, represents the spirit's victory over ignorance, signifying the perfection of wisdom and knowledge.

I used to think people with tattoos were rebellious and reckless. However, as I gained a deeper understanding of myself through life experiences, my perspective shifted, and I got my first tattoo in my mid-30s. My third tattoo was inspired by a photo I took on vacation in Maui, at the Garden of Eden Arboretum, where I saw a perfect blue lotus with a bright gold center in a pond. The tattoo wasn't just about the beautiful image, but also the powerful symbolism of the blue lotus and the bee. Over time, these symbols became deeply significant in my life, representing parts of my journey in ways I never could have predicted.

Like the blue lotus, I can write this book because of the strength, wisdom, and knowledge I have gained through overcoming adversities in my life and relationships. Like bees, I have always believed in hard work, generosity, nurturing others, and the blessings that come from those things. What I learned most recently were some of the other (and arguably the most impactful) lessons bees give us, that success in relationships comes from our ability to give and receive love based on soul connectedness.

Sections

The book is divided in three sections: (1) The Understanding; (2) The Preparation; and (3) The Application. Each section analyzes and explores the book's major themes in unique ways:

Section 1, subtitled "Lessons from the Soul," breaks down the elements of the term *Soul Reciprocity* itself and how it leads to Soul-Full Relationships. This section begins with defining "Relationships," which is what the book is all about.

Section 2, subtitled "Lessons from Bees," focuses on Soul Work, the necessary process a person must go through to uncover their Soul Identity and their Soul Needs and key revelations needed in order to understand and experience Soul Reciprocity. Section 2 also includes shortfalls that may impede the quest to Soul Reciprocity, eliminating or limiting our ability to attract a Soul Tribe. Each chapter makes reference to bees in its elucidation and how they model the concepts in some form.

Section 3, subtitled "Lessons from Life," focuses on the most significant relationships we have: romantic, family, friends, and work. It includes real-life anecdotes and targeted questions to help the reader better relate to and apply the book's main concepts.

Each section concludes with chapter summaries titled "Soul Reflections," allowing the reader to easily review the main points from each chapter. Finally, the book concludes with a resource and application section in the Appendix that includes questionnaires and sources referenced in the book.

Soul-Full

In the book, I use the term "Soul-Full" to describe relationships that are enriched by deep, meaningful connections grounded in mutual understanding and support. Unlike the standard term "soulful," which most often refers to a deep or sorrowful feeling, "Soul-Full" emphasizes the idea of being filled with the essence of the soul. These relationships thrive on instinctive reciprocity, where both parties nurture and nourish each other without the need for conscious effort or motive.

In a Soul-Full relationship, the give-and-take occurs naturally, creating an environment where both individuals feel valued and supported. This distinction highlights the unique quality of these connections, setting them apart from more superficial or transactional relationships.

As you read through this book, consider the relationships in your life that resonate with this concept. Are there connections that feel particularly Soul-Full to you? How do they differ from others?

SECTION 1:

THE UNDERSTANDING

Lessons from the Soul

1
THE BASICS PART I

RELATIONSHIPS

"There is a soul force in the universe, which, if we permit it, will flow through us and produce miraculous results."
~ Mahatma Gandhi

Soul Reciprocity is about relationships, both personal and professional. It's also about your relationship with yourself and how to understand, love, and nurture YOU so that you have a healthy, loving relationship with yourself first and then with others. Ultimately, this book mirrors the journey I took to understanding Soul Reciprocity and the need for it in relationships of every kind.

Relationships exist on different levels. Some are casual, others are peripheral or intermittent, and a few are deeply significant and constant. However, the most fulfilling connections are those born from a soul experience, as they hold the potential for Soul Reciprocity, offering a depth of mutual support and understanding that enriches our lives at the core.

We're going to delve into different "kinds" of relationships we have, how they are formed, and what our experiences are within them. As we examine our relationship with ourselves, we will take time to self-assess, ask the hard questions, and dig deeper into who we are so we can better understand what we need to do to take care of ourselves, insulate our souls, and connect with others. I hope you will gain new perspectives and skills that help you assess, discern, and ultimately deepen your most valuable relationships. In doing so, I will begin by providing definitions to get us on the same page, so there are no misunderstandings.

Because so many words in the English language have dual meanings or meanings that are tied to the context in which the words are used, it's easy to *think* you understand what someone is saying but you may completely *misunderstand* what they were "trying to say." With that, I'll begin with the definition of "relationship." We use the word so often that I wonder if we really stop to think about what it really means and what relationships really are. Since this book is all about relationships, I definitely need you to know what I'm talking about and in what context I am referring to them.

Relationship. "*The way in which two or more people are connected, or the state of being connected.*" (Oxford Learners Dictionaries n.d.)

Essential Meaning:
1. *The way two or more people talk to, behave toward and deal with each other.*
2. *A romantic or sexual friendship between two people.*
3. *The way in which two or more people or things are connected.*

Full Definition:
1. *The state of being related or interrelated.*
2. *a. The relation connection or binding participants in a relationship, such as kinship.*
   b. A specific instance or type of kinship.
3. *a. A state of affairs existing between those having relations or dealings.*
   b. Romantic or passionate attachment.
(Merriam-Webster n.d.)

The roots of the word "*relationship*" is "*relation*" and "*related.*" Among their definitions are:

Relation:
1. *A person connected by consanguinity or affinity (relative, kinship).*
2. *The state of being mutually or reciprocally interested.*

Related:
1. *Connected by a reason of an established or discoverable relation.*
2. *Connected by common ancestry or sometimes by marriage.*
(Merriam-Webster n.d.)

No matter what definition you find, "relationship," "relation," and "related" are all described as a connection between people that exists as a result of some interaction. From these formal definitions, there are two perspectives from which to view relationships, (1) relationships that result from circumstance, or what I call "Circumstantial Perspective"; and (2) relationships that result from the experiences we have around or within them, or what I call the "Experiential Perspective."

Although the definitions that formal authorities provide us describe relationships based on circumstance and experience, I believe there is yet a third category of relationships to be considered. But to understand this category requires looking at relationships from a "Soul Perspective." Observing relationships from a soul perspective necessitates the creation of the third category of relationships that I believe are those based on a "Soul Experience."

Circumstantial Perspective

Relationships viewed from a circumstantial perspective are those which result from the circumstances that connect people. So, if you are related, in the same class at school, "set up" on a date, or work at the same company, your connection to the other person is simply based on the circumstances that bring you together. There's no choice in the matter or conscious decision to introduce that person into your life.

Experiential Perspective

The experiential perspective of relationships stems from your actual encounters with the person. Not just the circumstance that arose for you to come to know someone, but actual experiences you may have with them in the course of your daily life (i.e., a school trip, a speed dating event, family holidays, or a team project at work). Experiential relationships are created from actual involvement and interaction with that person within a certain occasion, situation, or experience over a period of time.

Soul Perspective

Relationships that manifest from soul experiences originate from a place within us and not external factors, happenstance, or lineage. They are relationships that exist because of a soul connection that occurs as a result of two people being very clear about who they are, what they are capable of giving, and what they need. Each person's clarity about themselves allows them to "see" each other – meaning they recognize a like-mindedness and kindred spirit in the other. Thus, they are naturally drawn to one another in ways they are not with others. A relationship founded on a soul experience feels familiar from the beginning.

While formal definitions categorize relationships based on circumstance and experience, I propose a third category: relationships from a "soul perspective." This means recognizing connections that go beyond proximity or family ties, where a deeper, divinely guided force brings people together. Such connections form relationships based on a "soul experience." You'll understand this concept better as you continue reading.

Soul-based relationships arise from an internal connection rather than external factors like chance or family ties. These relationships form when both individuals have a deep understanding of themselves, allowing them to recognize a shared spirit and like-mindedness in each other. This natural connection often feels familiar right from the start, like meeting someone for the first time but feeling as though you've known them forever. From this connection, various types of relationships—romantic, friendship, familial, or business—may develop.

Every person will experience many relationships throughout life. These connections—whether with family, friends, romantic partners, or colleagues—shape who we are and how we view the world. Through them, we gain knowledge, form opinions, and find community. Our relationships bring both our best and worst memories, influencing our strengths, weaknesses, joys, and sorrows. Because relationships have such a profound impact on our lives, it's essential to assess who we surround ourselves with and how they entered our lives. Not all relationships will be equally close, but those founded on a soul connection and capable of Soul Reciprocity will be the most fulfilling

QUESTIONS

1. Think about the people in your life who you have relationships with. How did they get there? Who is in your life because of circumstances or experiences? Make a list of those people and indicate the way in which you became associated.
2. Do you think there is anyone in your life as a result of a soul connection? Who? How did your connection come about?
3. Is there a difference in the quality of the relationships you have with people based on how they came to be in your life? Circumstances vs. Experiences vs. Soul Experiences? What are the differences?

NEXT STEPS

For a deeper understanding of your relationships and how they align with the concept of Soul Reciprocity, I encourage you to complete the **Relationships Questionnaire** provided in *Appendix A*. This self-reflection tool will guide you through key questions to assess the quality and depth of your connections.

2
THE BASICS PART II

THE SOUL

*"We are not human beings having a spiritual experience.
We are spiritual beings having a human experience."*
~ Pierre Teilhard de Chardin

I coined the term "Soul Reciprocity" while searching for a concise way to explain the end of my marriage. From the outside, everything seemed perfect—and of course our social media painted an amazing picture. From the outside, we had a "couple goals" relationship, but something essential was missing. People naturally wanted to know what happened when it ended, and while I had long, exhausting talks with close friends and family, I needed a simpler way to explain it to others.

After years of soul-searching, I realized the root issue: a lack of deep, mutual soul connection. One day, the term "Soul Reciprocity" came to me, perfectly capturing what I had been missing. Despite all the positives in my marriage, the absence of this vital connection made the relationship unsustainable.

When I started using "Soul Reciprocity" to explain my decision, people seemed to immediately understand. It resonated with them, sparking self-reflection about their own relationships. My decision wasn't impulsive. It came from recognizing that the most important relationship in my life lacked the soul-level connection I needed. I then began to assess every area of my life, including my family, friends and even business relationships. What I learned through uncovering my true Soul Identity is that our Soul Needs must be mutually nurtured and nourished in any relationship.

It was a profound revelation: I realized I could answer people's questions with just two words. Despite all the positive aspects—the "pros"—of my marriage, the fact that it lacked Soul Reciprocity was a "con" that I couldn't overcome. That was it. My answer was simple: "I made the decision to end my marriage because it lacked Soul Reciprocity," and that is exactly what I said when asked.

I was amazed by how instantly people connected with the phrase. I received responses like, "Ahhh, I get it," "Oh, that's good," and "Whoa, that's deep, but I understand." It definitely sparked something. You could see the wheels turning as soon as they heard those words. They'd tilt their heads, nod slowly while processing, and then I'd see it click. It resonated.

Not only did they understand it within the context of my situation, but they also began applying it to their own lives. I'd hear things like, "Wait, I don't think I have Soul Reciprocity either!" and "I'm going to have to take a closer look at some of the people in my life!" It was a relief to know that my friends and family empathized with my decision. They knew me well enough to understand I wouldn't make such a major choice over everyday issues that come up. They understood my decision wasn't irrational or impulsive; rather, it stemmed from an irreconcilable deficit at the soul level in what was supposed to be my most significant relationship.

What Is and Why the Soul?

Although I had come up with a brief response to questions about my divorce, I eventually began asking myself, "What does Soul Reciprocity really mean to me?" When the phrase first came to mind, I felt an immediate, instinctive connection. It was as if I intuitively understood its significance — that it represented something I was missing and something essential for everyone. But as I repeated the phrase, I found myself reflecting on it more deeply. I paused to truly consider its meaning and decided to write down my thoughts. While we often use the word "soul" in everyday language, we rarely stop to think about what it actually means. We talk about "Soulmates" and being part of a "Soul Tribe." We say we feel things "deep in our soul" or describe artists as having a lot of "soul." We express love with all our "soul" and say that someone is, or has, a beautiful "soul."

What is the soul, and why do we describe people, places and things using the word soul? As it turns out, the soul can be a complicated thing to define or describe. There are many different explanations and interpretations of what the soul is (some competing), what it does, and what its importance is to our lives. How the soul is described varies based on perspective and viewpoint, including philosophical, religious, and spiritual views. Thus, it's important to note that perspectives on the soul vary across different cultures, religions, and belief systems. Some may not believe in the concept of a soul or may have different interpretations of its nature and origin.

Philosophical Views

Famous philosophers have described the soul in various ways. Socrates said not only that the soul is immortal, but also that it contemplates truths after its separation from the body at the time of death. He said, "Haven't you realized that our soul is immortal and never destroyed?" Socrates also sought to define justice as one of the cardinal human virtues, and he understood the virtues as "states of the soul." So his account of what justice is depends upon his account of the human soul.

The philosopher Plato, in the fourth century, believed the soul is made up of three parts: the rational, spirited, and appetitive. The rational part, like the guardians in a city, is responsible for decision-making. The spirited part, similar to the military, is associated with courage. The appetitive part, like the artisans or bankers, focuses on pleasure.

Plato's idea of the soul's three parts comes from his vision of an ideal city, which he divided into three groups: guardians, military forces, and artisans. He saw a clear connection between the structure of a city and the soul, with each part of the soul corresponding to a role in the city. This created an analogy between the two, with the rational part playing the executive role in both.

Aristotle, like Plato, described the soul as having "parts." Aristotle divided the soul into two parts: the rational and the irrational. Both philosophers agreed that the soul has at least two parts—one rational and one irrational. Their purpose in dividing the soul this way was both political and intended to explain human behavior.

Religious Views

In its most basic sense, soul means "life," either physical or eternal. (Although there are conflicting philosophies amongst religious beliefs as to the immortality of the soul.) Often, people use the words spirit and soul interchangeably. However, there are others who believe they are not the same thing. For example, in Christian scripture, the words "spirit" and "soul" are used to describe different things. "The primary distinction is that the soul is the animate life, or the basis of the senses, wishes, desires, affections, and emotions. The spirit is that part of us that connects (or refuses to connect) to God. Christians believe our spirits relate to God's Spirit, either accepting God's promptings and conviction, thereby proving that we belong to God (Romans 8:16) or resisting God and proving that we do not have a spiritual life (Acts 7:51)" (Compelling Truth n.d.). Unlike the soul, which may be alive both physically and eternally, the spirit can be alive (i.e., in the case of believers; see Peter 3:18) or dead as in the case of non-believers (Colossians 2:13; Ephesians 2:4-5) (Compelling Truth n.d.).

In evangelical Bible teaching, the trichotomy view describes people as being made up of three parts: the body, soul, and spirit. The soul includes intellect, emotion, and will. The Spirit is that part of us that is closest to God (Grudem 2018). In the religious realm, the soul was given to man by God after the body and breath. In Genesis 2:7, "the LORD God formed man of the dust of the ground and breathed into his nostrils the breath of life; and man became a living soul." From this passage, it can be understood that the body came from the dust, but it was the breath of God that made the dust live. And by making the body "live," it became a soul – a whole being. It was the soul that gave the body life and the two became interdependent and as one. Wolfe, Gregory (ed.) "the New Religious Humanists. The Free Press.

Both the Old and New Testaments of the Bible instruct that we love God completely, with our whole soul, meaning love God with everything that is in us that makes us alive (Deuteronomy 6:4-5; Mark 12:30; Luke 10:27). Therefore, a living soul equates with a living person. Some further expound by saying that a person does not "have" a soul but "is" a soul (Childs 1985).

In Hebrew, the word "Nephesh" has multiple meanings, one of which is "soul." It appears over 700 times in the Old Testament. For example, Psalm 42:1 reads, "As the deer pants for water, so my nephesh longs for you," and Psalm 42:2 says, "My nephesh thirsts for the living God." Besides "soul," nephesh is also translated as throat (its most basic meaning in Numbers 11:6; Psalm 105:18), living being, life, creature, mind, desires, heart, appetite, and persons (Genesis 46:15, Numbers 31:19). Although its primary meaning is "throat," the term extends to symbolize life itself, representing the whole human being. This broad definition suggests nephesh refers to the inner essence of a person, the core of their being. In Genesis, man became a living nephesh, brought to life by the breath of God, making each person a living reflection of God.

In Judaism, however, the soul is not immortal. Rather, the soul (nephesh) dies when the body dies. As noted above, one of the definitions of the Hebrew word nephesh is "a breathing creature," one in which life is present whether it be physical or mental life. The breath (which created the soul) dies with the body, disappears in the grave, and returns to God. A body without breath is called a dead nephesh. Thus, people do not "have" a nephesh, rather, we "are" a nephesh (a living, breathing, physical thing). (Jon Collins, Tim Mackey, "The Bible Project: "Soul"). It is not believed that the nephesh is the same as the spirit ("ruah"), which Hebrews (and others) believe will survive the death of the body. The ruah refers to powers and actions outside of the body. So, although the Hebrew Bible distinguishes between spirit and the body, it does not accept the dualism of body and soul as espoused in Greek and Christian teachings (Encyclopedia.com n.d.) .

Similar to other languages, the Arabic words for "spirit" and "soul" are translated as "wind" or "breath" and "self," respectively. Rūh relates to the spirit that comes from God (God's spirit). The term "nafs" refers to the human soul. The equivalence of life and soul in the Qurʾān, however, is not explicitly stated. Nor is there any explicit statement as to whether the soul is immaterial or material. The Qurʾān is primarily concerned with the moral and religious orientation of the human soul, its conduct, and the consequences of such conduct in terms of reward and punishment in the afterlife. This concern with the moral and religious disposition of the soul is reflected in the Qurʾanic characterization of the soul as either ammārah, the soul that commands what is evil, or the "carnal self" (12:53), lawwāmah, the soul that blames itself in its quest for goodness (75:2), or muṭma'innah, the tranquil soul that returns to God (89:27).

Regardless of denomination, a common religious belief is that one of the greatest gifts given to humanity is the breath of God, which granted us a soul and life itself. As a result, religious individuals believe it is their fundamental duty to love God with all their soul in gratitude for the gifts He has bestowed upon them.

Non-Religious Views

Whether from a religious perspective or not, most people believe in the existence of some form of a soul and have varying interpretations of what spirit is. Not all of what people believe about the soul and the spirit come from biblical or religious teaching. Many people have a dichotomy view and believe that people are made up of two parts: body and soul or spirit, and as such, believe that soul and spirit are essentially the same and can be used interchangeably (Grudem 2018). There are others who don't espouse an evangelical view at all and believe in monism: a view which sees a person as having one part, the body. In monism, the soul and spirit are just other words to describe a person or their "life" and not separate elements of a person's makeup.

Scientific Materialism is a philosophy wherein it is believed that "all phenomena in the universe, including the human mind, have a material basis, are subject to the same physical laws, and can be most deeply understood by scientific analysis" and that "any true and meaningful knowledge that we may gain about life, mind and the universe can be gotten only through the analytical methods of science" (Haught n.d.). As such, in scientific materialism, there is no belief in the soul – it's non-existent.

There are, however, other non-religious views of what the soul is and its relation to the mind, processing of information, and ultimately, the human experience. There are three dimensions of intelligence: IQ, EQ, and SQ. These scientific analyses are measures of how the human brain functions, the connection (or lack thereof) between the mind, body, and soul, and the relation of each to one's overall quality of life.

IQ

We've all heard about "IQ," or the intelligence quotient, a number derived from a standardized test used to measure a person's intelligence. The test score is compared to one's chronological age and is said to assess various mental processes, such as visual and spatial processes, knowledge, reasoning, and memory. One's IQ score is said to be the result of their mind's capabilities and an indicator of their potential for "success." IQ solely looks at the mind and body as its determining factors. Its processing occurs in the left side of the brain where intellectual intelligence resides.

EQ

Emotional intelligence ("EQ") is another form of intelligence that has been studied in an effort to uncover what determines a person's happiness and success in life. It is believed that the measure of one's EQ is just as important as IQ (Cherry 2021). Emotional intelligence refers to a person's ability to understand their own emotions in positive ways to relieve stress, communicate effectively, empathize with others, overcome challenges, build stronger relationships, and achieve personal and professional success. Emotional intelligence has four main components: 1. self-management (feelings, actions, adaptation); 2. self-awareness (emotions, thoughts, behaviors); 3. social awareness (empathy, understanding the needs of others); 4. relationship management (understanding of how to develop and maintain good relationships) (Jeanne Segal n.d.). EQ is developed on the right side of the brain where our emotions are processed.

Ego

In order to fully understand the third type of intelligence (SQ), we have to address the topic of ego. As stated above, IQ and EQ are associated with the state of our bodies and minds. Everything that humans are "aware of" comes from the IQ (thoughts) and EQ (emotions). We have awareness of parts of ourselves such as our self-image, thoughts, perceptions, emotions, memories, and beliefs. But when we go a step beyond our awareness of our thoughts and emotions and then identify with our state of mind and body, we are experiencing ego. The ego involves the layers of descriptions you attach to who you are, including your position and possessions

(Lechner 2016). This is when you believe what your mind tells you about yourself, which is typically grossly exaggerated in one way or another. Ego, by definition, is "a person's sense of self-esteem or self-importance." The key to the definition is "a person's SENSE." It's not a reality. Ego is not necessarily who we really are, although we often think it is. The ego is constantly seeking satisfaction and can never rest "in the now." It uses the present moment to get to the next. It reacts to events based on a sense of "lack" rather than responding from a place of fulfillment, whereas the soul is your authentic self who you *really* are at your core. The qualities of the soul are wisdom, compassion, integrity, joy, love, creativity, and peace. Unlike the ego, the soul doesn't seek satisfaction. It is already 'happy' because of its innate qualities. The soul can be in the now. It can also take its time to respond rather than hastily reacting to situations or emotions. Reacting comes from the ego. Responding comes from the soul. The soul is able to experience spiritual intelligence (where we experience ultimate fulfillment), whereas the ego cannot.

SQ

Spiritual Intelligence (SQ) is another recognized and studied dimension of intelligence. Spiritual Intelligence is a "higher dimension of intelligence that activates the qualities and capabilities of the authentic self (or the soul) in the form[s] of wisdom, compassion, integrity, joy, love, creativity and peace" (Griffiths, Ego and Soul 2011). "Experiencing one's SQ is said to result in a sense of deeper meaning, purpose, and improved life and work skills. It gives humans the capacity to ask questions about the ultimate meaning of life and the integrated relationship between us and the world in which we live" (Sahebalzamani M 2013). Spiritual intelligence is processed by activating the whole brain, combining our intellectual and emotional intelligence, to connect them to the soul.

The Spiritual Intelligence Paradigm ("SQ Paradigm") is the science of the soul, according to psychologist Robert Griffiths. It looks at the scientific make-up of humans while considering how the soul plays a part in one's overall thought processes, discernment, level of intelligence, and ultimate success and fulfillment. Whereas religious faiths teach that the accessibility to one's soul is tied to their belief in a supernatural power, the SQ Paradigm views the soul as a psychological "location" that is directly accessible to everyone and does not require reliance on religious faith in order to access it (Griffiths, The Spiritual Intelligence Paradigm 2012). However, the SQ Paradigm teaches that spiritual intelligence must be experienced in order to understand it and gain its benefits. Most people will encounter spiritual intelligence naturally from time to time throughout their life experiences. There are also teaching methods used to help people elicit the spiritual intelligence experience in order to train their minds to utilize spiritual intelligence as and when needed. In this regard, Dr. Griffiths developed 3Q Training, which is a combination of three dimensions of intelligence: IQ and EQ in association with SQ (diagram below). Basically, this training is a simplified version of meditation that shifts us from reacting from our egos to responding from our souls and utilizing both sides of our brains to optimize its function. The result: greater fulfillment, increased creativity, sharpened intuition, more empathy and compassion, and improved performance on a wide range of work and life skills (Griffiths, How to Experience Spiritual Intelligence 2012). In short, the SQ Paradigm combines our understanding of IQ, EQ, and SQ and shows us how to utilize our spiritual intelligence by shifting our mental thoughts from the ego to our souls in order to navigate through life in a way that allows us to achieve ultimate fulfillment.

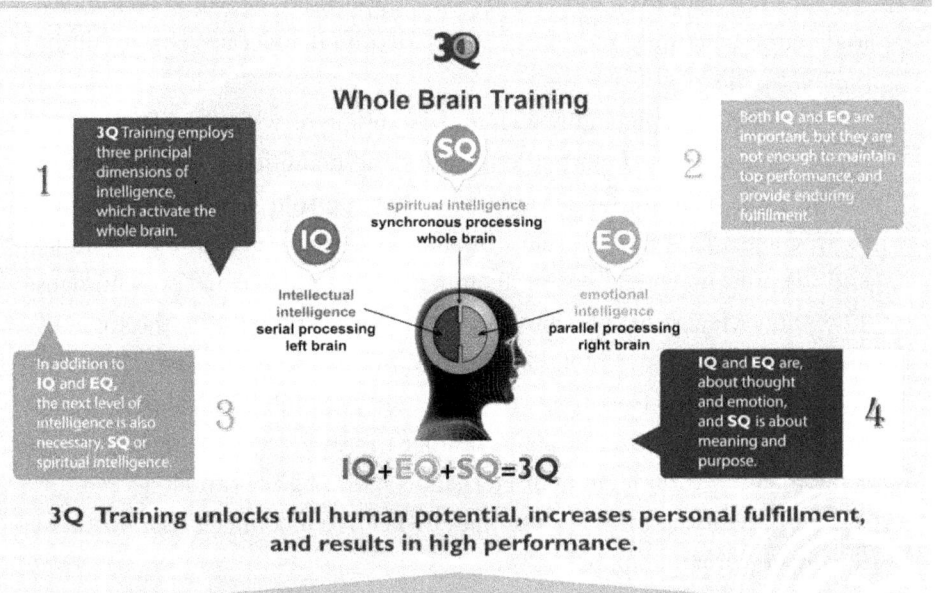

© 2012 – 2022, Richard Griffiths.

So, what does it all mean? Whether analyzed from a religious, spiritual, or scientific perspective, the soul is recognized as the core of who we are – our authentic selves. It is the part of us that holds the key to our ultimate happiness and fulfillment. It's the sounding board of our core desires and needs. It doesn't lie to us like our minds, emotions, and egos can. The soul is our connection to God, the universe, the synchronistic use of our brain, and the key to tapping into the highest level of our satisfaction and being.

Soul Reciprocity View

The phrase Soul Reciprocity came to me instinctively as a way to describe something I lacked but needed in my life. In fact, I realized that it's what everyone needs. What I didn't realize is that it was not a common phrase used to describe this "thing" I believed to be necessary at the center of fulfilling relationships. I didn't even know that it wasn't a "thing." And yet, whenever I used the phrase, it resonated immediately with people. It seems that no matter one's core belief system, people have heard the word soul, have an interpretation of what it means, and most seem to believe in the existence of the soul in one form or another. It was also abundantly clear that people gravitate to the concept of reciprocity and naturally desire it in relationships. However, most people have never used the word "reciprocity" to describe what they want from others, despite the fact it seems to hit the nail on the head!

When I contemplated my own understanding of what Soul Reciprocity really means to me, I started looking for the definition(s) or descriptions of the soul. It became quite apparent that the soul can be complicated to articulate. There are so many definitions of the soul (some competing), and varying interpretations of its function and impact on us as humans. The many viewpoints of what the soul is (or isn't) could be the topic of an entire book in and of itself, if not a life's work of research. Whether you define the soul from a spiritual, scientific, or philosophical perspective, the common consensus seems to be that the soul exists in some form or fashion, either for a lifetime or eternally. One thing we can all agree on is it is the "invisible part" of our human makeup that connects us to truth, or the divine (Santana 2003).

This book and my definition of Soul Reciprocity are based on the idea that the soul is the core of our being—our true essence and identity. It's who we are. The soul is a part of our human makeup, our humanity; it affects the quality of our lives and how we relate to ourselves and others. It is the basis of our emotions, senses, character, and desires. I also believe that the soul desires perfection and helps us evolve on that quest. The soul perceives wisdom, truth, beauty, and love, and the soul takes responsibility for its actions because it is within our souls that there is absolute truth. Further, it is my belief that every human has a soul and that our souls are the conduit through which we can experience deep levels of connection with one another.

I personally believe that the soul is both a part of every human's make-up while we are here and the effects of who we were which remain after we are gone. It is not the physical package you carry around, but it's a part of who you are. In short, I believe that the soul is a part of us that affects ourselves and others deeply. It is an almost indescribable place within us because it resides in a place so deep and so intricately woven into our physiology that it is buried in our subconscious, yet its power is so strong that it can drive us to make decisions and create connections between us. The soul can "see" for us and recognize like souls in others. It's pure and authentic and its lens is definitive and clear. Because our souls are such an important part of who we are, how we see the world, and how we can connect with others if we are in tune with it, I was compelled to take a look and analyze my relationships from a "Soul Perspective."

Importance of the Soul Perspective

As humans, we are made up of both physical and non-physical components. We often focus heavily on our physical health, appearance, and functionality, and recently, mental health has become a more prevalent part of public discourse. Even the connection between mind and body is now widely discussed and explored. However, we cannot overlook the importance of the soul, which, as discussed earlier, is the core of our being.

The soul is our foundation, and just like our bodies and minds, it requires attention and nurturing. A strong, fulfilled soul radiates through our entire being, promoting inner peace, balance, and overall wellness. When we can truly say, "all is well with my soul," we are able to live our best lives, fulfill our purposes, and positively impact others.

Think of someone who touched your life deeply but is no longer present. Reflecting on that person doesn't just bring back memories—you feel the emotions you experienced with them. That connection is their soul touching yours, resonating even after they're gone. Similarly, the people currently in your life have a profound impact on your soul. If a relationship doesn't affect you at the soul level, it raises questions about its depth and significance. How connected are you really?

We rarely think about the condition of our souls in everyday conversations. We ask each other how we're doing but often expect no deeper response than "fine." We focus on visible self-care, but soul care, especially after trauma or loss, is often neglected. Yet, the soul is crucial to our mental, emotional, and spiritual health, and tending to it should be a priority.

When we do the work to reveal ourselves at that natural, authentic level, what we find is the pure truth about ourselves and we are able to "see" and connect with others at a soul level, too. That's what makes thinking and observing our relationships from a soul perspective so special, necessary, and revealing. It's a deeper analysis than our minds and hearts can process. Our mind can rationalize things in ways we want to benefit us somehow. We can create a narrative that suits the situation and talk ourselves out of that which is "real" or "truthful." Our hearts can be swayed based on our emotional state, vulnerabilities, and external factors. Our souls, though, speak from a deeper, resolute place.

Whether your preferred definition and interpretation the soul comes from more of a spiritual or a philosophical perspective, the common consensus seems to be that the soul is a part of our human makeup. It is the basis of emotions, senses, character, and desires. We each have a soul and because of that, it is a conduit through which we can experience deep levels of connection.

In the world of Soul Reciprocity, the soul is seen as the foundation of who we are. It's a deep, instinctual place that, when nourished, reveals our true needs, which we call "Soul Needs." The soul doesn't lie, for it reflects our authentic selves and what we need to live a fulfilling life. When we engage with others at this level, we see the truth in our relationships, stripped of the filters that our minds and hearts might impose. Soul-level connections are the most honest and real, allowing us to view our relationships through a clear lens of truth.

QUESTIONS

1. How do you define the soul?
2. Have you ever thought about relationships from a soul perspective?
3. How do you nourish, nurture and feed your soul?

NEXT STEPS

To explore your connection with your soul and how it influences your relationships, please take the **Soul Questionnaire** in *Appendix B*. This tool will help you reflect on your inner needs, instincts, and how you align with your soul's desires.

3
THE BASICS PART III

RECIPROCITY

*"What you give is what you get. If you go out and give,
the universe will return that to you."*
~ Oprah Winfrey

Here we are, getting to the nitty-gritty: RECIPROCITY, a concept so simple in its definition, yet so challenging to apply in many relationships. However, reciprocity is the foundational principle this book explores and the basis for the revelations that have shaped this moment in my life and now yours.

I don't intend to bore anyone by including definitions and explanations of terms like "Soul Reciprocity," but it's all very necessary for context. My entire life changed when I stepped back, took a closer look, and reinterpreted words and concepts I thought I understood but had either misapplied or didn't fully grasp at all.

My new understanding and appreciation of the concept of *reciprocity* was a game-changer for me, and I assure you, it may very well be for you too. So, indulge me as I expound...

The Oxford English Dictionary defines "reciprocity" as "[t]he practice of exchanging things with others for mutual benefit, especially privileges granted by one country or organization to another."

Why Reciprocity

Reciprocity is critical in our relationships. It creates balance and stability. In meaningful relationships, **reciprocity** occurs when the contribution of each party meets the expectations of the other party. Knowing that there is a give and take in a relationship allows each person in it to have the confidence that they are safe in that relationship. Reciprocity is the foundation of trust. It provides an environment for each person to be transparent about who they are, what their fears are, what they need, and even what they don't know that they need.

There are two kinds of reciprocity: positive and negative reciprocity. **Positive reciprocity** occurs when an action committed by one individual that has a positive effect on someone else is returned with an action that has an approximately equal positive effect (Reciprocity 2013). For example, my girlfriend often takes care of my dogs when I travel. I have returned the favor by showing up with a small gift (flowers, souvenir from my trip, etc.) upon my return. There are also times when I watch her dogs when she travels. For there to be positive reciprocity, the reciprocated action should be approximately equal to the first action in terms of positive value. Otherwise, the result can be an uncomfortable social situation where one action is outweighed by the other, and the party who got the lesser result can feel an imbalance in the exchange. [19]

Negative reciprocity occurs when the action committed by one individual that has a positive effect on another is then returned by that person with an action that has an unequal, and therefore negative, effect. Imagine if my girlfriend took care of my dogs for a weekend and I returned the favor by buying her a car! I can only imagine the look on her face. She would look at me with disbelief and probably assume I had lost my mind, and she would likely even refuse it as a gift! Obviously, a car as the reciprocated gift for dog sitting would be grossly inappropriate because it does not equal the initial gesture. And because it would create an awkward situation, it would be negative, rather than positive, reciprocity. We expect our good deeds to be reciprocated by actions that are approximately equal in value. [17]

Conversely, what if my girlfriend took care of my dogs for the weekend and I didn't even so much as say thank you and instead asked her to bring them home to me without regard to the sacrifices she already made to her schedule and home routine to accommodate them? Nothing in return for something done for me that benefitted me is definitely negative reciprocity.

How many times have you given someone a gift or put together a surprise only to feel as though it is not received in the way you intended? It's not that you are looking for some grand display of gratitude in return, but rather you just want the person to recognize the meaningful effort you put into your gift.

I imagine every single person reading this has had that disappointing moment when an enormous amount of thought, planning, saving, strategy, logistics or sacrifice have gone into something you wanted to do for someone, and when the gift or surprise is revealed, it's received with far less energy than was expected. Perhaps the recipient was grateful but underwhelmingly so, or perhaps they were dismissive and moved on to the next gift without pause. Maybe they missed the point completely; they didn't at all comprehend the lengths you went through to make the moment happen and couldn't comprehend the effort and sacrifice that you made. This, too, is an example of negative reciprocity.

Sacrifice

Reciprocity is a form of sacrifice. To be willing to give yourself to someone else in ways that you know they need and want requires that you take time, exert mental, emotional, and physical energy, and even extend resources at times. The timing or circumstances are not always the most "convenient." People we love may need us any time of day or night; when we're tired or going through a tough time ourselves. They may require attention we may not think we have time to give or financial assistance when we are down to our last pennies.

If we are fully vested in the relationship, we should actively be thinking of the people we love. Being reciprocal doesn't mean waiting for someone to do for us and then we do something in return. Neither does it mean we only show up in times of need. Rather, reciprocity means thinking of others when they may least expect it and doing something that shows how much we care, without prompt or occasion.

But thinking of others before ourselves, or taking out time despite how overextended we may be, is the type of sacrifice that reciprocity is built on. By sacrificing ourselves, we show that we are truly vested in the relationship. We show that we care. We provide examples of how important the person is to us and that we are grateful for the connection and the relationship and all that they sow into it as well.

Showing up and demonstrating our love for another and/or commitment to the relationship and the fulfillment of the other within it, no matter what kind of relationship, is the foundation we must build for the longevity and success of it. Despite the fact that reciprocity requires sacrifice, when you are in a fulfilling relationship, you are willing to make the sacrifice and it doesn't feel like a burden. Instead, you WANT to make the sacrifice because it shows your commitment and gratitude for what that person contributes to you.

Reciprocal Expectations

Have you ever given someone something nice without any expectation of getting something in return, not even a "thank you"? If so, you expect no reciprocity. As it pertains to relationships, not having or expecting reciprocity is unlikely to yield a balanced or fulfilling experience. In fact, a relationship without reciprocity will always be unfulfilling and ultimately fail.

There's an irony about how I've felt about reciprocity in different situations in my life. I have known better than to not have expectations, but I haven't always been able to "do better." I always thought that focusing on what someone should do for you was a backwards thought process. I believed that you shouldn't have such expectations without first showing what you can bring to the table. It was as if I believed that I didn't deserve anything from anyone else unless I first demonstrated that I had something of worth to give them. However, if I'm honest with myself, I have also been in plenty of situations where I wasn't able to give what others expected of me. Ultimately, the pressure of what was expected would scare me and turn me away.

Since relationships are birthed from connectedness and interactions with others, just as we must be willing to "give" in relationships, there most certainly should also be something we "get" from the people we choose to have relationships with. We must have expectations of people closest to us. There's nothing wrong with that. Think about it: your parents were likely the closest people to you and loved you more than anyone you knew during your childhood. Yet, they came with an unending list of expectations of you and had no problem articulating them. They expected you to obey their rules, do your chores, complete your homework, and treat them with respect. You expected them to "parent" you, teach you, provide you with shelter, keep you safe, and love you unconditionally. Whether the expectations are spoken or unspoken, they are there. The invisible strings that make the relationship go two ways and feel mutually beneficial. By expecting reciprocity, you aren't expecting a specific "thing." Sometimes reciprocity lies simply in the response you get from the other person: a smile, a tear, a laugh, a look of love, an embrace. Reciprocity isn't tit for tat. It's literally just that constant exchange of energy that shows both parties are "in" the relationship.

Although I am now able to articulate the concepts of reciprocity, admittedly it remains a challenge at times to implement them in my own life. Especially when it comes to having reciprocal expectations of others. But the monumental lessons I've learned from relationships that lacked reciprocity (whether my fault or someone else's) have led me to writing this book about the importance of reciprocity.

Romantic Relationships

In romantic relationships, I often found myself stuck in a cycle of negative reciprocity. I would enter relationships not feeling worthy of expecting anything in return, only to end up feeling resentful and unfulfilled when the other person treated me as if I wasn't worth reciprocating.

When I was younger, I approached dating with the mindset that I had to prove my value first, without expecting much back. I'd even tell potential partners that I was going to show them how good of a girlfriend I could be, believing that women who expected more upfront had "entitlement issues."

Looking back, I realize I was wrong to think that way. I saw so many friends with long lists of what they expected in a partner—looks, income, certain behaviors—while I felt I had to give everything without asking for anything. One friend even had specific engagement ring requirements! While they felt entitled to ask for what they wanted, I believed I had to earn everything.

Think about your own relationship. Have you ever felt the need to give first without expecting anything in return? Or have you been in situations where the expectations placed on you felt overwhelming? How did these imbalances affect you over time?

In my experience, those imbalanced relationships were no one's fault but my own. The lack of positive reciprocity left me feeling empty. I thought I shouldn't expect anything, but I've since learned that expecting positive reciprocity isn't wrong—it's necessary.

Reflect on your relationship. Is it balanced? Do you feel fulfilled? The truth is, we *"should"* expect reciprocity in our most meaningful connections. Without it, there's no balance, peace or fulfillment. Without a sense of balance, there can be no true Soul Reciprocity.

Friendships

In my friendships, I often found myself in a cycle of giving without expecting anything in return. I prided myself on being the friend who sent birthday cards, flowers, and random texts of encouragement, never thinking my friends owed me anything back. I felt a sense of pride in that approach.

As I got older, I began to question some of these friendships. I realized certain friends had only ever received without giving, and I started wondering: *"Would the friendship survive if I stopped doing all the 'doing'?"*

On the flip side, I've also experienced friendships that felt overwhelming. Some friends gave so much—time, energy, support—that they expected the same from me in return. You know the type: friends who make you their top priority and expect you to do the same, even when you can't. No matter how much you give, it's never enough to meet their expectations. Their need for reciprocity becomes suffocating, and eventually, the friendship just can't last.

Looking back, I realize that I sought acceptance from friends, feeling the need to prove my friendship first and focusing more on what my friends need than myself. I convinced myself I didn't need anything in return, but in reality, the imbalance left me questioning the true value of these relationships.

So, I ask: Do you sometimes convince yourself that you don't need anything back in friendships? Have you ever reassessed the balance of give and take in your relationships? Have you ever had a friendship where no matter how much you try, it never seems to be enough? It's worth taking a moment to reflect on whether those around you reciprocate the energy and care you give them.

Family Relationships

We're often taught that we have obligations to our family simply because we share blood. The expectation is that we love and care for them without question. In reality, familial relationships are no different from any other. They require positive reciprocity to thrive.

My mother has always been the best example of positive reciprocity in my life. Our relationship is balanced; we give and take equally, and the love flows naturally. But not all family relationships are this way. For example, I have no relationship with my father. Blood alone couldn't create a bond, and he chose to leave my life early on. In this case, it wasn't negative reciprocity—it was the absence of reciprocity altogether.

On the other hand, there are family members I love, but we aren't very close due to distance, busy lives, or other factors. We don't invest much in each other emotionally, but when we do connect, the love is there, and we enjoy our time together. Sometimes, that's enough.

Then there are relationships I've truly wanted to work, but despite my efforts, they remained unbalanced. One in particular broke my heart. A family member I reconnected with later in life gave me hope that we could rebuild our relationship. Over time, I realized that she could only come to me in moments of crisis, asking for help or support. She never reached out just to check on me or invest in our connection. I don't think she meant to take without giving, but the imbalance became toxic, and I had to step back for my own well-being.

It was a painful decision, and I felt guilty, especially knowing the difficulties she faced. The truth is, without positive reciprocity, even family relationships can become draining and unsustainable.

Reflect on your own family relationships. Are there family members you feel obligated to care for despite a lack of reciprocity? When you think about your closest family relationships, do they feel balanced and fulfilling? Have you had to set boundaries with certain relatives to protect your emotional well-being?

Business Relationships

Reciprocity isn't just essential in personal relationships; it's equally crucial in business relationships. Trust and mutual contribution are the foundation of any successful business partnership. For example, when two people start a company, one might provide the financing while the other manages operations. If either party fails to fulfill their role, the business can't thrive.

As an attorney, I've seen many partnerships break down because expectations weren't met. In one case, a client invested a significant amount of money into a business, expecting their partner to manage operations and employees. However, as time passed, the partner didn't handle their responsibilities, resulting in poorly managed employees and no new business opportunities. Eventually, the investor had to sever ties because the partnership wasn't balanced. Just like in personal relationships, business success relies on positive reciprocity.

The same applies when working with colleagues on group projects. Team members often have different strengths and skills that complement each other, but if one person doesn't pull their weight, the entire project can be jeopardized.

Reflect on your professional relationships. In your work relationships, do you feel a balance in the give-and-take, or are you often left carrying more of the load? Have you ever been in a business partnership or team where you felt one person wasn't contributing equally? What steps can you take to establish clearer expectations and ensure positive reciprocity in your professional life?

Lessons Learned

The irony should be obvious. Lack of reciprocity creates a cycle of insecurity. The more we give without "receiving" from someone, the more we question their intentions, our worth, and ultimately the relationship itself. Whether consciously or unconsciously, we all expect reciprocity. No matter how much we tell ourselves that we do for others without expectation of something in return, the reality is, at the very least, we want to be appreciated and not taken for granted. It doesn't hurt for the person on the receiving end of our "giving" to "give back." However, reciprocity is a form of sacrifice that not everyone is willing or able to make.

Ultimately, the key to successful and fruitful relationships of all kinds – romantic, friendships, family, and business – is reciprocity. Regardless of the type of relationship, by not expecting, requiring, or even by refusing reciprocity, the only possible result is imbalance, lack of fulfillment or failure. Eventually, if we don't expect or demand reciprocity, we will become frustrated, blaming the other person for not doing their part. That frustration may then lead to feelings of being taken advantage of and, even worse, feeling like we are unworthy of love and affection. Desiring reciprocity does not mean you expect a specific "thing," but may lie in the response you get from the other person. Reciprocity is a two-way street. If you aren't capable of giving it, you shouldn't expect to receive it.

Some connections are simply deeper than others, often for reasons we can't fully articulate. These relationships feel easier to manage, more fulfilling, and stand out as distinctly different from the rest. We may find ourselves more drawn to certain people, forming bonds that feel unbreakable, while other connections remain fragile and, at times, dispensable. In these soul-deep relationships, reciprocity isn't something we consciously think about—it emerges effortlessly. We give and receive in ways that go beyond surface-level interactions. The connection runs so deep that both people are attuned to each other's needs without having to ask. The care, understanding, and support come from a place of mutual respect and an unspoken sense of responsibility to one another's well-being.

The latter are common relationships we have on a regular basis with most people. They may be enjoyable situations and include great people. However, they also may come and go with little overall impact on our lives. The former, however, are those rare, extra-special relationships that originate from a "soul-connection" and are sustained because they are authentically RECIPROCAL. These are relationships that have Soul Reciprocity.

Reciprocity from the Mind involves calculating the balance in a relationship, essentially keeping score. You might find yourself thinking or saying things like, *"I've done more for this person than they've done for me,"* or *"I need to do more for them because they've done so much for me."* This type of reciprocity is transactional, focused on ensuring the exchange is equal in a measurable way. While this mindset can bring awareness to imbalances, it can also lead to resentment if you constantly feel like you're giving more than you're receiving.

Have you ever caught yourself mentally tallying the things you've done for someone? Maybe you've noticed the effort wasn't returned, and it left you feeling unappreciated. On the other hand, have you ever felt obligated to give more because someone has given a lot to you? That sense of obligation can sometimes create pressure and turn a friendship into a task, rather than a bond.

Reciprocity from the Heart is driven by emotions and doing what feels right in the moment, regardless of the balance. In this case, you're more likely to act based on what you hope to receive in return—be it love, acknowledgment, or affection. You may find yourself thinking, *"He'll love me if I do this,"* or *"She upset me, so I'm not going to speak to her right now."* This approach is less about keeping track and more about how you feel at any given time. However, it can also lead to emotional highs and lows, as your actions become tied to expectations of how the other person will respond.

Think about a time when you acted purely out of emotion in a relationship. Were you seeking validation or hoping for a specific reaction? Or maybe you withdrew when you were hurt or angry, waiting for the other person to make the first move. This kind of reciprocity can sometimes make relationships feel unpredictable, as actions are led by feelings rather than consistency.

The next chapter discusses and explains reciprocity from the soul, or Soul Reciprocity, which creates a unique, special kind of relationship.

QUESTIONS

1. Before reading this book, how did you define "reciprocity"? Did it change at all after reading this chapter? If so, how?
2. Have you ever been in a situation where you were unable to give reciprocity to someone? Describe that circumstance and how you felt about it.

3. Have you ever rejected or been uncomfortable with accepting reciprocity in a relationship? Why? Describe that circumstance and how you felt about it.
4. Which type of relationship (romantic, friendship, family, business) in your life has the most reciprocity and which has the least or is it about the same across the board? Why?

NEXT STEPS

After completing this chapter on Reciprocity, I invite you to dive deeper by taking the **Reciprocity Questionnaire** in *Appendix C*. This questionnaire will help you reflect on how reciprocity shows up in your relationships and where growth is possible.

4

SOUL + RECIPROCITY =

SOUL-FULL RELATIONSHIPS

"Tell me who I've got to be to get some reciprocity"
~ Lauryn Hill, Ex-Factor

The ultimate goal of this book is for each person who reads it to understand how to obtain optimal fulfillment in the most important relationships in their life, especially with themselves. I believe the key to that fulfillment is "Soul Reciprocity." However, to have it, you have to understand what it is and how to achieve it. So far, I have laid out some foundational principles to enable us to speak the same language. I have defined various relationships, explored differing perspectives on the definition of "soul," and explained why I view relationships from a soul perspective. I have also explained the various meanings of "reciprocity" and why I feel it is an important foundational element for successful relationships. We've determined that relationships are connections between people that exist as a result of some sort of interaction: daily experiences (i.e. work or school) or circumstantial situations (i.e. kinship). I believe some relationships come from "soul experiences."

Soul experiences connect us on a deeper level and ultimately form our closest relationships. These relationships are formed because people are drawn to each other from a place of connectivity originating deep within them and not just because of kinship or the environment where they meet. Because the connection comes from souls being drawn to one another, other natural forces take over, such as a desire for each person to "give of" themselves and "give to" the other person and vice versa.

People in relationships with Soul Reciprocity do two significant things: *nurture* and *nourish*. When viewing relationships from a soul perspective, you can see why the most successful relationships are those birthed from soul connections between like-minded people who willingly nurture each other. The soul connection roots the relationship and produces positive reciprocity where each person feels nourished. Thus, Reciprocity is effortless because the willingness and inclination to reciprocate comes from each persons' soul and is, in many ways, instinctive. The cycle of mutual nurturing makes relationships with Soul Reciprocity fulfilling and long-lasting. As such, these types of relationships are called "**Soul-Full Relationships.**"

What Is Soul Reciprocity?

Reciprocity occurs among most people in various forms. If, for instance, someone opens one door for you, you may hold the next door open for them. If you are paid a compliment, it may compel you to return one by saying something equally nice. If someone refers you a new client, you may send a thank-you message, give a financial reward, or even refer business in return. Reciprocity is great and can create a wonderful dynamic between people, but it's a cerebral process. You may have to think for a moment about what compliment to pay or toil over what gift to give. A mutual exchange occurs with some thought.

However, Soul Reciprocity is a deeper experience than ordinary reciprocity. Soul Reciprocity is a state of being driven by passion, purpose or a deep connection with certain people who have the same mindset, motivation and level of evolution. Simply put, it's a soul-level inclination you have within for some people. When you have Soul Reciprocity with someone, your desire to give, do, be mindful, help, and attend to that person is automatic. The give and take aren't necessarily even in the same moment. You constantly offer yourself to that person and naturally do things for them, check on them, go out of your way to make their day or show extra support because you understand who they are and what they need. You don't overthink your actions. That doesn't mean if you are planning something special for them that you don't even have to think it through. It means that you don't have to think it through to think of them.

What makes it a Soul-Full relationship is that they would and have done the same for you without much thought.

Soul Reciprocity is a state of ultimate alignment in our relationships. It's synergistic, a relational utopia of sorts. Having it makes connectedness easy – even in tough situations. Soul Reciprocity motivates us to push through situational discomfort or temporary challenges inevitable in all relationships. It is the core of Soul-Full friendships, marriages, family relationships, or business partnerships. Soul Reciprocity is the glue that holds together our most important relationships. When we struggle to achieve or experience this in our relationships, we must do "Soul Work" to achieve Soul-Full relationships.

Soul Reciprocity is achieved or expressed in Soul-Full Relationships. It occurs when you can identify your Soul Needs, acknowledge the Soul Needs of others, and together, choose to nourish and nurture one another with those Soul Needs in mind. A Soul-Less Relationship, on the other hand, is a connection characterized by superficial interactions, a lack of emotional depth, and an absence of mutual support and reciprocity. These relationships often leave individuals feeling drained and unfulfilled, as they lack the authenticity and shared values that foster genuine connection and growth. In Soul-Less relationships, there is often a noticeable imbalance in give-and-take. One party may consistently give more while the other takes without offering support or understanding in return. These relationships often revolve around superficial topics and interactions. Conversations may be polite but lack real intimacy or understanding. There is little to no emotional investment. People in these relationships may not feel comfortable expressing vulnerabilities or seeking support from one another. Love or acceptance in Soul-Less relationships may be based on conditions or expectations rather than unconditional support and understanding. In such dynamics, one or both parties may feel more like an obligation than a valued companion.

By nature, I like to believe I am a reciprocal person. I believe everyone deserves to receive what they give to some degree. So, when someone shows kindness, I do so in return. For instance, if I'm at a restaurant, I tip the waitstaff well to show appreciation for their service. When people give me gifts, I take pictures or videos of the gift and send it to them with a thank you to show them I know they put effort into thinking of me and that I put effort into showing my gratitude. Again, those are examples of reciprocation in its basic sense. It's social etiquette, thoughtfulness, grace, not Soul Reciprocity. With those whom I have Soul Reciprocity, I know at any given time, they are going to show up for me in ways I will need and appreciate when it happens. This includes instances when it's just checking on me to see how I'm doing or noticing that I seem "off" and leaning in to see what I need or full-on, over-the-top planning of a surprise birthday. Big or small, people with whom I have Soul Reciprocity seem to know what I need and when even when what I need is nothing much at all. I feel the same way about them. These are Soul-Full Relationships. For people in my Soul Tribe (Chapter 9) with whom I have Soul-Full Relationships, I may get a thought in the middle of a day to shoot a text "just thinking about you" or to tell them "I'm proud of you". I love a video text of well wishes or encouragement just because. I love creating "love boxes" inspired by my closest friends' favorite things. I may see a card a year in advance of a birthday, but because I know it's perfect for a specific person, I'll get it and hold onto it until their birthday comes. I don't have to force myself to think about these things. I don't have to "gear up" to do for them. My love is pure, automatic, and second nature for those with whom I have Soul Reciprocity. These acts of reciprocation aren't an act at all. It's just something rooted in my soul that connects us in ways that I just do what I do to show I care and they do the same.

What Soul Reciprocity is NOT

Just as important as understanding what Soul Reciprocity *is*, it's equally as important to understand what Soul Reciprocity *is not*. Soul Reciprocity is <u>not</u> achieved at the surface level of relationships, where you simply have a desire to be with another person. It does not exist by simply having things in common such as shared educational experiences or geographic background. It's not about sharing socioeconomic status (or seeking a socioeconomic status that someone else may have), it's not found in job titles, where you live, what you wear or what you drive. It's definitely not the result of mere physical attraction, popularity, public opinion or statistics.

Some may consider karma as a form of ultimate reciprocity. Karma is originally a doctrine in Hindu and Buddhist religions that is based the premise that one's actions in this life carry over to their next life where they will reap the consequences. In mainstream culture, karma is usually summed up as "you reap what you sow" and is therefore used to describe the connection between your actions to others and what happens to you. Karma is a consequence that can be either good or bad depending on the energy you project. If you "do good," then good should come to you. If you "do bad," then bad things will come back on you. To an extent, experiencing Soul Reciprocity is similar to experiencing karma, at least as it relates to the good things that come as a result of the "good" you put into a relationship. However, with Soul Reciprocity, the exchange between action and consequence is direct between the people involved, not potentially other people in other comparable situations as with karma. So, what you put into a relationship with someone with whom you have a Soul-Full connection is going to come back to you from that person. The cause and effect are directly between the parties who are aligned at a soul level. With karma, the consequence is not always directly tied to the associated people or action. So, for example, you may do a good deed for someone, and the positive karma may manifest in a completely different setting, at a different time or from a different person. I recall a story about a homeless person who found a wallet with a lot of money and, rather than keeping it, turned it in for the owner to reclaim. Then, the story went viral, and the homeless person received donations of hundreds of thousands of dollars and was able to buy a home. The good deed that was done came back around in the form of good deeds from others.

Unlike karma, Soul Reciprocity isn't about negative consequences. If what you are putting out is "bad," you aren't likely to be in a relationship with Soul Reciprocity. A Soul-Full relationship isn't predicated on bad intentions or negative actions. In fact, Soul Reciprocity can't be built on a foundation of negativity. That doesn't mean there aren't challenging times or that bad things don't happen to people in Soul-Full relationships. Within the world of Soul Reciprocity, even if one person does something harmful to the other, the intrinsic force that connects them at a soul level will cause the person who did harm to admit fault, apologize, recognize the impact of their actions and rectify it. Together, the parties will be inclined to find a resolution. In Soul Reciprocity, the mutual respect and love between a couple begets the desire to work through tough situations and not with one person punishing the other or seeking revenge.

Soul Reciprocity is obviously not achieved by one person giving and the other just receiving. It can't come from one person sacrificing and the other not. It won't result from obligation. Soul Reciprocity does not exist in an environment where the parties involved don't know who they are or what they need (from the soul level). It can't occur in a place where one person has done Soul Work and the other has not (or where neither person has done any Soul Work). Soul Reciprocity doesn't manifest where there is no desire to nourish or nurture one another. While relationships are not always in equal balance, Soul Reciprocity can definitely not be achieved if the relationship is unbalanced. No matter how much love, admiration, respect, desire or effort exists within one party, if the other party does not feel and demonstrate the same, there is no Soul Reciprocity.

Experiencing Soul-Full Connections

Although I feel truly blessed to have several Soul-Full connections in my life, there are two relationships that stand out as undeniable examples of what Soul-Full love should look and feel like. The first is my mother, who I previously discussed (Chapter 3 – Family Relationships). The second person I recognize as embodying Soul-Full love is Cornell, the man in my life. I describe our relationship in this chapter and later in the book (Chapter 14), but to be completely honest, it is our connection that inspired the phrase "Soul Reciprocity." With Cornell, I discovered what other relationships were missing and how those voids could be filled. Our friendship is rooted in our souls, transcending mere companionship; he is family to me. We share the same philosophy about what family means, whether in work or personal life. Our bond extends to being each other's business advisors and partners, creating Soul Reciprocity in every aspect of our lives.

The journey to recognizing our connection as a soul connection has been long and winding, marked by disconnection and eventual reunion over nearly 30 years. We've often drifted in and out of each other's lives, each reunion happening in a different season, prompting us to rediscover who we are at that moment. Despite the changes life brings, our core understanding of one another remains intact. Reflect on your own relationships:

are there people you've reconnected with after years apart? How did those reunions feel, and what did they teach you about yourself or them?

Cornell and I have both experienced growth, and we can empathize, show grace, and exercise patience with one another. This reciprocal understanding allows us to foster and support each other's continued evolution. Our depth of connection creates a shared yearning for mutual well-being. At this stage in our lives, it's crystal clear what our love is about and how it differs from any other love we've encountered. It embodies the essence of Soul Reciprocity, Soul-Full Love, and Soul-Full Relationships.

From our very first meeting, there was an instant chemistry and draw, paired with a camaraderie and playful friendship. We genuinely enjoy each other's company, never complaining about our time spent together. Ask yourself: who in your life makes you feel this way? Who do you find yourself effortlessly drawn to, where every moment spent together feels like a gift?

By reflecting on these relationships, we can better understand the essence of Soul-Full love and how it enriches our lives.

Is Your Relationship Soul-Full?

Understanding whether you are in a relationship that has a soul connection can be a tough thing to discern. You won't know what soul connections feel like until you have them and recognize that what you have is something at a soul level. This discernment is like the first time you ride a roller coaster. In preparation, people may have told you what riding a roller coaster feels like, explaining the anxiety and nervousness you get as the train climbs the first steep hill. They may tell you all of the things that raced through their heads or how they may have broken into a sweat or how their heart started racing. Then they may describe that moment at the top where they look around and see how far up they are or maybe they close their eyes in anticipation and fear. They may describe that brief moment at the top as an eternity or not enough time to catch their breath before the descent. When people talk about the feeling they have as the roller coaster shoots down the hill, they describe a vast array of experiences and feelings. For some, it is exhilaration and euphoria, throwing their hands in the air and laughing all at the same time. Others are frozen in fear, feeling as if their heart dropped into their stomach. They typically keep their eyes closed, hold the handlebars or the person next to them as tightly as possible, and they may even hold their breath the entire time. Regardless of which end of the spectrum people experience – terror or thrill – the first experience is so significant that most people will come away with different determinations on whether they ever ride a rollercoaster again. Some will immediately get in line for the next rollercoaster ride while others may decide to wait and try again after some time. Others will decide the experience was not for them and avoid roller coasters at all costs.

If you've never ridden a roller coaster, you can only imagine what it's like based on other people's descriptions and examples. To give you some perspective on what riding on a roller coaster feels like, people may provide examples from other adrenaline-triggering experiences, such as riding on an airplane or going down a steep hill fast in a car. If, for instance, you've ever been on an airplane and felt butterflies in your stomach on the ascent or a sense of helplessness, nervousness or fear while in the air or landing, this may be likened to riding on a steep roller coaster. Still, no matter how many times you've heard people describe their experience on a roller coaster ride, you still won't know what it feels like to you until you actually do it. The same is true for relationships with Soul-Full connections.

People will tell you what it feels like when they're with their best friend or the first time they fell in love. They can describe the love they have for certain family members, and the connection they have with their team at work. They will distinguish their good relationships from their bad and what they've learned from each. There will be people who will be able to describe those few relationships they have or had with a unique connectedness that transcends all, such as the best friend, the *favorite* family member, the "work wife" or "husband" or the love of their life. They will describe these extra special people differently than others. For instance, the best friend since childhood who, no matter how far away he or she may live or how much the friends communicate, has always been connected. Every time the Soul-Full friends see each other or speak, it's like there's been no distance or lapse in time. They know each other so well that they truly root for each other in every way through every season of life. They don't have to explain themselves to each other because there's always been something about that connection that is instinctive and full of grace. Similarly, in a family dynamic, the relationship with a grandmother may be different from other family members, yielding a soul connection that was revered and nurtured the grandchild throughout life. Or maybe it was an aunt or uncle who provided a safe haven and became a confidant who also provided life lessons and stern guidance that impacted the decisions a person made. At work, some people will describe a colleague as a "work husband" or "work wife," a term of endearment representative of the time spent together, and not an indication of any romantic relationship. The connection with that colleague is one of partnership and collective goal-seeking. Even though the Soul-Full connection is in a work context, it stands out amongst the rest because it flows differently and energetically. The close friendship that is formed with the work spouse makes the work environment feel not so much like work. So, ultimately, this kind of connection results in emotional connectivity that supercharges work, productivity, success, and morale in the workplace. Meanwhile, I think we lean in the most with open eyes and ears when people speak about the love of their life. From the time we're children and our parents describe how they met to the conversations we have with friends in mid-life who say they have *finally* fallen in love for the first time, yet perhaps they were married previously or thought they had been in love before, we thoroughly enjoy love stories. So, we always pay close attention when people reference "the one" or the "soulmate."

Just like the roller coaster stories, other people's stories of soul connections vary widely. However, also like the roller coaster stories, there is a similar undercurrent. People who speak of having found "the one" romantically, for instance, distinguish the type of love they feel from other situations. They will say that the person is their soulmate or that it was just something about the person that was indescribable, unlike anything they've ever felt before. The connection is deeper and the communication flows freer. Upon first meeting, there was an attraction, not necessarily physical, but something that pulls them towards each other, and it's mutual. They both think about each other constantly, prioritize each other, demonstrate their love for each other with actions, not only words. They are consistent and reliable, and they make each other feel like no one else can. They may describe looking into the other's eyes and seeing the person's soul or feeling safe in their presence. Even in resolving differences or in difficult times when things become uncomfortable, they make a conscious effort to get through them together and reflect on what they can do differently to avoid the situation from recurring. There's a team spirit to those relationships, so they feel an obligation to meet the expectations of the other person because they know it's reciprocal. They have Soul Reciprocity. We all seem to have a basic understanding that there are levels in relationships, and having a Soul-Full Relationship is the deepest level. Just like a roller coaster ride, no matter how many people tell us about their Soul-Full relationships and what their soul connections have felt like, we still won't know for ourselves until we experience them or can even recognize them.

In Soul-Full Relationships, reciprocity is never a question or issue. Whether in love, friendship, family, or even business, reciprocity naturally flows without motive or thought. These relationships are grounded in soul connections. In relationships with Soul Reciprocity, there's an automatic, almost instinctive, inclination to nurture and nourish each other. This dynamic sets them apart from others, as the give-and-take feels effortless and requires little conscious effort.

Ultimately, Soul Reciprocity is actually a destination. It's a place that you get to in key relationships where you experience a mutual support of "Soul Needs" to achieve a "Soul-Full Relationship." Like bees and flowers that have a symbiotic relationship, so too are Soul-Full Relationships. To better understand this concept, Section 2 of the book uses lessons from honeybees to explain. Bees are essential for flowers to grow, and flowers are essential for bees to survive. Thus, they nurture and nourish each other's needs; their relationship is reciprocal and that is why the bee/flower relationship is nature's perfect example of Soul Reciprocity.

QUESTIONS

1. Knowing what you now know, what does Soul Reciprocity mean to you?
2. Do you have relationships where reciprocity feels effortless? How do these differ from other connections in your life?
3. Do you think you have any Soul-Full relationships? Who are they with? What things in those relationship(s) exemplify Soul Reciprocity?
4. What aspects of relationships with Soul Reciprocity most appeal to you? Do you think you can achieve Soul Reciprocity in more relationships in your life?

NEXT STEPS

As you reflect on the insights shared in this chapter about reciprocity, consider how these concepts apply to your own life and relationships. To deepen your understanding and facilitate your journey toward Soul Reciprocity, take the **Reciprocity Questionnaire**, located in *Appendix D*. This self-assessment tool will help you evaluate your current relationships and identify areas for growth, enabling you to foster deeper connections and a more fulfilling life.

SECTION 1 SUMMARY: THE UNDERSTANDING

S O U L   R E F L E C T I O N S

Chapter 1 - The Basics Part I: Relationships

Soul Reciprocity is about first cultivating a loving relationship with yourself, which then allows you to form deeper, more meaningful connections with others. Relationships can be understood through three lenses:

1. Circumstantial, shaped by external factors like family or work;
2. Experiential, built through shared interactions and experiences; and
3. Soul-Based, which arises from a deeper internal connection and mutual self-awareness.

By exploring these perspectives, the reader is encouraged to assess their relationships and understand the significance of connections that go beyond surface-level interaction. Ultimately, soul-based relationships, founded on a profound recognition of kindred spirits, are the most fulfilling and enduring.

Chapter 2 - The Basics Park II: The Soul

The phrase Soul Reciprocity came to me as a way to succinctly explain the unfortunate end of my marriage. Outwardly, everything seemed perfect, but something essential was missing—a deep, mutual connection at the soul level. After years of reflection, I realized that despite many positives, the absence of Soul Reciprocity made the relationship unsustainable. When I shared this phrase with others, it immediately resonated, sparking self-reflection about their own relationships.

At its core, Soul Reciprocity is about the deep, authentic bond between two people, where both truly see and understand each other at a soul level. This goes beyond surface connections or shared experiences, requiring mutual self-awareness and alignment with one's true self.

Looking at different perspectives on the soul helps frame this idea:

1. Religious views see the soul as a divine gift, connecting us to God and representing the essence of life. In Christianity, Judaism, and Islam, the soul is often tied to our emotions, life force, and connection with the divine.
2. Spiritual views focus on the soul as our true self, the source of wisdom, love, and fulfillment. It is the part of us that recognizes authenticity in others and forms deep, meaningful connections.
3. 3.Scientific views explore concepts like Spiritual Intelligence (SQ), which integrates intellect and emotion to tap into the deeper wisdom of the soul, guiding us toward greater fulfillment and connection with others.

Through this lens, Soul Reciprocity becomes the key to understanding the relationships that matter most—the ones grounded in authentic, soul-level connections.

Chapter 3 - The Basics Part III: Reciprocity

Reciprocity is simple in theory but often challenging to apply in relationships. It's the foundation of trust and balance, where both people give and receive in ways that feel equal and meaningful. Without it, relationships—whether romantic, familial, or professional—become unbalanced and ultimately unsatisfying.

There are two types of reciprocity in relationships: 1. Positive Reciprocity, where goodwill is returned equally, and 2. Negative Reciprocity, where an imbalance creates discomfort or resentment. True reciprocity requires sacrifice, which includes giving time, energy, and resources even when it's not convenient, all because we value the relationship.

It's natural to expect reciprocity, and when it's missing, it leads to frustration or feeling undervalued. Reflect on your own relationships: Do they feel balanced? Are you giving and receiving equally?

Reciprocity isn't about keeping score; it's about a mutual flow of care and support. In those rare, deep relationships where reciprocity happens naturally, without thought or calculation, the bond feels effortless and fulfilling. These are the connections that go beyond the surface, grounded in true Soul Reciprocity.

Chapter 4 - Soul-Full Relationships

Soul Reciprocity is the key to fulfilling, lasting relationships. Unlike ordinary reciprocity, which is often calculated, Soul Reciprocity is an instinctive, effortless connection where both people naturally nurture and support each other. This creates Soul-Full Relationships built on mutual respect and adoration between people who are drawn to each other from the soul. In contrast, Soul-Less Relationships lack depth and leave individuals feeling drained or unsupported.

Soul Reciprocity isn't about keeping score—it's about meeting each other's Soul Needs in a way that feels natural and fulfilling. Whether in friendships, family, romance, or business, this deep connection forms the foundation of meaningful relationships, where mutual support is instinctive and enduring.

SECTION 2:

THE PREPARATION

Lessons from Bees

5

THE BEES

UNDERSTANDING YOUR ROLE

"Your soul has become an invisible bee. We don't see it working, but there's the full honeycomb."
~ Rumi, An Invisible Bee

I've always been fascinated by bees, their behavior, their work and their symbolism. It just so happens that bees and their behavior are in many ways analogous to principles of Soul Reciprocity, where it comes from and what it looks like into the kinds and characteristics of bees. It may seem unusual to compare human relationships to those between insects and plants, but this analogy can offer valuable insights into forming deep, soul connections. We often struggle to understand others and ourselves, avoiding the hard questions about who we really are. However, to achieve Soul Reciprocity, you need to do Soul Work that requires self-analysis to discover your Soul Identity and Soul Needs. By using bees and their behavior as a metaphor, my goal is to help you reflect on yourself and your own relationships from the soul perspective. As you read, consider the parallels with your own life.

Bees are known for many admirable characteristics, traits and even spiritual and mythological symbolisms. Some of those traits and symbolisms. All which directly correlate to those found in humans. Some of those traits and symbolisms include:

- Hard work and endurance
- Intentionality
- Loyalty

- Consistency
- Reciprocate
- Cooperative nature
- Fertility and productivity
- Abundance
- Connection to soul

Like the relationship between bees and flowers, human relationships built from Soul-Full connections are natural and they draw from one Soul to the other in instinctive ways. While there are numerous ways people with soul connections find one another, they don't in fact have any specific overt path. Instead, the energy that attracts Souls to each other comes from each person's self-awareness, knowledge of self and their own needs, empathy for others, ability to sacrifice, one's nurturing spirit and the way one lives their life which is an example of who they really are at the Soul level. It's quite an amazing thing to experience when Souls recognize Souls. And it creates the perfect environment for relationships with Soul Reciprocity.

The Bee in You

Bees are found on every continent except Antarctica. According to the U.S. Forest Service, there are 49 species of bumblebees in the U.S. However, only one kind makes honey: **the honeybee**. Honeybees are the only type of bee that dies after stinging. They don't sleep; instead, they spend their nights motionless, conserving energy for the next day's activities. Honeybees travel up to 3 miles away from the hive in search of nectar and pollen and will visit between 50 and 100 flowers during their trip. They go to great lengths to take care of the hive/tribe. During the winter, some worker bees take on the job of "heater bees," where they vibrate their bodies in order to keep the hive at the optimal temperature of 95°F.

Interestingly, bees also have distinct roles, or follow an order, for everything they do, which is similar to the various ways people contribute to their communities, families, and personal lives. Just as honeybees play a vital role in their hive, people can have unique roles and contributions in their relationships, families, workplaces, and society as a whole.

A closer examination of the characteristics of bees reveals even more parallels to various types of people:

1. **Self-sacrifice**: Honeybees are known for their self-sacrificing nature. When they sting, the stinger gets embedded in the target, leading to the bee's death. Similarly, some people are incredibly selfless, putting the needs and well-being of others above their own. They are willing to make sacrifices for the greater good and the well-being of their loved ones or community.
2. **Diligence and hard work**: Honeybees are diligent and hardworking creatures. They tirelessly collect nectar and pollen from flowers, traveling long distances to gather resources for the hive. Likewise, some individuals exhibit a strong work ethic, dedicating themselves to their responsibilities and tasks. They show perseverance and a commitment to achieving their goals.
3. **Care for the collective**: Honeybees take care of their hive as a collective unit. They work together to maintain the hive's temperature and ensure its survival. Similarly, some people prioritize the well-being and harmony of their communities or families. They actively contribute to creating a supportive and nurturing environment, taking on responsibilities that benefit the collective rather than solely focusing on their individual needs.
4. **Conservation and energy management**: Honeybees conserve energy by remaining motionless during the night. This energy conservation allows them to be active and productive during the day. Similarly, some individuals recognize the importance of balancing rest and activity, managing their energy effectively to accomplish their tasks and goals while maintaining their well-being.

Kinds of Honeybees

Another Fun Fact: More than one half, about 80 percent, of all fruit and vegetable crops are pollinated by honeybees. Because they maintain a reciprocal relationship with human beings, the behavior of honeybees has been well-researched. Honeybees live in well-organized colonies and are best known for their production of honey, which they store in wax combs inside nests. There are three different types of honeybees in a hive: Worker,

Drone and Queen. Worker bees are always female and are the only bees to have stingers. Drones are always male, and only the Queen can reproduce.

Worker Bees

Tens of thousands of worker bees, all female, collaborate to build nests, gather food, and nurture larvae, while the queen lays eggs and drones assist in reproduction. A colony has one queen and thousands of workers, each capable of carrying nectar or pollen up to 80% of their body weight. Workers, although infertile, are essential to the hive's survival. Young workers care for larvae, while older ones collect and store food. As adults, they transition to foraging, where they gather resources for the colony.

Initially called "house bees," they clean, construct combs, and maintain the hive. As they age, they become "field bees," collecting nectar, pollen, and other materials. Worker bees have specialized body parts, including an extra stomach for nectar, pollen baskets on their legs, and glands that produce beeswax.

In relationships within a hive/colony (tribe), some people are like worker bees, and exhibit the following characteristics:

1. **Industriousness and productivity**: Worker bees are known for their tireless work ethic. They fulfill a variety of essential tasks within the hive, such as foraging for food, building and maintaining the hive, and caring for the young. Similarly, some individuals embody the characteristics of worker bees by being industrious and productive. They are diligent, responsible, and dedicated to their work, often taking on multiple responsibilities and actively contributing to their communities or workplaces.
2. **Teamwork and collaboration**: Worker bees thrive in a cooperative environment. They work together harmoniously, fulfilling their designated roles to benefit the hive as a whole. Likewise, some individuals excel in collaborative settings. They value teamwork, actively contribute to group efforts, and support the achievement of collective goals. Their ability to collaborate and cooperate with others enhances productivity and fosters a positive work or social environment.
3. **Adaptability and flexibility**: Worker bees are adaptable creatures. They adjust their activities based on the needs of the hive,

responding to changes in resources, environmental conditions, and the overall health of the colony. Similarly, some individuals possess adaptability and flexibility in their approach to various situations. They can easily adjust to changing circumstances, take on new responsibilities, and navigate challenges with resilience.
4. **Service-oriented mentality**: Worker bees have a service-oriented mentality. They dedicate their lives to the well-being of the hive, placing the collective needs above their own. Similarly, some individuals have a natural inclination to help and serve others. They are compassionate, empathetic, and find fulfillment in supporting and uplifting those around them. Their service-oriented mindset often leads them to pursue professions or activities that involve helping others.

People who exhibit characteristics similar to worker bees embody an industrious, collaborative, adaptable, and service-oriented mindset. Their contributions and efforts are valuable in creating thriving communities, workplaces, and relationships.

Drones

Drones, or male bees, are the minority in a colony and serve only one purpose: to mate with virgin honeybee queens. Soon after mating, drones die. These male bees are fed by the worker bees. To avoid wasting food on drones during the winter, the worker bees drive them out of the hive in the fall. This is pretty easy to do since male bees have no stinger.

In relationships within a hive/colony (tribe), some people are more like drones and exhibit the following characteristics:
1. **Self-Serving**: Drones in a bee colony have a specific reproductive role. Their primary function is to mate with the queen bee, they have very short lifespans, but while alive, they depend on nurse worker bees to feed them. Their focus is strictly on their (important) job to populate the hive. Similarly, some individuals may possess qualities associated with drones, where they may have a focus on their personal desires, interests, or pursuits. They may prioritize self-expression, personal growth, or the pursuit of their own goals.

2. **Limited tasks and responsibilities**: Drones have limited responsibilities within the hive compared to worker bees. They do not participate in tasks such as foraging, building the hive, or caring for the young. Their primary purpose is to mate, and once that is fulfilled, they do not contribute significantly to the overall functioning of the colony, but their role plays a key part in the colony's survival. Similarly, some individuals may have a limited scope of responsibilities or contributions within their social or professional circles. They may prioritize personal pursuits or be less engaged in collective responsibilities. Though their overall scope of work may be limited, because they are purpose-driven, their results can be impactful.

3. **Dependence on others**: Drones rely on worker bees for their sustenance and maintenance. They do not possess the same level of self-sufficiency as worker bees and depend on the collective efforts of the hive for their well-being. Similarly, some individuals may rely heavily on others for support, guidance, or resources. They may prioritize relationships or external sources for their needs, rather than actively taking initiative or self-sufficiency.

4. **Individuality and uniqueness**: Drones, being male bees, possess distinct physical characteristics that differentiate them from worker bees and the queen bee. In this sense, drones can represent individuality and uniqueness. Some individuals may value and embrace their unique qualities, expressing their individuality through their thoughts, actions, or personal pursuits.

Like drones, certain people have similar characteristics, such as individuality, self-focus, selfish and lack of self-sufficiency. At the same time, people with these traits can be of extreme value to the world at large by their contributions through their "purpose."

Queens

Queen honeybees mate with drones, establish new colonies, and lay eggs. She can use her stinger more than once. Queens produce pheromones that unite the bee tribe socially under their rule. Thus, they unite the tribe and keep the colony going.

In relationships within a hive/colony (tribe), some people are more like queen honeybees and exhibit the following characteristics:

1. **Leadership and authority**: Queens bees are the central figure in a bee colony. They are responsible for leading and guiding the hive. Similarly, some individuals metaphorically associated with queens exhibit leadership qualities. They possess natural charisma, influence, and the ability to inspire and guide others. They may take on leadership roles in their communities, workplaces, or relationships.
2. **Fertility and reproduction**: Queen bees are the reproductive core of the colony. They lay eggs and ensure the survival and growth of the hive. Similarly, some individuals may embody the characteristics of queens by having a strong focus on family, nurturing, and the continuation of lineage. They prioritize relationships, parenting, or caretaking roles.
3. **Confidence and assertiveness**: Queen bees exude confidence and assertiveness. They command respect and establish their presence within the colony. Similarly, some individuals possess a confident and assertive demeanor. They are self-assured, vocal about their needs and desires, and are comfortable taking charge in various situations.
4. **Influence and impact**: Queen bees have a significant influence on the behavior and dynamics of the colony. Their pheromones affect the behavior and productivity of worker bees. Likewise, some people have a strong impact on the people around them. They possess the ability to inspire, motivate, or influence others positively

The concept of queens in bee colonies may not directly align with human social structures because leadership and authority can manifest in different ways, and individuals may exhibit leadership qualities in various contexts. Furthermore, societal roles and expectations can vary, and each person's contributions, strengths, and impact may differ based on their personal aspirations, values, and circumstances.

Human Complexities

It's important to recognize and appreciate the diverse capabilities and potentials individuals possess. Just as bees can switch roles based on the needs of the colony, individuals can demonstrate a range of qualities and behaviors depending on the circumstances they find themselves in, allowing them to contribute in different ways.

Ultimately, while some honeybees serve a specific purpose within a colony, in human societies, the roles and contributions individuals make can vary greatly based on immediate needs and occurrences, and societal expectations are diverse and ever-evolving. Individuals can exhibit different qualities and behaviors based on the circumstances they find themselves in. While someone may typically embody characteristics metaphorically associated with a drone, there may be situations where they can display qualities akin to a queen bee.

People have the capacity to adapt and adjust their behavior depending on the context and their roles and responsibilities. Just as a drone bee may have limited tasks within the hive but can exhibit unique qualities during specific events, individuals can tap into different aspects of their personality and abilities as needed. For example, someone who usually takes a more passive or supportive role in a group may step up and assume a leadership position when the situation calls for it. They may display confidence, assertiveness, and the ability to guide and inspire others when necessary, similar to a queen bee.

This dynamic nature of individuals highlights the versatility and complexity of human behavior. It also emphasizes that individuals are not limited to a single role or set of traits. The ability to adapt and take on different roles is a reflection of the multifaceted nature of human beings

Wannabees

While some people may exhibit traits similar to honeybees, others may align more with the characteristics of other types of bees or have unique qualities that make them bee-like, or "wannabees." Some harmless insects mimic bees to trick predators into thinking they're armed with a sting. Others are relatives that have a convincing family resemblance. What kinds of bees or insects look like honeybees but are not? These are some: hover flies, bee flies, yellowjackets, hornets, paper wasps, and hummingbird moths.

Hover Flies

Insects such as hover flies that mimic the appearance of honeybees belong to different species. In fact, most honeybee look-a-likes are hover flies. These harmless flies cannot sting. Some hoverflies resemble solitary bees or honeybees such as drone flies. There are also hairy species that mimic bumblebees called a bumblebee hoverfly.

Some individuals operate like these "wannabees" in the context of their behavior or characteristics in the following ways:

1. **External appearance**: Hover flies have evolved to resemble honeybees in their appearance, benefiting from the honeybees' defense mechanisms that deter predators. Similarly, some individuals may adopt certain behaviors, attitudes, or appearances to imitate or align themselves with a particular group or ideal. They may seek to gain acceptance, recognition, or advantages associated with that group.

2. **Imitation without substance**: While hover flies may visually resemble honeybees, they do not possess the same attributes, behaviors, or roles within the ecosystem. Similarly, individuals metaphorically referred to as "wannabees" may attempt to emulate the characteristics or accomplishments of others without truly embodying them. They may lack the depth, substance, or authenticity that comes with genuinely embracing and developing their own unique qualities and contributions.

3. **Lack of individuality**: Hover flies, as mimics, may struggle to establish their own distinct identity and may be overshadowed by the presence of the bees they imitate. Similarly, individuals who exhibit "wannabee" behaviors may find themselves lacking a genuine sense of self or struggling to express their own individuality. They may prioritize conforming to others' expectations or standards, compromising their authenticity and personal growth.

4. **Missed opportunities for self-discovery**: Hover flies that mimic honeybees miss out on fulfilling their own ecological roles

and potential contributions. Similarly, individuals who consistently emulate others may miss opportunities for self-discovery, personal growth, and the realization of their own unique abilities and aspirations. By focusing on imitation, they may limit their own potential and hinder their own journey of self-actualization.

Bee Flies

Another fly in bee's clothing is the bee fly. These brown, hairy flies look rather like brown carder bumblebees and male hairy-footed flower bees. Masters of disguise, they also feed from the same flowers with a jerky, hovering flight.

While bee flies are another example of insects that resemble honeybees, they are not actual bees. Some individuals operate like these "wannabees" in the context of their behavior or characteristics in the following ways:

1. **External appearance and imitation**: Bee flies mimic the physical appearance of honeybees, likely for their own protection or to gain advantages associated with bees. Similarly, individuals metaphorically referred to as "wannabees" may imitate certain aspects of a particular group or individual to fit in or gain benefits, recognition, or acceptance. They may adopt similar behaviors, styles, or attitudes to project an image of belonging.

2. **Lack of substance and authenticity**: While bee flies may visually resemble honeybees, they do not possess the same biological characteristics, behaviors, or roles within ecosystems. Similarly, individuals labeled as "wannabees" may lack the depth, substance, or authenticity that comes from developing their own unique identities, talents, and contributions. They may prioritize external appearances or conformity, compromising their ability to express their true selves.

3. **Shallow engagement and missed opportunities**: Bee flies, as mimics, may not engage in the same behaviors or fulfill the ecological roles of honeybees. Likewise, individuals who exhibit "wannabee" tendencies may miss out on authentic experiences and meaningful connections. By focusing on imitation rather than genuine engagement, they may limit their own growth, hinder

their personal development, and miss opportunities for genuine connections and self-discovery.
4. **Lack of individuality and self-expression**: Bee flies that mimic honeybees may struggle to establish their own distinct identity and may be overshadowed by the genuine bees they imitate. Similarly, individuals labeled as "wannabees" may find themselves lacking a genuine sense of self or struggling to express their own unique perspectives and talents. They may prioritize conforming to others' expectations or imitating others' accomplishments, limiting their ability to cultivate their own individuality.

Wasps

Wasps are bee's closest relatives. In fact, bees are really like a vegetarian group of wasps. Say what? There are many species of social wasps. They may seem annoying and even scary, but they are useful because not only do they pollinate, but they also hunt pests like caterpillars, aphids and planthoppers.

Wasps may bear a striking resemblance to honeybees, but they belong to a different species. Some individuals operate like these "wannabees" in the context of their behavior or characteristics in the following ways:
1. **Deceptive appearance**: Wasps may share visual similarities with honeybees, which can serve as a form of protection or advantage. Similarly, individuals metaphorically referred to as "wannabees" may adopt certain traits or behaviors to project an image that aligns with the perceived benefits or recognition associated with a particular group or role.
2. **Aggressive or opportunistic behavior**: Wasps are known for their more aggressive nature and opportunistic behaviors compared to honeybees. Metaphorically, individuals labeled as "wannabees" may exhibit similar characteristics, such as adopting aggressive or opportunistic approaches to achieve their goals or secure personal gains, often at the expense of others.
3. **Lack of genuine purpose or contribution**: Wasps, unlike honeybees, do not play a significant role in pollination or honey production. Similarly, individuals identified as "wannabees" may

lack a genuine sense of purpose or a meaningful contribution to their communities or relationships. They may focus more on personal gains or self-interest rather than actively participating in and benefiting the collective.
4. **Disruption and negative impact**: Wasps can be disruptive and may cause harm, both physically and in terms of ecosystem balance. Similarly, individuals metaphorically associated with "wannabees" may bring disruption or negative influence to their social circles or communities. Their behavior or actions may undermine harmony, cooperation, or the overall well-being of those around them.

Hornets (Yellowjackets)

Hornets and yellowjackets are types of wasps. Hornets nest above ground, and yellowjackets nest in the ground. They defend their nest aggressively by stinging when their colony is threatened. Unlike with the honeybee, they can sting more than once. They resemble honeybees but belong to different species called vespidae. Similar to honeybees, they are social creatures that live in colonies.

Some individuals operate like these "wannabees" in the context of their behavior or characteristics in the following ways:
1. **Visual resemblance**: Hornets or yellowjackets share similar physical features and coloration with honeybees. Similarly, individuals metaphorically referred to as "wannabees" may adopt behaviors, styles, or attitudes to imitate the perceived benefits or recognition associated with a particular group or role.
2. **Aggressive or confrontational behavior**: Hornets and yellowjackets are known for their more aggressive and confrontational nature compared to honeybees. Similarly, individuals labeled as "wannabees" may exhibit similar characteristics, displaying aggression, confrontational tendencies, or an overly competitive approach in their interactions with others.
3. **Self-centeredness and self-interest**: Hornets and yellowjackets primarily focus on their own survival and interests rather than contributing to the greater ecosystem. Metaphorically, individuals associated with

"wannabees" may prioritize their own gains, self-interest, or personal agenda over the collective well-being or the needs of others.
4. **Disruption and negative impact**: Hornets and yellowjackets can be disruptive and pose a threat to other organisms, including honeybees. Similarly, individuals metaphorically identified as "wannabees" may bring disruption, negativity, or harm to their social circles or communities. Their behavior or actions may undermine cooperation, harmony, or the overall well-being of those around them.

Similar to wannabees, people may engage in imitation or emulation for various reasons. For instance, some individuals may temporarily adopt certain traits or behaviors as part of their self-discovery process or exploration of different identities. Ultimately, though, embracing one's own individuality, strengths, pursuing personal growth, and cultivating genuine connections with others (and not imitation) are essential for personal fulfillment and building meaningful relationships and communities.

Once a person reaches a point of self-acceptance that results from the process of self-discovery, they can make a difference in their own lives of others and the world around them. This is the primary reason we engage in Soul Work and why it's so important to do so.

Busy as a Bee - Soul Work

We've all heard the saying "busy as a bee," meaning that someone works extremely hard or continually. Bees are some of the hardest working, most diligent insects. Their work is, in fact, critical to the existence of many plants and the survival of their species. Similarly, Soul Work is critical to achieving Soul Reciprocity and the creation and maintenance of Soul-Full relationships with others.

Soul Work is the process of self-reflection, self-identification, assessment (of yourself and others) and self-discovery. It's the work you have to put in order to enable yourself to give and receive Soul Reciprocity. I'll talk about it in more detail in Chapter 6.

You will notice that I repeat this phrase multiple times in this book: Soul Reciprocity is a destination." In order to get there, you have to do the

WORK, not just any kind of work. In order to achieve Soul Reciprocity, you must do SOUL WORK, which entails the following:
1. Discover Your Soul Identity (Chapter 6)
2. Identify Your Soul Needs (Chapter 7)
3. Producing Reciprocity (Chapter 8)

Everyone should do Soul Work as a matter of creating healthy, balanced Soul-Full Relationships. These are a few signs that you don't have this type of relationship at home, work, church, social groups, and so forth:
- You are doing all the "work"
- You feel unfulfilled or unhappy
- Your needs are ignored or minimized
- You get no acknowledgment or appreciation
- You invest most of the resources, such as money
- The communication is toxic or abusive
- You feel obligated instead of motivated to spend time with certain people

Where do you go from here? First, you prepare yourself to do Soul Work. Just like any other journey, you take time to get prepared. Think about a flight. In order to get ready for take-off, the flight attendant gives you a list of things to do: look around, seat back up, tray table locked, items stowed away, window shades up. The same is true for preparing to do Soul Work. You have to do a self-check and assess your surroundings so that you know you are ready for the journey. Do you really know yourself at the soul level? Are you clear about your Soul Needs? What are you missing? Ask yourself questions like those above. Once you have the answers to the preparatory questions, you will likely determine that you have more questions and that there are voids in your life that have you in a state of confusion or unfulfillment. With this presence of mind, we do Soul Work, the work that assists you in finding your Soul Identity, discovering your Soul Needs, and removing all impediments to Soul Reciprocity. Sometimes, we also need to do Soul Work to recommit to Soul-Full principles we have abandoned or forgotten. Once you've done the work, you will receive the ultimate reward, you will discover your Soul Tribe.

UNDERSTANDING YOUR ROLE

How often do you do Soul Work? As much as is necessary to ensure you have a thriving Soul Tribe, people who reciprocate and fill you as much as you fill them.

Once you complete the process, you will know who you are like never before, reap the benefits of your work and understand your core needs with clarity and conviction. You will know who should be in the tribe and will be ready to experience the beauty of Soul Reciprocity in your closest relationships. But if you haven't taken the steps and done the work, you won't know how to give or receive Soul Reciprocity in your life.

The reality is that it's impossible to experience Soul Reciprocity without doing the work and going through a process of self-discovery first. Once you have done that work, you will see yourself and the world around you differently. And the world will see you differently as well. The people who are supposed to be in your tribe will seem to just appear because your Souls can "see" each other. These are the special people who are capable of Soul Reciprocity because they too have done the Soul Work.

QUESTIONS

1. Which type of "bee" best represents your role in relationships? Do you see yourself as a self-sacrificing worker bee, a nurturing queen bee, or more like a drone, focused on your own needs?
2. What qualities do you share with bees, such as being hardworking, adaptable, loyal, or consistent? How do these traits show up in your relationships?
3. Can you relate to "wannabees"—insects that resemble honeybees but aren't? If so, how? How do you perceive your interactions with those who engage in imitation or emulation?

6

THE MEADOW

DISCOVERING YOUR SOUL IDENTITY

"The greatest discovery in life is self-discovery. Until you find yourself, you will always be someone else. Become yourself."
~ Miles Munroe

Achieving Soul Reciprocity means reaching the ultimate destination—a place where your most important relationships thrive because they nurture and nourish you at the deepest, soul level. However, to get there, you must embark on a journey of self-discovery, one that covers many terrains. Along the way, you'll encounter challenges, revelations, and growth.

Imagine that in your quest for Soul Reciprocity, you approach a meadow. This meadow represents a space of personal exploration and transformation. Just like the wildflowers and grasses that bloom each year, your soul is growing and evolving. Bees, symbolizing the connections and support from others, help the meadow flourish. Similarly, the relationships you nurture along the way will contribute to your soul's evolution.

The meadow is a place where you discover your Soul Identity—where self-awareness takes root. Individuals may have revelations about themselves, gaining insights into their true nature, purpose, and identity. Just as wildflowers may bloom and reveal their beauty in different ways, individuals may have unique experiences and realizations about their soul's identity and path.

Each different type of wildflower represents the unique aspects of yourself, and through Soul Work, you tend to both your strengths and weaknesses. This work, like cultivating the meadow, allows you to grow into the best version of yourself. But it's not just about your individual journey; it's also about the interconnectedness with others, just as wildflowers grow together and thrive through mutual support.

As you journey through this meadow, you get closer to Soul Reciprocity, a place where your relationships bloom and your soul is nourished.

Soul Identity: Discovering Who You Really Are

Understand this: If you don't know who you truly are, how can you know what you really want? The answer is simple. You can't. It's impossible.

There are seemingly infinite resources all around us for self-improvement and self-help. We are encouraged by books, apps, programs and motivational speeches to identify what we want out of life, who we want to be, and to seek out what we need. We set goals to eat better, lose weight, make more money, reduce stress and live our best lives. We're given recipes, meal plans, workout regimens, career advice and all kinds of programs to join and products to buy. All of those things are great and help us to set goals and be better, but where is the emphasis on the importance of knowing our "WHY"? Why are we in need of losing weight? What got us there? Why don't we make or have enough money? Why are we stressed and why aren't we living our best lives? It's one thing to want to improve ourselves, but it's something else to take the time to face the reality of who we are so we can understand why we are in the place where we need the improvements we seek to make. If we don't take time to look at ourselves and how we have contributed to our situations, the chances are that we will eventually end up right back where we started no matter how many self-improvement road maps we follow.

I believe that understanding who you really are is the only way to optimize a self-improvement journey, to know what you want, who you want to be or what you need. Most importantly, knowing who you are is the only way to get to your "why." And quite frankly, until you are clear about who you are, you can't optimize your journey to self-improvement and fulfillment in life.

That is why the first step to achieving Soul Reciprocity in your life is to understand your Soul Identity. To discover your "Soul Identity," you have to go through a process of self-discovery that requires a level of honesty and reflection you may have never been willing or able to do before. But it's necessary. So often, we are afraid to turn the mirror around and look at ourselves honestly and without a filter.

Without blaming external circumstances or other people for how or why we are who we are. But if we are being honest, really honest, with ourselves and are fully open to the change that can come if we are, this is the lens through which we need to look in order to understand who we really are. So, the journey begins here. A journey into self-realization, self-awareness and self-discovery.

The Crossroads

Maybe you've reached a critical moment, a crossroad, where a decision will significantly impact the course of your life. These moments signal a turning point where you must choose a path, often related to career, relationships, personal growth, or major life transitions. Crossroads can bring feelings of uncertainty, even anxiety, but they also present opportunities for growth, self-discovery, and positive change.

In 2015, I found myself standing in my walk-in closet, compelled to take a "before" picture in my sports bra and biker shorts. I had promised myself countless times that I would lose weight, hoping this image would serve as accountability. Behind me were designer clothes and shoes—evidence of indulgence not just in food but also in material possessions. I snapped the photo and thought little of it at the time.

At that point, I was overwhelmed by both home and work responsibilities. My law practice was flourishing, and I felt I had no right to complain. However, the lifestyle I had grown accustomed to was financially draining. My ex-husband, whom I had encouraged to return to the music industry, was struggling to find work, leaving me to cover all household expenses, including support for his three kids from previous relationships. As the primary breadwinner, the pressure mounted, especially since we had relocated to Los Angeles, significantly increasing our living costs.

Adding to the chaos, one of the children faced severe personal challenges. I worked with my ex and his ex-wife to find solutions to help. I thought we were working collectively to find professional help to ensure his daughter received adequate support. Yet, without my knowledge, a unilateral decision was made for her to move in with us. And I discovered this plan just five days before her scheduled arrival and first day of school! To add insult to injury, my ex didn't tell me this change of plan. Instead, I found out while browsing the family computer. I felt blindsided and overwhelmed. This was my breaking point. Not even two weeks prior, I had cried to my ex about needing more help carrying the load. Rather than finding solutions to help, even more responsibilities were added to the household. I was at a crossroads in my life, and I had no idea which way to go.

I chose flight over the fight. I booked a one-way flight to Florida and left to stay with my mother indefinitely. For weeks, I had begged my ex to help me manage the household responsibilities, but the pressure of being the breadwinner and catering to his needs and the needs of his children was too much to bear. At the same time, I did not want my breakdown and the state of our relationship to affect the transition of an innocent child, so I left. I was constantly solving problems for my clients, my family, and myself, often feeling unappreciated and unsupported. I was a "fixer," overwhelmed by my obligation to help others, yet feeling as if no one was there for me in return.

Upon arriving at my mother's, I was assured that everything was fine, the transition was smooth for his daughter. However, when I returned home a few weeks later, I was met with even more chaos. He lied to lure me into returning, and again, I had to take charge to create structure and manage the household. Meanwhile, the narrative created was that I abandoned the family in a critical time of need while he was portrayed as the hero-father.

This experience, while overwhelming, forced me to confront my reality. I realized I could either lose myself entirely or embark on a journey of self-discovery. I chose the latter. I began asking myself hard questions: Who was I? What was my purpose? Why was I fulfilled in some areas of life yet empty in others? I sought therapy, enrolled in a mind-body-spirit boot camp, and turned inward to find the answers I desperately needed.

For any of us seeking deeper fulfillment, there's a moment—that moment—when you know you need change. It's a time to pause and reflect.

Often, it's uncomfortable, even painful, as you confront the reality of your circumstances. You may want to blame others, the world, or even God for what has happened in your life. But when you're ready to take ownership of your situation, to stop playing the victim and start moving toward your true self, that's when the real journey begins.

In Soul Reciprocity, this pivotal moment—when life's demands feel overwhelming and you feel distanced from your true self—is described as a crossroads, an invitation to evolve. This moment acts as a doorway to self-discovery, where stepping forward allows you to enter a vast "meadow" of potential and reconnect with your Soul Identity, the authentic self beneath all societal expectations and internalized noise. Embracing this moment is a profound opportunity for personal transformation, aligning your life with what holds real meaning and rediscovering what genuinely resonates with you at your core.

Making Changes

Human beings are creatures of habit, so changing deeply ingrained habits can be difficult. Breaking away from familiar patterns and establishing new routines requires conscious effort, discipline, and persistence. Whether it's a career change, relationship transition, or relocation, navigating the unknown can be daunting. The lack of a clear road map or immediate answers can create anxiety and make change feel overwhelming. However, when the negative impact of not making necessary life changes outweighs the fears, uncertainties and complexities of making those changes, the decision becomes compulsory. That was my situation.

The decision to begin to make changes in my life came during what seemed like an ordinary day. I was sitting in a hair salon with one of my dearest friends, feeling completely disconnected from myself. I had returned from "running away from home" and found myself back on the hamster wheel. So much had changed in my mind, but nothing was changing in my day to day experience and I had no idea what to do to change any of it. I told her how lost I felt—overweight, overextended, burdened, helpless, lacking confidence, and wondering when I had lost my "mojo." I also had no idea how to solve the imbalances in my marriage or what to do if there were no solutions.. Despite having much to be grateful for, I was struggling internally. I had lost myself, and I had no idea how to get back to that place of self-assurance and peace.

As I poured my heart out, my girlfriend, who seemed to have it all together—fit, beautiful, successful—looked at me and said, "Sister, you should join my trainer's next boot camp with me! We'll do it together. It'll be just what you need!" I was stunned. My girlfriend who was the picture of fitness, was inviting me to a boot camp? I thought boot camps were for people like me—"fluffy" girls who needed a serious push to get back on track. What was she doing in a boot camp?

Nevertheless, I decided to give it a try. This was my "ah ha" moment. I realized that to make a real change. I had to do something different, something that felt uncomfortable but necessary. While sitting under that dryer, I signed up before I could talk myself out of it. When I got the confirmation email, to my surprise, it welcomed me to the "Mind-Body Fitness Challenge." It instructed us all to come as we are, but to bring a towel, yoga mat, water, and a journal. I was definitely nervous and a bit confused. On the first day of boot camp, I showed up ready, with my brand-new outfit, yoga mat covered in positive affirmations, and a never-used journal that my mother had given me. When I walked in, my heart sank. The room was filled with women who looked like they had just stepped out of a high-end athleisure catalog—thin, toned, and confident. Then there was the trainer, Ashley, a blonde bombshell with a radiant smile, perfect physique, and a calm, joyful energy. They were all clones of my girlfriend!

I wanted to turn around and leave. There was no way I belonged there, but I stayed. Something inside me knew this was my crossroads leading me to changes. I had to push through the discomfort and fear of not fitting in, not being enough. It wasn't just about weight or fitness—it was about reclaiming "myself." This was about more than shedding pounds; it was about shedding the self-doubt, the guilt, the chaos, the confusion and the shame. It was about stepping back into my power, my confidence, my Soul Identity.

November 10, 2015, was the first day of bootcamp and it was the beginning of many revelations to come. Ashley explained that the bootcamp was designed not only to kick our butts, but also to challenge our mindsets. It was about the connectivity between our outward appearances and projection of ourselves to the world and our states of mind, what we think and why. The Challenge was physical and mental with the goal of strengthening us from the inside out on all levels. One day of each week, after the workout, the class gathered in a circle to discuss a topic related to wellness and to review "homework" assignments we were given to journal about. The first assignment came on November 11 (11/11 for those who follow Angel numbers). It was a 10 year visualization exercise coupled with goal setting for our careers, health, personal/family goals and a dream big question. The purpose was to start the process of getting "unstuck" and to reevaluate ourselves on a physical, emotional and spiritual level. Ashley encouraged us to get inspired, set goals, and "journal so that [our] intentions [for the bootcamp] come from a really honest place".

That first day of bootcamp and the first assignment marked the beginning of real change for me. I realized that decisions to make change aren't always grand or dramatic—they can happen in the midst of everyday moments, like a conversation with a friend or a decision to edit your routine and try something new and unknown. But the significance lies in how you respond to the opportunity to make a change. Do you turn around and walk away, or do you lean into the discomfort of the challenge and see where it leads?

This experience of finding myself at a crossroads and making a decision to make changes in my life led me to rediscover my true Soul Identity and marked the beginning of my quest for Soul Reciprocity. Instead of blaming others for my situation, I looked in the mirror and, although I didn't know who I had become or how, I asked myself how I had contributed to my own unhappiness. I knew the answers could only come from within. It was time to do some deep reflection, nourish my soul and learn what it truly desired and needed. To accomplish this, I knew I had to make some serious life changes. I knew it wouldn't be easy, but I forged ahead nonetheless.

In general, making life changes can be challenging for several reasons:

1. **Comfort zone**: Humans tend to gravitate towards familiarity and routine because it provides a sense of stability and security. Stepping out of our comfort zones to make changes often involves uncertainty, fear of the unknown, and the risk of failure. This psychological resistance can make change difficult.

2. **Fear of failure**: Change often involves taking risks and venturing into uncharted territory. The fear of failure and the potential consequences

can be paralyzing. People may worry about making the wrong decision, facing setbacks, or not achieving their desired outcomes.

3. **Emotional attachment**: We can develop emotional attachments to our current situations, even if they are not ideal. This emotional attachment can make it challenging to let go of familiar circumstances, relationships, or habits, even if they are holding us back from growth and happiness.

4. **Limited belief systems**: Our beliefs and perceptions shape our reality. If we hold limiting beliefs about ourselves, our abilities, or the world around us, it can hinder our motivation and confidence to make changes. Overcoming these self-imposed limitations requires introspection, challenging our beliefs, and cultivating a growth mindset.

5. **Lack of support**: Having a support system, whether it's friends, family, mentors, or a community, can make a significant difference in successfully navigating life changes. Without adequate support, individuals may feel isolated, overwhelmed, or discouraged, making the process more challenging.

Despite the challenges, making life changes can also bring growth, fulfillment, and new opportunities. It requires self-awareness, resilience, and a willingness to embrace discomfort. Seeking support, surrounding yourself with like-minded people, setting realistic goals, breaking down changes into manageable steps, and cultivating a positive mindset can help overcome the challenges and increase the likelihood of successful life changes.

Rediscovering Authenticity

Discovering your true identity and purpose can be a transformative experience, but the journey to embrace and enact those changes is often fraught with challenges. After finding yourself at a crossroads, making initial changes, and gaining clarity about who you are and what you desire, you may feel inspired to make more significant shifts in your life. However, the path is rarely straightforward. Rather, it's long, winding and crosses many terrains. After years of experiencing bumps and detours in my own road, it wasn't until a moment of genuine reflection in my 40's, (that day standing in front of my closet mirror), that I began to see my life through a new lens of truth.

In my mid-30s, I was shocked to find myself feeling "lost," despite believing I knew myself well. I considered myself self-reflective, acknowledging my faults and weaknesses without hesitation. I felt confident, in control of my life, and optimistic about my future. I believed I was generally liked and comfortable in my own skin. I even thought I was kind of cute—not the best-looking girl in the world, but not the worst either—and I was someone who comfortably celebrated the beauty in others. I thought I had balance and perspective, so how could I possibly feel adrift?

Years earlier, one of my best friends told me to "stop trying to be Picasso." We were discussing an invitation I was given to take a trip to Hawaii for my birthday. I found myself hesitating, burdened by feelings of unworthiness and the fear of what others might think. My friend interrupted my spiraling thoughts and pointed to a painting hanging above my mantle. She urged me to see it for what it was—complete and beautiful as is. Her advice was clear: Stop trying to rewrite my life's narrative and appreciate it for what it already was.

In that moment, she wasn't discouraging my dreams but rather urging me to stop forcing an idealized vision onto my reality. I was often the one giving in relationships and felt unworthy of receiving. Yet, here was someone offering me a trip to a place I'd long wanted to visit, an opportunity I was considering rejecting. I ultimately accepted the offer, but I didn't fully embrace her wisdom because I continued to paint a picture in my mind of what my life was supposed to look like. This image fueled my desire to be married. However, once I embarked on my Soul Identity journey, this provided the clarity that ultimately led to my divorce.

Reflecting on that experience now, I see that my friend was right. When we forcefully paint pictures of our lives based on external expectations or perceived needs, we risk crafting partial fairy tales. We might dream of how we want things to come together without digging deep enough to discover our true selves and desires. We often tell ourselves things like:

"I need a partner who is/has _____."
"I need ___ kids, a dog named _____, and a white picket fence."
"I need a _____ house in the suburbs and a luxury _____ _."

"I want a job doing _____ with a huge salary and all the perks."

"I want the looks and body of a model, actor/actress, or athlete like _____."

Sometimes, the things I believed I needed were true for that moment, but they weren't rooted in my authentic self. They were projections of desires influenced by societal norms, not my own truths. Like a movie playing in my head, I envisioned a fairytale life without questioning the origins of those dreams.

You might recognize this in your own life. Have you ever thought you needed something, only to later realize that it wasn't truly what you wanted? Conversely, there are likely desires you never considered before that later became essential to your happiness. Uncovering these truths requires a willingness to explore your inner self, moving beyond surface-level wants and understanding what truly resonates with your soul.

Surrounding yourself with supportive individuals—your Soul Tribe—can significantly ease this journey. Their encouragement and understanding will help you navigate the emotional ups and downs, reminding you of your worth and purpose when doubt creeps in. Ultimately, while the road to embracing your true identity may be difficult, the rewards of living authentically and in alignment with your purpose are immeasurable. Each step you take, no matter how small, brings you closer to a Soul-Full Relationship with yourself and others.

The Key: Self-Examination

It's worth saying again. To truly understand what you want and need, you must first know who you are. This requires deep soul searching, an exploration that goes beyond recognizing your strengths and achievements. While you likely have a good sense of what makes you feel good about yourself, such as your appearance, social status, and accomplishments, true self-discovery also involves confronting the less flattering aspects of your identity.

We often celebrate our lives through social media, sharing our adventures and successes, but seeking your Soul Identity means acknowledging the parts of yourself that are less admirable. You might discover feelings of anger, fear, or sadness lurking beneath a confident exterior. It's essential to recognize these traits, even if they challenge the self-image you present to the world.

This journey may unearth forgotten moments or decisions you regret, revealing aspects of yourself you've ignored or denied. Facing these truths requires a level of honesty that many people struggle to achieve. Admitting your faults can be one of the hardest parts of this process. We often criticize others for the very traits we possess but fail to see in ourselves. How many times have you observed someone lamenting the behavior of another, unaware that they, too, exhibit those same flaws?

For example, at a family gathering, an elder relative—let's call them Sam— was criticizing one of their siblings— who was accusing them of being selfish, needy, and demanding attention. Ironically, Sam was also known for those same traits, often being the subject of family complaints. We've all been "Sam" at some point, unable to recognize our own shortcomings yet critical of someone else who exhibits the very thing we can't see in ourselves.

Embarking on the path to uncovering your Soul Identity means you can't escape your true self. Accepting the qualities you might want to ignore is crucial. This isn't about self-punishment; it's about gaining a deeper understanding of who you are and why you are that way. This clarity allows you to evaluate what you might want to change, what you wish you could change but can't, and what you might be willing to work on over time.

Interestingly, part of this journey can reveal strengths you didn't know you possessed. Often, others see qualities in us that we overlook or undervalue. By opening yourself to self-discovery, you can uncover these hidden gems and embrace the full spectrum of your identity.

Getting Feedback

Feedback is essential for identifying potential pitfalls and areas for improvement, enabling you to correct your course before problems escalate. Constructive feedback reveals your strengths and weaknesses, helping you gain a clearer understanding of how your actions impact others. This self-awareness is crucial for personal development and enhances your effectiveness in various aspects of life.

Part of my journey in uncovering my Soul Identity involved soliciting opinions from others about how they perceive me. Sometimes this took the form of structured exercises during retreats or journaling sessions, while other times it emerged naturally in conversations with friends. Regardless of the context, the insights I received were often uncomfortable and confusing; at times, I didn't even recognize the person they described.

For example, my partner frequently shares what he appreciates about me alongside some less flattering observations. He tells me that many people are both overwhelmed by my presence and deeply moved by my stories. While I strive for confidence, I often feel self-conscious, worrying about my appearance or wondering if I'm communicating effectively. Despite my intentions, I struggle to see myself as someone who changes lives; I think of figures like Oprah and Tony Robbins as truly inspirational.

My partner also challenges me to acknowledge traits I might not be aware of. I have a tendency to speak my mind without fully considering the impact, often resulting in moments of lapse in judgment. My tone can sometimes come off as harsh or dismissive, and jokes I intend to be lighthearted are occasionally misinterpreted. This disconnect leaves me puzzled, as these traits don't align with how I see myself.

Facing the consequences of these unfiltered moments has been eye-opening. Recently, I learned that something I allegedly said years ago about a friend's mourning led to long-lasting hurt. During a couple's cruise, I made a comment expressing my desire to enjoy the trip without negativity, which was misinterpreted as insensitivity toward someone grieving a loss. While I can't recall the exact words I used, I know I would never intentionally belittle someone in mourning. Nonetheless, the pain my words caused—and the awkward dynamics it created among friends—has been a harsh lesson in the importance of mindful communication.

Understanding how others perceive us is just as vital as the insights we gain through self-discovery. Feedback plays a critical role in both personal and professional growth. While not all feedback will resonate or be accurate, it's essential to assess the source and approach it with an open mind. Maintaining a growth mindset and seeking diverse perspectives can help you build a more comprehensive understanding of your strengths and areas for improvement.

The Right Questions

The road to Soul Reciprocity is a road of self-discovery. First, you reflect on the people who affected your life and circumstances the most, especially those who have helped shape you into who you are – both good and bad. Maybe these people have done you wrong or they know the difficult circumstances that you have endured and failed to help, support or protect you. Maybe this involves a long-term or close relationship that went bad. No matter the situation, look at it through a lens of self-analysis, asking: What did I learn from that experience about myself? What did I contribute to that situation if anything? What truths must I accept and what things should I avoid as a result? Again, it's looking at those circumstances through a lens of self-reflection so that you get a better understanding of you, not just passing blame for those circumstances to the other person.

By understanding all aspects of yourself—the good, great, amazing, bad, ugly, disappointing, dark, conscious, and subconscious traits—you begin to uncover your Soul Identity. This includes recognizing what you love and hate about yourself, and even what others see in you. Through this self-awareness, you get to the root of your Soul Needs, beyond what your mind or heart may desire or think you need. These realizations are key to understanding many aspects of your life and relationships. You'll gain insight into how you contribute to your successes and failures, and how your identity shapes your circumstances, both positive and negative. You'll also find new reasons to love yourself as you're forced to see yourself through the eyes of others. Yes, you'll become even more certain about the amazing qualities you already knew you had. To reach this point, you must ask yourself meaningful questions—not just surface-level queries, but ones that challenge you to see yourself from the outside in, and then reflect inwardly. I know from personal experience that this is easier said than done, which is why I've written this book—to kickstart your journey with thoughtful questions, exercises, and other tools.

The Right Steps – Soul Work

You can't expect to find someone who mirrors you if you don't truly know yourself. A key component to Soul Work involves self-discovery. Once you understand who you are, you naturally attract people whose friendship and love are reflective of what your soul needs. That's what Soul Reciprocity is all about. This journey of self-discovery isn't just personal; it can involve others as well. Here's a breakdown of what it typically involves:

1. **Self-Discovery**
   - Introspection: Engage in reflective practices to understand your thoughts, feelings, and behaviors. This can include journaling, meditation, or quiet contemplation.
   - Feedback Gathering: Seek insights from others about how they perceive you. This can provide valuable perspectives on your strengths and areas for growth.

2. **Awareness of Identity**
   - Recognizing Strengths and Weaknesses: Acknowledge what you love about yourself as well as traits you may want to improve. Understanding both sides fosters a more complete self-identity.
   - Uncovering Blind Spots: Be open to recognizing aspects of your personality or behavior that you might not be aware of, which can lead to important revelations.

3. **Emotional Healing**
   - Addressing Past Experiences: Confront and process past experiences, mistakes, or traumas that may affect your current behavior and perceptions. This step is crucial for emotional growth and healing.
   - Forgiveness: Work toward forgiving yourself and others, which helps release negative emotions and creates space for positive growth.

4. **Connection with Others**
   - Building Relationships: Foster authentic relationships that encourage vulnerability and open communication. This is a cornerstone of Soul Reciprocity, where mutual respect and understanding thrive.
   - Practicing Empathy: Develop a deeper understanding of others' experiences and feelings, which can strengthen your connections and foster a sense of community.

5. **Reciprocity and Balance**
- Mutual Support: Engage in give-and-take relationships where both parties benefit and grow. This balance is essential for sustaining healthy connections.
- Sharing Insights: Be willing to share your own insights and experiences while also valuing the contributions of others. This exchange enriches both parties' journeys.

6. **Intentional Living**
- Aligning Actions with Values: Ensure that your actions reflect your core values and beliefs. This alignment fosters authenticity and purpose in your life.
- Continuous Growth: Recognize that Soul Work is an ongoing journey. Commit to continual self-reflection and adaptation as you evolve.

7. **Cultivating Gratitude**
- Recognizing Contributions: Appreciate the support and love you receive from others, acknowledging their impact on your growth and well-being.
- Being Present: Practice mindfulness to stay grounded in the moment, allowing you to fully engage with your own experiences and the experiences of those around you.

In essence, Soul Work is about gaining an understanding of oneself while simultaneously acknowledging and nurturing the interconnectedness of relationships. It encourages a balanced approach to personal growth, where the insights gained about oneself contribute positively to the collective journey of those you engage with. Keep in mind, sometimes Soul Work must begin or be done entirely alone. Don't be ashamed of the process, for being transparent will attract resources and like-minded people to you.

The Right Setting

As previously stated, the quest to Soul Reciprocity will take you on a path that crosses many terrains, The Soul Work that you do as you trek along will take on many forms From solitary exercises like journaling to immersive activities like group therapy, there are a myriad of ways to engage in Soul Work One of my favorites are retreats. A retreat represents the meadow where individuals or groups withdraw from their normal routines and responsibilities to engage in activities that promote self-reflection, personal growth or spiritual exploration. Like the differing meadows (e.g. wet, dry, prairie, coastal), retreats can vary in setting, content and duration, taking place in various settings such as centers, nature or monastic environments. They typically provide participants with a supportive and focused environment to engage in practices such as meditation, mindfulness, yoga, workshops, seminars, therapeutic activities, or silent reflection. They offer individuals an opportunity to step away from the busyness of daily life, detach from technology and external distractions, and create space for inner exploration and rejuvenation.

Soul Reciprocity Retreats focus on attendees discovering their Soul Identity, providing tools and guidance for self-discovery and growth. The purpose is to create an intentional and nurturing space that allows individuals to recharge, gain clarity, deepen self-awareness, and cultivate a sense of inner peace and alignment. It is a dedicated time for self-care, reflection, and personal transformation.

They provide an opportunity for individuals to reconnect with themselves in several ways:

1. **Space for Reflection**: Retreats offer a break from daily routines and distractions, providing a dedicated time and space for self-reflection. Away from the demands of everyday life, individuals can delve deeper into their thoughts, emotions, and personal experiences.
2. **Mindfulness and Present Moment Awareness**: Retreats often incorporate mindfulness practices and encourage participants to be fully present in the moment. This heightened awareness helps individuals tune into their thoughts, feelings, and sensations, fostering self-awareness and a deeper connection with oneself.
3. **Solitude and Silence**: Many retreats provide opportunities for solitude and silence, allowing individuals to detach from external stimuli and engage in introspection. This solitude can facilitate a deeper understanding of oneself, personal insights, and inner clarity.

4. **Personal Growth and Exploration**: Retreats offer workshops and therapeutic activities focused on personal growth and self-exploration. Through these activities, individuals can gain new insights, learn valuable tools for self-discovery, and engage in practices that facilitate personal transformation.
5. **Connection with Nature**: Retreats often take place in serene and natural environments, allowing individuals to reconnect with nature. Spending time in nature can have a calming and grounding effect, fostering a sense of connectedness and harmony within oneself.
6. **Supportive Community**: Retreats often bring together like-minded individuals seeking similar experiences. The supportive community and shared journey can provide a sense of belonging, understanding, and acceptance, which can foster self-acceptance and self-compassion.
7. **Healthy Lifestyle Choices**: Many retreats promote healthy habits such as nutritious meals, physical activities like yoga or meditation, and self-care practices. These activities can promote overall well-being and contribute to a sense of inner balance and self-care.

Overall, retreats create a conducive environment for individuals to step away from their daily routines, explore their inner landscape, and cultivate a deeper connection with themselves. The combination of intentional practices, solitude, nature, and community support can contribute to a transformative and rejuvenating experience.

Besides attending an organized retreat, you can create a makeshift retreat at home. At my house, I have a Moroccan room that is designed specifically to be a retreat and a place to escape the world. It's a very zen space where I light candles, burn incense, dim the lights, and relax on my comfy couch with blankets and diffusing oils. I like to create a retreat environment if I'm at home, and I need that type of time for reflection and self-discovery. Sometimes I pull out my journal and just jot my thoughts that I have about a particular topic, something I need to resolve or something that's reared its head that I'm unsure about. I compose notes so that I can come back and actually reflect on them again, usually with more clarity. I have also been recording voice notes in my phone so I can notate a significant issue or thought I'm having at the moment. Later on, I usually go back and listen, contemplating and addressing anything that requires deeper reflection. Nature has always provided solace for me. I feel safe and calm when I'm in a natural environment, especially near the water. Sometimes I just listen to water fountains for a sense of serenity. I have a fountain in my Moroccan room for that reason. All of these things help to calm the noise of everything else in the world so that I can hear myself for Soul Work.

Remember, Soul Work has to be done in order to know your Soul Identity, and if you haven't done that work, you're not going to get it. You're not going to understand me. You're not going to understand my message or even why I'm talking about it. In fact, this message is going to make you uncomfortable because you aren't there with yourself. I can't get you there if you're not willing to do the work. If you are ready and willing, realize that discovering your soul identity is a process that takes time and patience no matter your method. Be open to exploring new experiences and perspectives, and trust that you will find your way to your true self as long as you're persistent and passionate about it.

NEXT STEPS

To deepen your understanding of your Soul Identity, I encourage you to complete the **Soul Identity Questionnaire** located in Appendix E at the back of this book. This questionnaire is a powerful tool designed to guide you through a series of reflective questions that will help you explore the core aspects of who you are.

As you work through the questionnaire, take your time to answer each question thoughtfully and honestly. Your responses will provide valuable insights into your values, beliefs, and the unique traits that define your Soul Identity. After completing the questionnaire, spend some time reflecting on your answers. Consider how your insights can inform your choices and interactions in your life. Embracing your Soul Identity is a crucial step toward living authentically and aligning your life with your true self.

7

THE NECTAR AND POLLEN

IDENTIFYING SOUL NEEDS

*"Your soul knows the geography of your destiny.
Your soul alone has the map of your future."*
~ John O'Donohue

Bees are essential for flowers to grow, and flowers are essential for bees to survive. They have evolved over time to ensure they attract one another to fulfill their mutual needs. Thus, they nurture and nourish each other. Their relationship is reciprocal; bees seek nectar (the basis of honey) to feed themselves and their colony (and of course their queen), and in the process, they provide fertilization through pollen enabling flowers and plants to reproduce. This natural exchange mirrors Soul Reciprocity, where two people meet each other's Soul Needs, creating a balanced, nurturing and nourishing relationship.

There are two kinds of "needs": basic life needs and Soul Needs, and both are critical to our existence. Basic life needs include things like food, water, and shelter. Soul Needs go beyond basic life needs. While basic life needs are essential for physical survival, Soul Needs are tied to our emotional, spiritual, and psychological well-being. These include the need for truth, faith and love. Basic life needs support our survival and keep us alive, whereas Soul Needs nourish the deeper aspects of who we are, helping us find meaning and fulfillment. Deprivation of basic life needs can result in our physical demise. Failure to have our Soul Needs met results in "Soul-LESS" relationships. For instance, if your unique Soul Need is for intimacy but it is not being met, you will feel that your partner doesn't love or care about you. The result will be a "Soul-LESS" relationship that leaves you feeling alone and unfulfilled. Doing your Soul Work is all about identifying and learning to honor your Soul Needs. To understand your Soul Needs and if they are being met, ask yourself:

- What are my unique Soul Needs?
- Are these needs being met? By whom?
- How do unmet Soul Needs (universal and unique) affect my life?
- What can I do to get my Soul Needs met?

These questions are an example of Soul Work that will help you understand and honor what you need beyond basic life necessities. With that clarity, you will see the interconnection between your Soul Identity and your Soul Needs. And I guarantee that once you have the epiphanies that will follow, you will adjust your life to ensure you have what your soul requires because when your Soul Needs aren't respected or met, Soul-Less relationships and unfulfilling experiences are guaranteed. If you neglect someone's Soul Needs, the outcome can take one of three paths: the person may leave to find fulfillment elsewhere, seek to satisfy their needs through other means or, in a more damaging scenario, they might stay while consciously or subconsciously withholding what you need. This final dynamic often leads to an unhealthy emotional stalemate, where neither party's needs are met, fostering frustration and disconnection. This chapter examines not only your Soul Needs (**Nectar**) but also the needs of others (**Pollen**).

NECTAR: Identifying Your Soul Needs

Nectar is a food source that bees get from flowers which they use to make honey and provides them the energy they need to travel from plant to plant for cross pollination. The type of flower a bee takes nectar from determines the flavor of the honey it produces. Like bees that need nectar to thrive, what exactly does your soul need? It will vary depending on the person (flower). Our Soul Needs come from deep within, a place our minds or bodies alone are unable to comprehend. Some of these needs are universal, and others can be as diverse as we are physically. They emerge from an authentic place that triggers our so-called "gut reactions" to circumstances.

Most of us think about what we "need" from a practical and basic sense. We describe our basic life needs in terms of physiological, physical, emotional, and psychological things. However, Soul Needs are different because they are not material things or created in our minds from our egos or feelings. Rather, they are basic and natural, originating from our subconscious minds deep within us. A review of the examples below of basic life needs and Soul Needs will help to make the comparison clearer. These are some common basic life needs:

- **Physiological** = Food, Sleep, Air, Water
- **Physical** = Clothing, Shelter, Touch, Sex, Movement
- **Emotional** = Belonging, Security, Attention
- **Psychological** = Autonomy, Competence, Relatedness
- **Soul** = Truth, Unconditional Love, Faith, Balance, Peace

Our Soul Needs can be both universal among us all and unique to each individual. There are certain fundamental needs that are shared by all human beings, such as the need for love, connection, belonging, meaning, and fulfillment. These needs are rooted in universal principles and are essential for our overall well-being and thriving. At the same time, our Soul Needs can also be shaped by our individuality, including our purpose, personality, and perspective. Our purpose, which is our unique reason for being and what gives our life meaning, can deeply influence our Soul Needs. For example, someone who has a purpose centered around creativity may have a strong need for self-expression and innovation, while someone with a purpose focused on service may have a strong need for compassion and altruism.

Similarly, our personality, which encompasses our unique traits, characteristics, and tendencies, can also impact our Soul Needs. For instance, an introverted person may have a greater need for solitude and reflection, while an extroverted person may have a greater need for social interaction and stimulation.

Furthermore, our perspective, which is shaped by our beliefs, values, experiences, and worldview, can influence our Soul Needs as well. For example, someone with a spiritual perspective may have a greater need for connection with the divine or inner peace, while someone with a scientific perspective may have a greater need for knowledge and understanding.

Our Soul Needs are complex and multifaceted, and they vary from person to person. Understanding and honoring our unique Soul Needs, while also recognizing the universal aspects of human nature, can help us cultivate a fulfilling, meaningful life that aligns with our authentic selves.

Basic (Universal) Soul Needs

Our Soul Needs are fundamental, basic, and rooted in truth; they aren't something we can invent or convince ourselves of. We can't force them upon ourselves, unlike the things we might tell ourselves we "need" because of societal expectations—like, "I need a bigger house," or "I need a luxury car," or "I need my best friend to always agree with/validate me." These are external expectations, not true Soul Needs. Basic Soul Needs include: **Truth**, **Faith** and **Love**.

Truth (Path)

Inner truths are the beliefs and values that reflect who we really are deep down. They guide how we think, act, and make decisions based on what we truly feel, without being influenced by others or society. The truth of the soul comes from a place beyond you. The idea that the truth of the soul comes from a place beyond an individual suggests that it originates from a source or realm that is beyond someone's conscious understanding or control. This truth is something that children honor but adults often ignore because of many factors, usually trauma and fear. Inner truths are what we believe to be true with our whole being. It's the personal framework from which we view life.

Truth In Love

Sometimes in life, we have experiences which cause us to detach from what we once believed to be true. We reach a point of confidence in our beliefs, but then life challenges them, and we lose faith, with our actions following suit. We convince ourselves that what we thought was an inner truth was really a lie. I've disconnected from my inner truths many times, as I think we all have. I believed in fairytale love, that people are inherently good, hard work always pays off, and kindness is reciprocated. But I've had to step back from those beliefs when reality proved otherwise.

For example, in high school, I thought I'd found my first love. Busy with academics and tennis, I had little time for socializing, so he spent his time with other girls. When I found out, he justified his actions by pointing out all the things they had that I didn't, making comparisons primarily to physical attributes. This left me struggling with body image, hair texture, and confidence issues, disconnecting me from my self-worth and belief in fairytale love for years.

Reconnection after the disconnect is a process that takes time and courage. Typically, people have to heal from that which caused them to disconnect in the first place. For some, the healing never happens because the cause was so painful that they are scarred and choose to avoid the situation again. Think of people who go through ugly divorces that last years and reveal the worst of each person. After they argue through every single issue, including their children, they forget why they ever were in love or got married. Often, they vow never to marry or even love again. They give up on their belief in a forever partnership and thus disconnect permanently from their prior inner truths about love and marriage.

Reconnecting with inner truths is possible once we confront and heal from the lies that disconnected us. The key is being open to the healing process, whatever that may involve. After my first love, I wasn't afraid to love again—I knew it was possible. But the damage to my body image and self-worth was harder to overcome. It wasn't until my mid-20s that I began regaining confidence, and even then, it fluctuated. Even though I wasn't afraid to fall in love, in romantic relationships, my self-esteem remained fragile.

Healing required deep soul searching. While I didn't follow any formal program, positive relationships, personal achievements, and maturity helped rebuild my sense of worth. Graduating college and law school, passing the bar, and receiving affirmation from others gradually boosted my confidence. My friends were vital, offering encouragement, constructive criticism, and unwavering support.

As I became more invested in my growth, I deliberately confronted the lie that I wasn't enough. Journaling, self-help books, the world of Oprah, positive affirmations, retreats, and therapy all played a role in my healing.

And honestly, the healing journey continues to this day. True recovery from the scars that disconnect us from our inner truths of confidence and worth takes time and effort—it's what Soul Work is all about.

Truth within Families

Children are often believed to have a natural connection with their inner selves, and are often more in tune with their intuition, emotions, and spiritual awareness. They may exhibit qualities such as curiosity, innocence, and a sense of wonder, which are often associated with a deeper understanding of the soul or inner truth. Children deal with sensory overload in that, every day, they experience some new and uncharted territory that they navigate as best they can with the limited information they have at the time. They haven't developed their full brain functionality, and thus, their discernment and decision-making skills are not yet refined enough to guide them through all that they encounter. Yet, children are curious and inquisitive. They want to know more, see more and do more. Inevitably, they are also insecure, rebellious, and intimidated to an extent because there is such a big world out there, but there are also so many rules of engagement that seem to limit their exploration.

As children grow into adulthood, they may become more influenced by societal norms, responsibilities, and external pressures, which could lead to a distancing or neglect of their inner truths or soul. The pursuit of materialistic goals, societal expectations, and rational thinking may take precedence over honoring and nurturing the deeper aspects of the self. A young boy, naturally sensitive and empathetic, may be in touch with his emotions and openly expresses them. He comforts others, cries when upset, and shares his feelings freely. However, as he grows, his family tells him "boys don't cry" or to "toughen up." His father or siblings may tease him for being too emotional, pushing him to suppress his feelings.

Over time, he internalizes these messages, disconnecting from his inner truth—that it's okay to express emotions. To fit in, he hides his sensitivity, adopting a tougher exterior. As he matures, this disconnection from his natural empathy makes it harder for him to understand and connect with his emotions, all due to his family's influence.

Truth at Work

In the context of work, inner truths are the core beliefs, values, and principles that define how we approach our work, make decisions, and interact with others. These truths might include a commitment to integrity, passion for creativity, dedication to quality, or the desire to contribute meaningfully to a team or mission.

However, these inner truths can become disconnected due to external pressures. Colleagues might prioritize short-term gains over long-term value, clients may push for unethical practices, or superiors could reward behavior that conflicts with personal values. Additionally, a toxic or highly competitive work environment might force someone to compromise their principles to fit in, gain approval, or advance in their career. Over time, the disconnect between personal values and the external environment can lead to disillusionment, job dissatisfaction, or burnout, as the individual strays from their authentic self.

As an entertainment attorney, I approach my work from my place of passion for advocacy for creatives, individuals who support them and companies who provide opportunities for them. My commitment to my clients is to work with integrity and zeal to preserve and protect the legacies they create. And I believe it's possible to do so even within an industry known for greed, corruption and unfair dealings. However, I have witnessed those who have succumbed to the high-pressured nature of the industry where quick wins and high profile deals have caused them to prioritize financial gain over fairness, cut corners of ethics, and otherwise compromised their principles to meet the expectations of their clients or their firm.

Truth in Life

The idea that the truth of the soul comes from a place beyond our consciousness suggests that it is something deeper and inherent, which may be more evident in children but can be overlooked or ignored by adults. This highlights the importance of introspection, self-awareness, and reconnecting with our inner truths, regardless of our age or background. As we get older, we develop inhibitions and fears that keep us comfortable in being unaware and inauthentic, or disconnecting from the truth. Vulnerability is about being authentic, speaking your truth and allowing someone to see you completely without any pretense or defenses. Some may see it as weakness, but it is a strength that empowers and encourages others to be more emotionally expressive or authentic. Thus, vulnerability is a soul truth that will trigger soul truth in another person, or reciprocity. It challenges the lies we tell ourselves and may be telling others in an effort to protect our image. This is, again, why Soul Work is so important, because it allows us to break down the barriers we've built over time—whether from societal expectations, past traumas, or self-imposed limitations—and reconnect with the essence of who we are. Soul Work encourages us to face the discomfort of self-examination and to confront the lies we've accepted about ourselves in order to rediscover our authentic selves. By embracing vulnerability and speaking our truths, we create deeper, more meaningful connections with others, as authenticity invites authenticity. This reciprocity of openness fosters stronger relationships and helps us live more aligned with our inner truths, allowing us to grow and evolve in both personal and professional realms. Ultimately, Soul Work is about returning to the core of our being and living in a way that honors our true self.

Faith (Action)

Faith is hope in action. It transcends mere feelings and thoughts, moving an individual from a passive state of contemplation into a state of active engagement. It can propel individuals to take action based on their beliefs, manifesting their notions into tangible actions in the world. This can include acts of kindness, charity, advocacy, service, or other forms of positive expression that are aligned with their faith. Moreover, faith can provide solace and resilience during challenging times, as it can serve as a guiding light and a source of hope, courage and strength. It can help individuals persevere through difficulties, navigate uncertainty, and find meaning even in the face of adversity.

My faith has its roots in my upbringing in the church. Raised in a Catholic household, I attended church almost every Sunday and participated in Sunday School, where I was first introduced to God's Word and how it could be applied to daily life. Over time, though, the strict tenets of the church began to clash with some of my own personal beliefs—my inner truths. I found it difficult to reconcile the literal teachings with the real-life experiences I observed. This inner conflict led me on a journey of spiritual discovery, where I explored different religious institutions and their practices. I visited various Christian denominations, such as Seventh-Day Adventist and Baptist churches, and even explored a Bahá'í Temple with Buddhist influences. Despite this exploration, the foundation of my faith remained strong. I believe deeply in God's promises and in His sacrifice of sending His only son for the forgiveness of our sins—principles that were instilled in me from a very young age.

When people understand and express their faith, it can bring their soul into a state of presence in the natural realm, allowing them to be more authentic and sincere. It can awaken a sense of awareness and alignment with their innermost convictions, values, and beliefs, giving their soul a sense of vitality and purpose. Faith can ignite a sense of passion, motivation, and inspiration to act in accordance with one's deeply held convictions and beliefs.

My journey of spiritual growth has led me to a deeper understanding of living in the present and embracing principles of righteousness. I've learned that it's not just about interpreting words from religious texts but integrating those teachings into daily life. As I've merged the foundations of my faith with lessons from other cultures and spiritual practices, I've embraced values like peace, love, compassion, empathy, patience, and gratitude. Regardless of labels, I am, without a doubt, a woman of faith. This means I strive to live each day in alignment with Godliness and righteousness, guided by spirit and understanding that my blessings flow from how I live my life. I believe what I give is what I receive, that the energy of the universe connects with me, and that God sees me in all that I do. I carry myself as a servant and vessel, even down to this book and brand. From the beginning, I've said Soul Reciprocity is a purpose project. I didn't set out to be an author or a relationship expert—life pushed me to adapt and grow. What I learned through my healing process became so clear that I felt compelled to share it with others. Over time, I realized that true understanding of oneself comes through Soul Work, where you connect with your soul, take heed to your soul's intuition, and where pure intention and truth live.

Love (Energy)

Everyone talks about love, but not often where it originates within us. The soul is where a love is birthed. And love is a Soul Need we all have in common. The concept of love, often associated with the soul, is deeply ingrained in our understanding and has been described in various ways. The idea that love is connected to the soul and is personified in its purest form implies that it is a foundational aspect of human existence that transcends boundaries, cultures, and beliefs. It is a unifying force that has the potential to bring people together, foster understanding, and promote positive change in the world. Interpretations and understandings of love may vary depending on cultural, philosophical, and personal beliefs. However, the notion that the soul is the birthplace of love, and that it inspires selfless actions and reactions, is a perspective that resonates with many people and has been reflected in various spiritual and philosophical teachings throughout history.

In the Christian tradition, the Bible is often referenced for its teachings on love. 1 Corinthians 13, also known as the "Love Chapter," describes love in its purest form, highlighting its qualities and importance. It speaks to the idea that love originates from the soul, and that it is a motivating force for selfless actions and reactions. According to 1 Corinthians 13, love is patient, kind, not envious, not boastful, not proud, not rude, not self-seeking, not easily angered, and keeps no record of wrongs. It rejoices in truth, protects, trusts, hopes, and perseveres. It is described as a force that transcends mere feelings and actions and is a fundamental aspect of human nature that has its origins in the soul. The idea that the soul knows and personifies love in its purest form suggests that love is not just a superficial emotion or action, but a deeper, intrinsic aspect of our being. It implies that love goes beyond superficial expressions and encompasses a profound connection that originates from within ourselves. Furthermore, the motivation for selfless actions and reactions, as described in 1 Corinthians 13, suggests that love is a driving force that inspires individuals to act in ways that are compassionate, caring, and considerate towards others. It can lead to acts of kindness, empathy, and self-sacrifice for the well-being of others, and it can be a guiding principle for moral and ethical behavior.

You know that love is coming from the soul when it's pure and effortlessly given. Love from or at the soul level is an oddly natural thing. It actually involves less pomp and circumstance than people expect. It's "easy like Sunday morning" as Lionel Richie formerly with the Commodores sang. You see, love from the soul level comes from a place of intrinsic understanding of another soul. You can't fake it or force it through antics or gamesmanship. Love from the soul level expresses connectivity that is undeniable. Think of a magnet being placed inside your stomach. You could walk past a million people who don't have a magnet within them and nothing would happen. If, however, you walk past another person with a magnet, you would feel a pull from deep inside of you that would draw you towards that individual. It would literally be something inside of you that you can't control or explain. You would each be equally guided towards one another, and when together, there would be an inexplicable sense of attachment. If you tried to pull away, you would be lured back in that direction. And even if you broke away, you would nonetheless always have a draw in that direction. That's what love emanating from the soul feels like, and there really is nothing like it. The frustrating part is that you won't know what this Soul-Full love feels like until you have it. However, there are many signs that alert you when you don't have it. And the tools in this book such as the questionnaires will help you determine if you have it or not in your relationship.

Diverse (Unique) Needs

While some of our Soul Needs are fundamental, basic and similar, rooted in universal principles, they can also be unique, based on our purpose, personality and perspective. We can't cultivate them because they are us, part of our Soul Identity. These needs are truly beyond our control and based on use of our talent, traits and time.

Talent

Our natural giftings are sometimes seen as genetic or generational. However, they are never exactly the same level or expression, no matter how similar they may be to someone else's. These natural abilities or talents can include musical aptitude, artistic skills or intellectual capabilities, which are also considered part of an individual's inherent endowments. The concept of natural giftings, talents, or abilities being passed down through generations is often associated with the idea of genetic or generational traits. It is commonly believed that certain characteristics, skills, or talents may run in families due to genetic inheritance or cultural upbringing. However, the perspective that these giftings ultimately come from the soul suggests that they are not solely determined by genetics or external influences but are intrinsic to an individual's being. According to this perspective, the soul, often understood as the inner essence or core of a person, is believed to be the source of one's natural giftings. It is seen as a unique and individual aspect of a person that transcends genetic or generational influences. While there may be similarities in talents or abilities among family members, the belief is that each individual's giftings are ultimately shaped by their soul, which is distinct and unique to them.

Talent, skill and aptitude are, by definition, natural abilities. Because these things are intrinsic, they emanate from the soul. It's what we do (or don't do) with our talents, skills and aptitude that can affect the path our lives take. Our use of these gifts may lead us closer to our purpose. Our failure to use them may take us off course or further away from opportunities. Underutilization may slow down progress in our lives. We can all think of an example in our own lives where we didn't nurture a talent we have and instead focused on other things. For me, it was tennis. At a very young age, I was introduced to tennis by my stepfather. He recognized very early that I had an athletic ability that was enhanced by the fact that I was a pretty smart kid. I started playing tennis at about 10 years old. By the time I was 12, I was playing in junior circuit tournaments. In eighth grade I played on a high school varsity team where I was in the starting lineup. My freshman year of high school I went to the state championship, the youngest ever to go in the history of my school. At my peak, I was ranked third in the Midwest USTA rankings. Tennis was a huge part of my world. Yet, despite the obvious, natural ability and talent I had, I nonetheless had a love-hate relationship with the sport. Ultimately, I quit when I was 16 years old, seemingly at the top of my game. I knew I was disappointing a lot of people, but the fact was that I wasn't sure if I was playing for myself or to meet the expectations of other people. Although I had this athletic gift, I did not have the passion for it. Lucky for me, God gave me a few other gifts and I used them to focus heavily on scholastic achievement. People have asked me if I think my life would have been different if I stuck with tennis or if I have any regrets about quitting. Honestly, I don't think about it in that way. I suppose I could have selected tennis scholarships instead of academic scholarships or even turned professional if I continued improving. However, I always envisioned a life where my job would be my passion. Even at a young age, I was aware of how many adults complained about their jobs and didn't like the work that they did. So, I prayed that I would be able to be a person who loved what she did professionally and could make a good living at it. Even though I didn't know exactly what I wanted to do in my teens, I did know that playing tennis was not the vision I had for my life. At the same time, I don't regret a day of it. I learned so much about myself, pushing past what I thought was my limits, the thrill of working towards something and accomplishing it, and even the heartache of failure. Maybe most significantly, I learned that we can contribute to our own failure.

Many factors can encourage people to explore and cultivate their natural talents and abilities. Personal agency and individuality mean that individuals have the ability to develop and express their unique giftings in their own way, separate from familial or social influences. Talent, skill and aptitude emerge from our souls, but because we also have free will, the decisions we make with regard to those gifts determine whether we nurture and develop those gifts. Thus, the decisions we make in that regard can change the trajectory of our lives. That doesn't mean the outcome will always be negative if you choose not to utilize a talent, but it definitely will alter a path that was available to you.

Perspectives on the soul and the origins of natural giftings may vary across different cultural, philosophical, and spiritual beliefs. Some may attribute talents to genetics or environmental factors, while others may emphasize the role of the soul or other metaphysical concepts. Ultimately, the understanding of natural giftings and their origins is a complex and multifaceted topic, and different individuals may hold different perspectives on this matter.

The needs related to a specific talent can vary depending on the nature of the talent and how it is expressed. However, some common needs that may be associated with specific talents include:

1. **Need for Self-Expression**: When a person has a talent in a creative field, such as art, music, dance, or writing, they may have a strong need for self-expression. This can involve the desire to

communicate their thoughts, emotions, and ideas through their chosen medium, and to share their unique perspective with others.

2. **Need for Mastery**: Many talents require a certain level of skill and expertise to be fully realized. Therefore, individuals with specific talents may have a need for mastery, which involves developing and honing their skills to achieve a high level of proficiency in their chosen area of talent. This can include a desire to continually learn, improve, and challenge oneself to reach new levels of excellence.

3. **Need for Recognition**: Talent often involves a certain level of recognition or validation from others. Individuals with specific talents may have a need for recognition, appreciation, and acknowledgment of their skills and achievements. This can come in the form of praise, awards, accolades, or simply being acknowledged for their unique abilities.

4. **Need for Impact**: Some talents, such as leadership, public speaking, or advocacy, may involve a need for making a positive impact on others or the world around them. Individuals with such talents may have a desire to use their abilities to make a difference, create positive change, or contribute to a greater purpose or cause.

5. **Need for Challenge**: Talents often require pushing boundaries, taking risks, and stepping out of one's comfort zone. Individuals with specific talents may have a need for challenge and novelty, as they seek to continually stretch themselves, overcome obstacles, and explore new possibilities in their area of talent.

6. **Need for Connection**: Talents that involve collaboration, teamwork, or social interaction, such as acting, sports, or music, may also be associated with a need for connection. Individuals with these talents may have a desire for social bonding, camaraderie, and meaningful relationships with others who share their passion and interests.

7. **Need for Autonomy**: Some talents, such as entrepreneurship, invention, or innovation, may involve a need for autonomy and independence. Individuals with these talents may have a desire for freedom, autonomy, and the ability to create and pursue their own vision or ideas.

The specific needs associated with a talent can vary widely depending on the individual and their unique personality, background, and perspective. Not everyone with a particular talent may have the same needs, and it's important to recognize and honor the individuality of each person's experience with their talents.

Traits

In the context of the human body, "traits" typically refer to the natural or inherent characteristics or features that a person possesses. It can encompass various aspects of the body, such as physical attributes, genetic traits, or physiological capabilities, that are present from birth or developed during early stages of life. These endowments can include things like height, body composition, metabolism, strength, agility, sensory abilities, and other inherent qualities that are unique to each individual. My racial background "mixed", as my mother is Caucasian, and my father is African American. Although being of mixed race was (and is) far more common in Minneapolis where I grew up than most places in the country, there were still environment in Minnesota with more homogeneous families, and where I stood out. I was my maternal family's only "other" grandchild, so I stood out in that regard as well. My grandmother adored me, so I never really felt like I was being treated differently from my white cousins and other relatives. I was self-conscious about it… I don't feel as if I was hampered or helped by my physical traits, although, at times, I felt I had to try harder to fit in with different groups. I learned that the people who did and ultimately would be part of my Soul Tribe would be people who were open and accepting, not necessarily those who looked like me.

The way we look, think and move may be things we can alter, but these characteristics also represent things with which we were created to use as a means to execute our life's purpose. Indeed, our physical appearance, thoughts, and movements are integral aspects of our individuality, and they can play a role in how we express and fulfill our life's purpose or soul's destiny. These characteristics are part of our unique makeup and can influence how we engage with the world around us:

1. **Physical Appearance**: Our physical appearance, including our body type, features, and overall appearance, is something we are born with and cannot easily change. It is a part of our identity and can impact how we interact with others and how we perceive ourselves. Our physical appearance can be a tool for self-expression, as it can reflect our personality, culture, and style. It can also influence how others perceive and respond to us, which can impact our opportunities and experiences in life.
2. **Thoughts**: Our thoughts, beliefs, and perspectives shape our mindset and worldview. They influence how we perceive ourselves, others, and the world, and they can guide our actions and decisions. Our thoughts can be a powerful tool for shaping our reality and manifesting our life's purpose. Positive and empowering thoughts can inspire us, drive us forward, and help us overcome challenges, while negative or limiting thoughts can hold us back and hinder our progress.
3. **Movements**: How we move and express ourselves physically, such as our gestures, posture, and mannerisms, can also be a unique aspect of our individuality. Our movements can convey our emotions, intentions, and personality. For example, someone with a talent for dance may use their movements as a means of artistic expression, while someone with a talent for sports may use their physical abilities to excel in their chosen field. Our movements can be a vehicle for embodying our purpose and expressing ourselves authentically.

Honoring and embracing our unique traits can allow us to leverage them as tools for fulfilling our life's purpose, or soul's destiny. While we may have the ability to alter some aspects of ourselves, our inherent characteristics are also part of our unique identity and can serve as powerful vehicles for expressing ourselves and living in alignment with our authentic selves. Embracing our individuality and utilizing these characteristics can help us navigate our life's journey and fulfill our soul's purpose with authenticity and purpose.

Some Soul Needs related to our endowments may include:

1. **Acceptance**: Self-acceptance without judgment or comparison to others is a fundamental soul need. This involves embracing our unique features, perspectives, and ways of expressing ourselves in cultivating self-acceptance and self-love.
2. **Authenticity**: Being true to ourselves and expressing our physical endowment in an authentic way is another soul need. This involves honoring our thoughts, beliefs, and perspectives, and expressing them genuinely without trying to conform to societal or external expectations. Embracing our unique physical appearance, thoughts, and movements as part of our authentic self allows us to live in alignment with our true nature.
3. **Connection**: Our attributes can influence our ability to connect with others and the need for social connection is a fundamental soul need. This may involve using our appearance, thoughts, and actions to build meaningful relationships, connect with others who share our perspectives, and cultivate a sense of belonging and community.
4. **Growth and Development**: Our characteristics can be a vehicle for personal growth and development, and the need for continuous growth and improvement is a soul need. This may involve using our thoughts to expand our knowledge, perspectives, and understanding of ourselves and the world, and using our physical movements to challenge ourselves, develop new skills, and reach our full potential.
5. **Purpose and Meaning**: Our physical and emotional identities can be connected to our sense of purpose and meaning in life, and the need for purpose and meaning is a fundamental soul need. This may involve aligning our physical appearance, thoughts, and movements with our life's purpose and utilizing them as tools for fulfilling our unique path and destiny.

The Soul Needs related to our characteristics can vary from person to person, and individuals may have unique needs and desires based on their individuality, background, and perspective. It's essential to honor and respect our individuality and to cultivate self-awareness and self-acceptance in our journey of fulfilling our Soul's Needs and living authentically.

Time

Our Soul Needs related to time, or longevity, are often connected to our perception of time and our understanding of the fleeting nature of life. As the saying goes, "tomorrow is not promised" to anyone, and this is what makes our Soul Needs diverse in terms of our longevity. The uncertainty and impermanence of life can greatly influence our Soul Needs and how we perceive our own longevity. The awareness that tomorrow is not promised to anyone can lead us to prioritize certain Soul Needs related to time and longevity, such as finding purpose, fulfillment, and connection in the present moment. It can also serve as a reminder to make the most of the time we have and to live authentically in alignment with our own unique Soul Needs and values. The understanding that life is finite can inspire us to reflect on our priorities, set meaningful goals, and cultivate a sense of meaning and impact in our lives. Embracing the diversity of our Soul Needs in relation to our longevity can lead us to live with greater intention, purpose, and appreciation for the preciousness of time.

Some Soul Needs related to time or longevity may include:
1. **Purpose and Meaning**: The need for a sense of purpose and meaning in life is a fundamental Soul Need. We may seek to understand the purpose of our existence and the meaning of our lives in the context of the limited time we have on Earth. This may involve exploring our passions, values, and beliefs, and aligning our actions with our sense of purpose and meaning.
2. **Fulfillment and Satisfaction**: The need for fulfillment and satisfaction in life is another Soul Need related to time or longevity. We may strive to make the most of the time we have, seeking experiences and activities that bring us joy, fulfillment, and a sense of accomplishment. This may involve setting and pursuing meaningful goals, creating memories with loved ones, and making a positive impact on the world.
3. **Legacy and Impact**: The desire to leave a lasting legacy and make a meaningful impact is another Soul Need related to time or longevity. We may seek to create a positive and lasting impact on the world, leaving a legacy that extends beyond our limited time on Earth. This may involve contributing to our community, making a

difference in the lives of others, and leaving behind a positive legacy that inspires future generations.

4. **Awareness and Mindfulness**: The need for awareness and mindfulness of the present moment is also related to our perception of time and the fleeting nature of life. We may seek to cultivate mindfulness, being fully present in each moment and appreciating the preciousness of time. This may involve practices such as meditation, reflection, and being fully present in our relationships and experiences.

5. **Reflection and Self-Examination**: Our perception of time may also lead to a Soul Need for reflection and self-examination. We may seek to reflect on our lives, examine our thoughts, emotions, and actions, and gain insight into ourselves and our existence. This may involve practices such as introspection, self-inquiry, and self-reflection to deepen our understanding of ourselves and our place in the world.

6. **Transcendence and Connection to Something Greater**: The need for transcendence and connection to something greater than ourselves is also related to our perception of time and longevity. We may seek to connect with something beyond our individual selves, such as nature or our higher power, to find meaning, purpose, and a sense of interconnectedness with the universe.

Our Soul Needs related to longevity may vary for each individual and can be influenced by our personal beliefs, values, and perspectives. It's essential to reflect on our own understanding of time and how it impacts our Soul Needs, and to strive to live in alignment with our own unique perception of time and the fleeting nature of life.

The Path to Purpose

According to some spiritual and philosophical beliefs, each person is thought to have a unique life-defining purpose or mission. Consequently, people have specific Soul Needs aligned with this purpose, making these needs distinct from person to person. Each individual's path may call for different types of support, experiences, and connections, all designed to fulfill the unique mission of their soul.

The concept of a life purpose or mission suggests that each individual has a unique reason for being on this Earth, and that their soul has specific goals, lessons, or experiences to fulfill during their lifetime. These goals or purposes may vary greatly from person to person, and may encompass different areas of life such as relationships, career, personal growth, or spiritual development.

Based on this perspective, it is believed that the needs of the soul, which may include emotional, psychological, spiritual, or existential needs, are aligned with its unique purpose. These needs may manifest as desires, longings, or yearnings that are specific to each individual, and may guide their choices, actions, and life path.

For example, if someone's life purpose is believed to involve creative expression, their soul may have a need for artistic inspiration, self-expression, and opportunities to create. On the other hand, if someone's life purpose is believed to involve service to others, their soul may have a need for compassion, empathy, and opportunities to help those in need.

The understanding of Soul Needs and life purpose is often subjective and may vary depending on one's beliefs, culture, and personal perspectives. Some may interpret Soul Needs and life purpose in a spiritual or religious context, while others may approach it from a philosophical or existential perspective. It's important to note that these concepts are open to interpretation and may be understood in different ways by different individuals.

Both unique and universal Soul Needs can guide us towards fulfilling our life purpose. The understanding is that the soul has both individualized and shared needs that are aligned with its purpose.

On one hand, unique Soul Needs are considered to be specific to each individual, based on their unique nature, experiences, and life path. These unique Soul Needs may include personal desires, longings, or yearnings that arise from an individual's inherent nature and life experiences. These unique Soul Needs can serve as guides or indicators of an individual's personal path and purpose, leading them towards experiences, opportunities, or choices that are aligned with their individual journey.

On the other hand, universal Soul Needs are considered to be shared by all individuals, regardless of their unique nature or life experiences. These universal Soul Needs may include fundamental aspects of human existence, such as the need for love, connection, meaning, purpose, and spiritual fulfillment. These universal Soul Needs are often seen as common to all human beings and are believed to be inherent aspects of the human condition.

According to this perspective, both unique and universal Soul Needs can work together to guide individuals towards fulfilling their life purpose. Unique Soul Needs can provide individualized guidance, taking into account an individual's unique nature and life circumstances, while universal Soul Needs can provide shared values and principles that guide individuals towards experiences and choices that are aligned with their higher purpose.

Based on our unique life's purpose, our Soul Needs can vary. For example:

- Politician - wisdom, cause
- Athlete - movement, achievement
- Visual Artist - exposure, inspiration
- Mechanic - malfunction, symptoms
- Musician - sound, inspiration
- Speaker - dialogue, concepts
- Teacher - understanding, information
- Lawyer - dispute, injustice

The Bottom Line

Once you have reconciled your Soul Identity and have done your Soul Work, your Soul Needs are easy to identify. Your Soul Needs have a zero-tolerance policy. They are non-negotiables because they are born from your authentic self and the natural state of your perfect peace. They are fundamental requirements for your life, and the people who are closest to you should recognize, respect and be able to serve those needs. If, for example, you've been hurt by people's dishonesty and your Soul Work reveals that it's caused you to become distrustful and cynical, then you know one of your Soul Needs is honesty. As a result, your best friend can't be someone who constantly embellishes the truth, exaggerates her experiences, or never gives you a straight answer. Your significant other shouldn't be the person who lies about where he is or what he is doing. Dishonesty in any form, omission or commission, may seem intolerable to you.

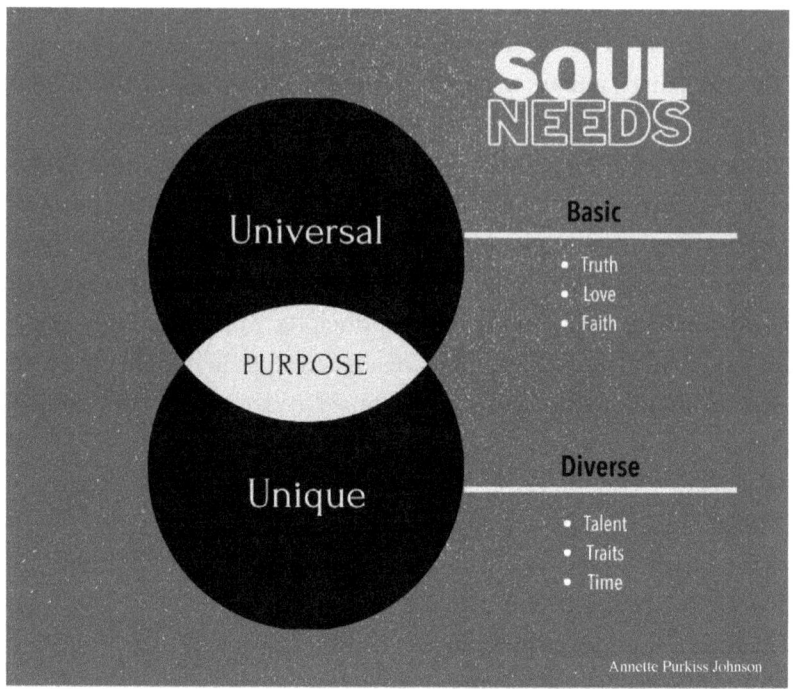

POLLEN: Identifying Others' Soul Needs

Bees use the process of pollination in which they gather pollen from a "male reproductive organ" of a flower and later transfer that pollen on to a "female reproductive organ" of another flower with tiny hairs on their bodies. Pollen plays a vital role in the reproduction of life for both the flower and the bee. Flowers rely on bees to cross-pollinate their female plants. Pollen acts as the flower's fertilization and helps flowers to continue to grow, which is of course mandatory for the survival of that flower species. Pollen is also a major part of the bee's diet, and when water is combined with a flower's sugar, it creates nectar, which is also essential for bee's survival.

Thus, bees and flowers have a symbiotic relationship because they mutually benefit each other's existence and actions. Although they are not considered "intentional" pollinators, bees have evolved over millions of years to gather and transport pollen more efficiently. Likewise, certain species of flowers who require bees for pollination have evolved to essentially "reach out" to bees to attract them through color, nectar and even ultraviolet characteristics to invite bees to them.

Bees collect nectar from flowers as a food source, while inadvertently transferring pollen from one flower to another, which helps in the process of pollination, allowing flowers to reproduce and produce seeds. In turn, flowers provide bees with nectar, which serves as a source of nutrition for their survival. Similarly, the idea of supporting each other's needs and fostering mutual benefit is often emphasized in human relationships and communities. Just as bees and flowers rely on each other for their survival and reproduction, humans can also benefit from working together, supporting each other's needs, and promoting mutual well-being.

In human interactions, supporting each other's needs can involve acts of kindness, empathy, cooperation, and collaboration. It can mean offering help and support to those in need, showing understanding and compassion towards others' challenges and experiences, and working towards common goals that benefit everyone involved. It can also involve fostering a sense of community, inclusivity, and belonging, where everyone's needs are considered and respected.

Promoting mutual benefit and supporting each other's needs can contribute to the well-being and harmony of individuals and communities. It can create positive relationships, foster cooperation and collaboration, and promote a sense of interconnectedness and interdependence among people, just as bees and flowers rely on each other for their mutual benefit.

However, it's important to note that human relationships and communities can be complex and multifaceted, and not always perfectly analogous to the simplicity of symbiotic relationships in nature. People have diverse needs, perspectives, and experiences, and finding a balance between individual needs and collective well-being can sometimes be challenging. Nonetheless, the idea of mutual benefit and supporting each other's needs is often promoted as a positive principle for fostering healthy and harmonious relationships among individuals and communities.

Recognizing Others' Needs

Recognizing the feelings and needs of others is the first step towards empathy and connection (Rumie.org n.d.). We can detect emotional cues by paying attention to other people's body language, including their posture, tone of voice, facial expressions, and other nonverbal cues. This can provide valuable insights into their emotional state and needs. Nonverbal cues can communicate a lot about a person's emotions, thoughts, and feelings, sometimes even more than their words.

Here are some examples of how body language can provide clues about other people's emotional needs:

1. **Posture**: A person's posture can reveal a lot about their emotional state. For example, slumped shoulders and a downcast gaze may indicate sadness or low energy, while an upright posture and open body language may indicate confidence or engagement.
2. **Tone of voice**: The tone of voice, including pitch, volume, and pace, can convey a lot of emotions. For example, a raised voice and fast pace may indicate anger or frustration, while a soft tone and slow pace may indicate sadness or calmness.
3. **Facial expressions**: Facial expressions, such as smiles, frowns, raised eyebrows, or wrinkled foreheads, can provide insights into a person's emotions. For example, a genuine smile may indicate happiness or joy, while a furrowed brow may indicate concern or worry.
4. **Eye contact**: Eye contact or lack thereof can also communicate emotions. For example, avoiding eye contact may indicate shyness, discomfort, or lack of confidence, while direct eye contact may indicate attentiveness, interest, or assertiveness.

By paying attention to these nonverbal cues, we can become more attuned to other people's emotional needs and better understand how they may be feeling. This can help us respond in a more empathetic and supportive manner, as we can adjust our approach based on their emotional cues.

Interpreting body language can be subjective and context-dependent, however. Different people may display different body language cues based on their cultural background, personality, and individual differences. Therefore, it's crucial to approach body language interpretation with sensitivity, empathy, and a willingness to communicate and clarify if needed. This can facilitate better communication and understanding in relationships and interactions with others.

In general, recognizing other people's needs requires empathy, active listening, and observation. Here are some tips on how to best recognize other people's needs:

1. **Empathy**: Put yourself in the other person's shoes and try to understand their perspective and emotions. Empathy involves not only understanding someone's situation cognitively but also emotionally connecting with their feelings. Try to imagine how you would feel in their situation and show genuine compassion and understanding.
2. **Active Listening**: Actively listen to what the other person is saying, both verbally and nonverbally. Pay attention to their words, tone of voice, facial expressions, and body language. Avoid interrupting or assuming, and instead, focus on truly hearing and understanding their perspective. Ask clarifying questions to ensure that you have a clear understanding of their needs.
3. **Observation**: Observe the other person's behavior and actions. Notice any changes in their behavior, mood, or demeanor that may indicate their needs. For example, if someone appears withdrawn or less communicative, it may signal that they are going through a tough time and may need support.
4. **Communication**: Open up lines of communication and create a safe space for the other person to express their needs. Encourage open and honest communication and be non-judgmental and non-critical in your responses. Be willing to listen without offering solutions or advice unless asked for, and respect their perspective and feelings.
5. **Ask directly**: Sometimes, the best way to recognize other people's needs is to ask them directly. You can inquire about their well-being, ask if there's anything you can do to support them, or simply express your willingness to listen and be there for them.
6. **Be present**: Be fully present in the moment when interacting with others. Avoid distractions and give your full attention to the other person. This shows respect and validates their feelings and needs.
7. **Practice cultural sensitivity**: Recognize that people from different cultural backgrounds may have unique ways of expressing

and perceiving their needs. Be culturally sensitive and respectful of their norms, values, and communication styles.

Remember that recognizing other people's needs requires genuine care, understanding, and effort. It may take time and practice to develop this skill, but it is essential for building healthy and supportive relationships with others. By actively engaging in these practices, you can develop a better understanding of others and respond to their needs with compassion and support that will be reciprocated by those in your Soul Tribe (Chapter 9).

Respecting Others' Needs

Just because we can recognize the needs of others doesn't always mean we respect them. This is why "recognition" and "respect" are distinct concepts. While recognition involves acknowledging the existence or presence of someone or something, respect goes beyond mere acknowledgment and involves showing consideration, honor, and esteem towards others.

Recognition can be a preliminary step towards respect, as it involves acknowledging the existence, identity, or needs of others. However, respect goes beyond recognition by encompassing a deeper appreciation and valuing of others as individuals with their own inherent worth, rights, and dignity.

For example, you can recognize the needs of others by acknowledging their feelings, thoughts, or perspectives, but respect goes further by actively honoring and valuing their needs, opinions, and boundaries. Respect involves treating others with consideration, kindness, and empathy, and showing reverence for their inherent worth as human beings.

It's important to note that respect is not dependent on agreement or approval of others' beliefs, choices, or actions. It is possible to respectfully disagree with someone or have different opinions, while still treating them with dignity and consideration.

In relationships, workplaces, and communities, recognizing the needs of others without respecting them can lead to misunderstandings, conflicts, and lack of harmony. Respect is an essential aspect of healthy and positive relationships, as it fosters mutual understanding, trust, and cooperation.

Essentially, while recognition is an important step towards understanding the needs of others, respect goes beyond recognition by involving a deeper appreciation, consideration, and valuing of others as individuals. Recognition and respect are distinct concepts, and cultivating respect towards others involves actively honoring and valuing their inherent worth, rights, and dignity.

Here are some ways to show your respect for others' needs:
- Actively Listen (e.g. nod)
- Be Present (e.g. focus without multitasking)
- Address Needs (e.g. get food)
- Acknowledge Actions (e.g. say "Thank You")
- Make Mutually-Beneficial Decisions

Model of Soul Needs

Young children provide the purest demonstration of Soul Needs. They love without restriction or judgment, freely offering fellowship and forgiveness. They tell the unvarnished truth, especially to those they love most. Their faith empowers them to act instinctively, without overthinking or fearing failure. Though they quickly learn from missteps, they never stop believing in the outcomes they seek, for they are determined and focused. In contrast, adults often give up quickly or avoid trying if they perceive difficulty. We filter our truths, saying only what fulfills a desire or withholding information that might lead to rejection. The truth is often avoided if it could cause discomfort or disruption, becoming optional or masked rather than a necessary, liberating force. As we age, judgment creeps in, and love becomes conditional, meted out based on perceived worthiness. Relationships fracture and fail when love is treated as negotiable, contingent on moods, merit, or momentary mindset, rather than being rooted in unconditional care or steadfast commitment. This is why young children are the best representation of universal soul needs; as we grow older, these needs are often neglected or reshaped to fit our desire for acceptance and conformity.

Our unique Soul Needs, like our universal ones, are often more clearly expressed in young children. In environments that allow uninhibited creative expression and exposure to diverse social or cultural settings, children reveal their unique Soul Needs through natural skills, interests, and personality.

These needs are expressed simply in conversations and play, often through questions or requests. Children will openly share what they do and don't like or what they want more or less of. While some children express desires verbally, others communicate their Soul Needs through affection (a hug), body language (a smile), or gestures (a small gift). Each action indicates their need for more or less of something: affection, affirmation, specific activities, or exposure to particular experiences.

Matthew 18:1-4 reminds us to adopt the qualities of children, including:
- Delight in simple things
- Willingness to forgive easily
- Humility
- Submission
- Trust, unburdened by fear of disappointment

This is why children represent Soul Needs in their purest form. By learning to recognize these needs in children, we can become better equipped to perceive and support them in adults, fostering Soul-Full relationships grounded in genuine understanding and connection.

NEXT STEPS

As you reflect on your unique Soul Needs, it's important to take actionable steps toward understanding them more deeply. To assist you in this journey, I invite you to take the Soul Needs Identifier Survey in Appendix E at the back of the book. This survey is designed to help you uncover and articulate your individual Soul Needs, guiding you toward a clearer understanding of what truly drives you and fulfills you.

Once you've completed the survey, take some time to review your responses. Reflect on the insights you've gained and consider how you can begin to integrate your identified Soul Needs into your daily life. By doing so, you'll be better equipped to align your actions with your true purpose and passion, paving the way for a more fulfilling existence.

8

THE HONEY

PRODUCING RECIPROCITY

"When a man is guided by the principles of reciprocity and consciousness, he is not far from the moral law. Whatever you don't wish for yourself don't do unto others."
~ Confucius

As with honey, which is always sweet no matter the type, reciprocity is always sweet to the soul. It can emerge from the same type of reciprocal relationship that bees have to flowers. The bees carry pollen to fulfill a plant's germination needs. Meanwhile, the bees use a plant's nectar to produce honey to fulfill their needs. Everything in the process wins! Similarly, reciprocating other people's needs involves responding to their needs in a supportive and caring manner.

Here are some tips on how to effectively reciprocate other people's needs:

1. **Show empathy**: Acknowledge and validate the other person's emotions and experiences. Let them know that you understand and care about their needs. Show compassion and provide emotional support.
2. **Take action**: Once you have recognized someone's needs, take appropriate action to address them. This may involve offering practical help, providing resources, or simply being there to listen and support them. Be proactive in finding ways to assist them based on their expressed needs.

3. **Communicate openly**: Keep the lines of communication open and maintain an open and non-judgmental attitude. Encourage the other person to express their needs and feelings openly, and be willing to listen without interrupting or criticizing. Respond in a compassionate and supportive manner.
4. **Be reliable and dependable**: If you commit to helping someone with their needs, follow through on your promises. Be reliable and dependable in your actions. Show up when you say you will, and do what you say you will do. This builds trust and reinforces your commitment to supporting their needs.
5. **Respect boundaries**: While it's important to be supportive, also respect the other person's boundaries and autonomy. Avoid imposing your own solutions or opinions on them without their consent. Respect their choices and decisions, and be mindful of their comfort levels and preferences.
6. **Practice reciprocity**: Just as you are reciprocating other people's needs, be open to receiving help and support when you need it. Allow others to reciprocate and support you in return. Building mutually supportive relationships involves a balance of giving and receiving.
7. **Be non-judgmental**: Avoid judging or criticizing the other person's needs or choices. Everyone has their unique experiences and perspectives, and it's important to approach their needs with empathy and understanding, even if you don't fully agree or understand their situation.
8. **Be patient and understanding**: Recognize that everyone has their own pace and process in addressing their needs. Be patient and understanding and provide support without pressure or expectation. Respect their journey and be there for them consistently, regardless of the timeline or outcome.

Reciprocating other people's needs requires active effort, genuine care, and respectful communication. By being supportive, reliable, and understanding, you can effectively reciprocate other people's needs and contribute to healthy, reciprocal relationships based on mutual respect and support.

Types of Reciprocity

There are more than 300 different types of honey, according to the National Honey Board. Each type of honey is unique based on factors such as color, texture and flavor. However, the basic difference in most all varieties is which plant the nectar comes from, which also determines the name of the honey. Here are some examples:

- Clover Honey: one of the most popular honey varieties among consumers and is often actually considered the baseline
- Wildflower Honey: mild taste typically from a mix of flowers and flavors
- Acacia Honey: comes from the false acacia tree, otherwise known as the black locust
- Alfalfa Honey
- Buckwheat Honey: the darkest honey, ranging from purple to almost black
- Orange Blossom Honey: renowned as the sweetest honey
- Manuka Honey: can only come from the North Island in New Zealand; potency not found in other varieties
- Eucalyptus (Blue Gum) Honey: native to Australia, some varieties have an almost menthol-y aftertaste
- Tupelo Honey: tree blossoms only last two to three weeks, so it is a prized rarity

After completing your Soul Work, you've undergone a transformative process, thus you should produce honey (reciprocity). The variety of reciprocity is much like in nature, where different types of people will yield slightly different varieties of reciprocity based on their personality. Popular author, speaker, teacher, and psychotherapist Ian Morgan Cron has written extensively on the Enneagram, a personality system that categorizes individuals into nine different types, each with its distinct patterns of behavior, motivation, and coping mechanisms. Here are the Enneagram types delineated by Cron and the American Journal of Psychiatry:

1. *Perfectionists:* based on integrity and excellence
2. *Challengers*: based on protecting self and others
3. *Peacemakers*: based on conflict avoidance
4. *Helpers*: based on genuine concern or care

5. *Achievers*: based on drive for success
6. *Loyalists*: based on desire for mutual respect and trust
7. *Individualists*: based on unique ideas and insight
8. *Investigators*: based on expression of capabilities
9. *Enthusiasts*: based on desire to remain positive and happy

(Booth 2023)

For example, a person with a "Perfectionist" orientation (Type 1) might express reciprocity through acts of conscientious care and high standards in their interactions, striving to do what's "right" for others. In contrast, a "Loyalist" (Type 6) may show reciprocity through steadfast commitment and protective support, creating a sense of security in their relationships.

Shortcuts

Reciprocity is a mutual exchange of something, such as privileges, support, benefits, where both parties contribute and receive something in return. Soul reciprocity is also a mutual exchange of something, but the distinguishing factor is where the inclination to do so develops. When you have Soul Reciprocity with someone, the desire to reciprocate emanates from within you and is more instinctive and automatic than planned or calculated. It's automatic in a way that doesn't just come from a good upbringing, for instance. It's an inclination you have within you for some people. In addition, when it comes from within, driven by passion, purpose or a deep connection, it tends to be more enduring. External factors like getting gifts or compliments might trigger a temporary reciprocal action, but Soul Reciprocity leads to more sustained, fulfilling relationships. So, you can't just work on reciprocity itself and still have a Soul-Full relationship.

Like there are no shortcuts to the production of honey, there are no shortcuts to Soul Reciprocity. Understanding reciprocity by definition or ideal, some people may believe they already live in a manner that represents Soul Reciprocity. For instance, those who say, "I treat others the way they treat me," may believe they are exemplifying Soul Reciprocity. These reciprocal acts, though, are most often shortcuts to true Soul Reciprocity.

These are common types of reciprocity:

- **Physical**: Doing what is done to you
- **Mental**: Believing people should reap what they sow (karma)
- **Social**: Choosing friends and activities that are mutually beneficial
- **Emotional**: Caring about people who have shared experiences

Here are a few examples:
- Giving someone a compliment because the person complimented you
- Giving people a free item with hopes that they will purchase your product
- Doing a favor for someone who had helped you in the past
- Agreeing to mutual-respect in a relationship

These are all shortcuts and don't represent Soul Reciprocity.

Empathy is a form of emotional reciprocity, but it is not Soul Reciprocity. Empathy is the ability to understand and share the feelings of another person. It involves putting yourself in someone else's shoes, recognizing their emotions, and responding with understanding. I often say that "empathy is a lost art form." I say that because I feel so strongly that most people just go through life unaware of the people around them. We are in a very narcissistic era with our selfies, social media posts, filters, and editing tools that enhance our personal appeal. So much of our messaging today is to brand ourselves, love ourselves, strive to succeed at all costs, and protect ourselves – all of which are messages of "me, me, me." It just feels like the more advanced we get with technology, the more disconnected we get from each other. And if you are disconnected, you cannot even begin to be aware of others' thoughts and feelings let alone "vicariously feel" what someone else is going through. Empathy is definitely something that you must have or know how to tap into in order to be capable of Soul Reciprocity, but empathy is not Soul Reciprocity. Soul reciprocity takes empathy a step further and utilizes the awareness you have of others' feelings and experiences and uses that knowledge to nourish and nurture them. There are actions beyond understanding and awareness that make Soul Reciprocity what it is, and those actions have to be mutual. Someone with whom I was very close with for a very long time had no capacity for empathy. It took me years to put my finger on what was missing in that relationship, and then one day it literally occurred to me that this person was completely unaware of what I was feeling or how I think. Because of that gap, I felt misunderstood and underappreciated. Even though there was great camaraderie in the connection, there was no depth, no common ground beyond a good time and socializing. There was never a time when this person leaned in and considered what I might be thinking or how her actions might affect me. As a result, many things this person did actually hurt me in one way or another, even if that was never the intention. At one point, I explained, "The consequences of their actions and inactions become harmful to me when there is no regard for me." What that means is that someone can actually not intend to hurt you. They may not even be thinking of you really. However, it's that very state of disregard that creates the harm, especially if it's supposed to be someone you "love." It's a lonely place to be in any kind of relationship. We all desire to have connections with people who are connected. There is nothing fulfilling about a one-way street or disconnected energy with someone. So, if someone isn't capable of empathy, they aren't capable of being in a Soul-Full relationship. Empathy is a foundational element of Soul Reciprocity, so you must be able to give it as well as find those who have the capacity to do the same.

Shortfalls

When bees gather nectar, there is still no guarantee that they will produce honey. Similarly, you can do the Soul Work and not achieve Soul Reciprocity because of personal shortcomings, such as low self-esteem, bad habits, second-guessing, and fear.

They say the first step to "recovery" is realizing you have a problem. Well, the same philosophy holds true for being successful in Soul Work. You won't be able to achieve Soul Reciprocity or even make a genuine effort to go through and complete the process if you don't acknowledge or recognize that there is something missing in your current relationships. Why don't we want to admit and face the problems in our relationships? Well, for many of us, including myself, the thought of making changes in our lives that remove or reposition people who are there now can be scary or uncomfortable. Some people dread change. Others can't handle the truth. For many people, we have difficulty facing hard facts about those we care about. We can't handle the thought of someone you love (or think you love) 1) not being worthy of their position; 2) doing us more harm than good; 3) not being able or willing to provide our Soul Needs or 4) not being there (even if they shouldn't be). Let's be honest, we often don't want to admit problems in relationships because we just might have to admit that WE ARE THE PROBLEM. So, rather than being honest with ourselves that something is missing, we just let time pass and get progressively frustrated and dissatisfied. As a result, we move through life with Soul-Less connections and miss out on the beauty of Soul-FULL ones. I believe that we find ourselves stuck in relationships that don't serve us because we just don't know what to do or we don't know what the possibilities really are for something better. This is why Soul Reciprocity is a destination, a place of mutual consideration, shared sentiments, and a deep connection. Reaching the point of Soul Reciprocity is a meaningful, fulfilling destination.

By this point, you should have a fairly good understanding of what Soul Reciprocity is. The question now becomes then: Do you want it? The answer should be "Yes! I need it!" When you realize that you have actually suffered without Soul Reciprocity, you will understand that you need it. Why would anyone want to be in a relationship that is one-sided? Why would we choose a mate who doesn't consider our needs and wants as much as we prioritize theirs? Why would we have friends who only take and demand and not seek friends who provide us with the companionship and connectedness we desire in a friendship? Why would we allow family members to remain close who lack respect and understanding simply because they have the title of "family"? Why would we choose business partners with whom we don't have trust or synergy? There is no one answer to the question of why we go through our lives without experiencing Soul Reciprocity, but the following are some factors that are worth considering.

Low Self-Esteem

It's a tough truth: many of us feel we don't deserve better, which affects our relationships. We often struggle with feelings of unworthiness—believing we aren't worthy of love, trust, or belonging. This self-criticism can lead us to withdraw from opportunities before others even have a chance to include us. Such feelings stem from various sources, and when they creep in, they hinder our chances of achieving Soul Reciprocity.

One mistake I've repeatedly made is feeling obligated to prove my worth to others. This stems from a fear of abandonment, rooted in my childhood. My parents divorced when I was two, leaving my mother to navigate life as a single parent with a biracial child. My father was absent, having gone off to the military shortly after my birth. My mother, still a teenager, had little to no support and ultimately called it quits after enduring years of inconsistency and neglect.

As a child, I waited for my father to visit, hoping he would take me to the park, only to be left disappointed time and again. I never understood how someone could bring a child into the world and walk away. I've often questioned my worth, wondering, "Was it me? Why didn't he want to know me?" Those unanswered questions linger.

This absence has plagued me throughout my life, manifesting as a fear of abandonment. The result: I feel the need to prove my worth to earn love, respect, and presence in my relationships.

Bad Habits

Many relationships in our lives become habitual rather than conscious choices. We find ourselves connected to family members we've known forever, childhood friends, long-term partners, and spouses with whom we've made lifelong vows. How often have you heard someone say it's "too late" to change a relationship, or that blood ties create an automatic obligation to maintain closeness?

I've witnessed several relationships like this, including one couple who had been together for decades. They experienced a passionate romance; she uprooted her life for him, and he ended a long-term relationship to be with her. Despite their seemingly perfect partnership, she wanted marriage and children, while he did not. Years passed with them breaking up and reconciling multiple times. They clung to the idea that love was enough, yet their relationship lacked the fundamental elements of Soul Reciprocity.

This made me realize that some relationships resemble bad habits—patterns we fall into without consciously choosing them. Just like habits, they can become ingrained in our daily routines. Not all habits are bad;

some, like enjoying a morning coffee or walking the dog, enrich our lives. However, bad habits—such as excessive drinking, smoking, or lying—are detrimental to our well-being and challenging to break.

Breaking a bad habit requires readiness to endure discomfort and face fears of the unknown. For example, overcoming an addiction often involves withdrawal, bringing physical and emotional pain. You may experience sickness, anxiety, or deep sadness during this process. The struggle forces you to confront weaknesses you'd rather ignore and examine how the habit formed in the first place.

It's daunting and can feel impossible, so many prefer to remain trapped in these unhealthy cycles, often to their detriment and that of others around them.

Capability

This book is not about blaming others for our shortcomings; it's about facing reality and acknowledging that many of our dysfunctions stem from within. We often create our own obstacles to achieving Soul Reciprocity. This concept requires us to look inward, understand who we are, and prepare ourselves to engage authentically with others. We cannot ask for what we aren't ready to give.

I had a painful realization about my own capability for Soul Reciprocity through a deep friendship. I thought this friend was a core member of my Soul Tribe, embodying the kind of relationship that arises from genuine connection. We bonded over our independence, love for cooking, shared free spirits, and mutual support. We even took an impromptu trip together, further solidifying our connection.

However, when I moved to Atlanta and my friend faced a serious health crisis, I found myself falling short. While in Los Angeles working, I received the call from her husband that she was in an induced coma due to a surgical error. Though I panicked and offered help, I eventually returned to Atlanta without following up or providing the support she needed. Days turned into months, and guilt consumed me. Where was the evidence of my growth?

When I finally visited her, the conversation was awkward yet honest. I admitted I had failed her during a critical time in her life. She echoed my entiments, expressing disappointment and confusion over my absence, especially given our commitment to supporting each other.

Then, a breakthrough occurred. During a conversation with another friend, she pointed out that my absence wasn't a choice but a reflection of my own struggles. My friend recognized that she had also been unavailable for me during that time. This moment brought me grace and understanding.

The revelation was clear: we must be both emotionally and physically available to give and receive Soul Reciprocity. When we lack it in relationships, we should examine our own capacity to contribute.

In this case, my friend and I were mutually incapable but still desired a connection. Perhaps, in some way, we never truly lost our Soul Reciprocity; instead, we learned the importance of understanding our limitations and supporting each other through them.

Refusal

Many people struggle with accepting reciprocity, often viewing it as a burden rather than a gift. For some, there's an underlying belief that accepting help or affection means inviting expectations or strings attached. This mindset can lead us to refuse the very love, respect, or support that others wish to offer.

I've found myself in this position numerous times, rejecting generous offers from people who wanted to provide me with grand experiences, expensive gifts, or deep emotional connection. You might think this is why I struggled to find reciprocity and fulfillment, and you'd be right. However, it's more complicated than just turning it away.

I often felt that such generosity came with too many strings attached. My mind raced with fears of negative reciprocity, influenced by stories of women in relationships with powerful men who seemed to have it all but were often trapped in toxic dynamics. They faced infidelity, neglect, or abuse, all while feeling they had to choose between their fulfillment and their luxurious lifestyles. Witnessing these struggles left me wary; I began to equate anyone's willingness to give too much with potential negative consequences.

In my attempts to prove my worth, I would eagerly invest in relationships, hoping that my efforts would impress others and secure their affection. I expected nothing in return, yet I often received very little, if anything at all.

Even now, I sometimes wrestle with these thoughts. I recognize that believing "proving worthiness" is a one-sided endeavor has led to imbalanced relationships in my life. It's essential to understand that reciprocity should flow both ways, creating a healthier connection for everyone involved.

Apathy

The reality is that experiencing Soul Reciprocity is impossible without engaging in self-discovery and overcoming apathy. A lack of emotional investment or engagement in your own life prevents you from identifying your true needs for happiness and peace. When you fail to reflect honestly on yourself, you risk rejecting the very reciprocity that can fulfill you.

Apathy can manifest as indifference or emotional disengagement, causing you to overlook the importance of nurturing relationships and investing in your own growth. This mindset not only stunts your personal development but also blocks meaningful connections with others. When you operate from a place of apathy, your ability to reciprocate—emotionally, spiritually, and socially—diminishes.

It's a difficult truth to confront, but your own unfulfillment may stem from this lack of engagement. Acknowledging that you are the cause of your own disconnect is a crucial step toward growth. This introspection may feel uncomfortable, but it's necessary to uncover your true Soul Identity and understand your Soul Needs.

Once you commit to this work, you will begin to see both yourself and the world differently. As your energy shifts, you will naturally attract those meant to be in your tribe, as Souls recognize one another. Your Soul Tribe will then consist of individuals who are also capable of Soul Reciprocity, having engaged in their own self-discovery and emotional investment.

Ultimately, overcoming apathy allows you to cultivate relationships rooted in genuine connection and mutual respect, creating a vibrant community that nurtures your soul.

Unforgiveness

I had to learn to forgive my absentee father to heal from the hurt he caused, and it took some time. Forgiveness requires a willingness to let go of pain, but many people resist this step. They often struggle because forgiveness means confronting feelings of disappointment, betrayal, or hurt, which can be deeply uncomfortable.

Unforgiveness interferes with our authenticity; it keeps us in a reactive mode where we allow the infractions of others and even our own mistakes to plague our psyche and aura. When our hearts and minds are filled with negativity, such as revenge, we cannot genuinely experience or achieve Soul-Full Relationships.

While it's possible to move past these emotions, it demands a conscious choice. This isn't easy; the sadness and anger that accompany the need for forgiveness can lead us to shut down and avoid those situations altogether. Embracing forgiveness, however, is essential for reclaiming our peace and fostering healthy, authentic relationships.

NEXT STEPS

To gain deeper insight into how you typically approach reciprocity and to identify common shortfalls that may be holding you back from practicing Soul Reciprocity, I encourage you to take the Reciprocity Test in Appendix G. This test will help you reflect on your current reciprocity style and guide you toward cultivating deeper, more meaningful connections.

9

THE BEE TRIBE

FINDING YOUR SOUL TRIBE

"The only way to have a friend is to be one."
~ Ralph Waldo Emerson

Now that you have done your Soul Work, discovered your Soul Identity and recognized your Soul Needs, you're ready to assess who in your life does and does not provide you with Soul Reciprocity. You are ready to meet your Soul Tribe, or Bee Tribe! The good news is that this is the easiest part of the process. Well, sort of...

Bees are classified into various families including honeybees, bumblebees, and digger bees. Tribes are used to further classify bees within a family. Within the family Apidae, you can find various tribes such as the Apini tribe (which includes honeybees), Bombini tribe (which includes bumblebees), and many others, each with its own unique characteristics and species. Different tribes within a family may have distinct features or adaptations. Bees within a tribe share certain evolutionary characteristics and are more closely related to each other than to bees outside of the tribe.

While bees have several interesting and admirable traits, of particular import is how they maintain a cooperative and reciprocal relationship between themselves and with nature. They nourish and nurture. They live, work and die together in a beehive. The social nature of bees is a reminder of how important it is for us to make connections, form friendships and establish solid relationships and networks in our own lives.

Let's liken your Soul Tribe to an actual bee tribe, which is quite different from a beehive. A beehive is a physical structure where a bee colony resides, while a bee tribe is a taxonomic classification used in the study of bees to group closely related genera within a particular family. They represent different aspects of bees: one is a habitat, and the other is a scientific classification. A beehive is restricted to a geographic place and contains bees from the same family. A bee tribe means you may be related or similar, but you don't have to be in the same location or even look exactly alike. This, too, is like your Soul Tribe.

It really becomes obvious because once you know you it's easy to know what you need and want from others in your life. You can actually see the people who fit the description of those who will become part of your bee tribe. Many of them may have been there all along, but you didn't recognize them for who they are. You may not have been ready for all they had to offer in your life. You may not have felt worthy of the love they were offering. Some will be new discoveries. Souls recognize souls. Even if you thought (like me) that you weren't looking for new friends in your life, you may find that there are people you actually need. You just didn't know what those relationships could look and feel like, so you didn't find them necessary.

Types of Friends

The people in our lives with whom we have things in common, understand, socialize, are like minded and for whom we have mutual affection. From our friends we receive support, share our feelings, exchange opinions, spend quality time and experience a level of connectedness that goes beyond that which we experience with mere acquaintances or others who may be in our lives, but do not share the same level of intimacy as someone we consider a friend. Too often people are quick to call someone their friend without really understanding the significance of the title and the obligations that come with it. I think the casual approach people take at times is a key contributing factor to them being easily disappointed and hurt by people they have deemed friends, but who did not in fact ever meet the definition of what a friend is.

There are different types of friendships that can vary in terms of their depth, duration, and the nature of the connection. Some common types of friendships include:

1. **Casual Friends**: These are acquaintances or people you interact with occasionally, such as colleagues, neighbors, or classmates.
2. **Close Friends**: These friendships involve a deeper level of trust, mutual understanding, and emotional connection. Close friends are typically supportive, share personal experiences, and can be relied upon for advice and assistance.
3. **Childhood/Long-term Friends**: These friendships are formed in childhood or early years and can often last throughout one's life. They are characterized by shared history, memories, and a deep sense of familiarity.
4. **Best Friends**: These friendships represent the closest and most intimate bonds. Best friends often know each other extremely well, share deep secrets, and provide unwavering support and companionship.
5. **Work Friends**: These friendships develop within a professional or work setting and involve camaraderie, shared experiences, and support related to work-related challenges.
6. **Online Friends**: These friendships are formed and maintained primarily through online platforms and social media. Online friends can offer companionship, emotional support, and shared interests despite physical distance.

Friendships can also be categorized based on shared activities or interests, such as hobby friends, sports friends, travel buddies, or book club friends. Each type of friendship brings its own unique dynamics and benefits, contributing to a rich and diverse social network. Based on my experience, the only category missing from this list are "Soul-Full," or Soul Tribe Friends.

Identifying Your Soul Tribe

We can't be everything to all people. It's impossible. Yet, people in our lives have a lot of needs and demands from us. Quite frankly, as do we for others. We need people in our lives for a lot of things. We need advice, we need help, support, someone to talk to, companionship, and so many other things. But the reality is there is only so much time in a day and we each only have so much physical and emotional bandwidth because we also have to take care of ourselves. The concept of Soul Reciprocity is not one which requires us to be all things to all people. Instead, Soul Reciprocity is about balancing the needs and demands people have for each other with the reality that we can't be all things to all people. And because we need to have people in our lives we can rely on and those closest to us deserve to be able to count on us as well, we need a way to determine who those people should be. So by doing Soul Work and figuring out our soul identity and were able to determine what we can give and identify to whom we should give it to.

You see, the Soul Tribe is a very select group of people. Everyone can't come. This is the people that you naturally gravitate to because of who you are and vice versa. They are the people so you can rely on to be there for you in time of crisis, and time of need and when you desire companionship. And if you pick them wisely, you will be able to expect and experience the same from them. This is also not to say that there aren't others in your life who will contribute to your overall happiness and fundamental needs along the way. Remember, the process of finding Soul Reciprocity in your life is not designed to eliminate everyone from your life except a select few. It's about your inner circle and most intimate connections.

Finding someone who can be part of your Soul Tribe or closest friend group can be a special and fulfilling experience. While the dynamics of friendships can vary, some key signs that indicate a strong connection and potential for a Soul Tribe or close friend group include:

1. **Authenticity**: You feel comfortable being your authentic self around them, without judgment or pretense. They accept you for who you are and create a space where you can be vulnerable.
2. **Trust and Loyalty**: There is a high level of trust and loyalty between you. You can rely on each other for support, confidentiality, and mutual understanding.
3. **Shared Values and Beliefs**: You have similar values, beliefs, or a common worldview. This shared foundation can foster deeper understanding and meaningful conversations.

4. **Emotional Intimacy**: You can openly express your emotions, fears, dreams, and challenges without hesitation. There is a sense of emotional safety and genuine empathy in the relationship.
5. **Mutual Growth and Support**: Your Soul Tribe friends inspire and encourage each other's personal growth. They support you in pursuing your goals and aspirations, offering constructive feedback and motivation.
6. **Deep Connection**: There is a profound sense of connection and understanding between you. Conversations flow easily, and there is a natural rapport and mutual appreciation.
7. **Shared Interests and Activities**: You have common interests, hobbies, or passions that you enjoy pursuing together. Engaging in shared activities strengthens the bond and creates memorable experiences.
8. **Time and Effort**: Both parties invest time and effort in maintaining the friendship. There is a mutual commitment to nurturing the relationship and creating meaningful shared experiences.

It's important to note that the formation of a Soul Tribe takes time and cannot be rushed. Building deep connections requires mutual investment, open communication, and shared experiences. Trust your intuition and allow relationships to grow organically, while also being open to cultivating and nurturing connections with those who resonate with your soul.

The Revelation

What I noticed most as my Soul Tribe began to reveal itself to me was that there are certain people in my life who, after having had some contact with them, make me feel GOOD! People who, after a phone call, having lunch, a meeting, a weekend retreat, or working out with, left me feeling exhilarated, renewed, happy, hopeful, inspired and generally fulfilled. I'd wondered why I never noticed how good some people made me feel? Was I just not open? Was I avoiding experiencing the whole moment of being around them? Was I so arrogant or closed that I missed the amazingness of so many people I come in contact with? Or was I so cut off from living, that I wasn't inserting myself into situations where these beautiful people existed? I guess in hindsight, it was a bit of all of that.

What I definitely learned through the process is that once you have taken the time to find your Soul Identity and do the Soul Work, you will find that your Soul Needs will be met naturally by a Soul Tribe that is out there just for you. You will have an entirely new outlook and perspective on life. You will walk with a different walk and emit a different energy. And that energy and renewed spirit will attract people to you who's souls mirror yours!

This is a completely different experience from the tribe you attract when you don't know who you really are and have not found your Soul Identity. When you are lost in your own bad habits of accepting less than enough, don't know yourself fully or what you need and are instead projecting a false image and energy. The people you attract in that state of being are completely different and those relationships don't feel at all the same. Those relationships are challenging, difficult and riddled with complexities that are unhealthy and likely don't last or simply lack fulfillment. They definitely don't feel as good as the relationships that feed your Soul Needs and have Soul Reciprocity.

And what is abundantly clear once you have truly tapped into your Soul Needs and Soul Identity, is who DOES NOT belong in your Soul Tribe. It's so obvious, it's a bit scary. Because what is revealed can't be ignored. It's so loud and clear. The relationships in your life which lack Soul Reciprocity are so easy to identify that you almost feel silly that you didn't see it before. And, quite frankly, to rid yourself of these relationships can be quite easy.

This is actually a point where you need to be extremely careful. The epiphany of who you are and who you want to be is a very strong one. Once you have done all of this soul searching and all of the Soul Work, you will come out on the other side ready to get to all the good things your life has in store. You will crave relationships with Soul Reciprocity. You will seek to spend more time with those from whom you receive it. You will want to rid yourself of anything that doesn't feel the same, and you will want to do it FAST!

However, many of those relationships you may want to purge from your life may have been the longest you've had. They may be the most complicated to rid yourself of. They may even be worth investigating whether or not they can be salvaged. You must not forget that you have gone on a journey to get where you are now. You have done a lot of work that most people never get to. You have to realize that many people don't do that work because they don't want to- it may be that they don't know how. They may never have thought about it. They too may be where you were and just haven't had the strength to face the facts of why they are unhappy in some of their closest relationships. And they definitely may not have been ready to break their bad habits and endure the discomfort of what comes from doing the work to do so. Most importantly, most people do not know how to hold that mirror up to themselves and admit that the reality of their circumstances begin with themselves.

So, as you enter this amazing phase of your life in seeking out Soul Reciprocity in your closest relationships, you must also do so with grace. Grace for those in your life who may not have yet seen the light or had the benefit of the work you have done. There is actually another phase of work that you must do in sorting through who stays and who goes.

And remember, the entire point of this Soul Reciprocity thing is to achieve it with the people who you keep CLOSEST to you. You will not and should not have this threshold for everyone in your life. It's impossible. In the words of some of my favorite Soul Tribe members "everyone can't come"! There are many people in your life who will remain, come and go who don't have to care regularly about your innermost needs and wants. Nor will you have that level of connectivity to them. But that doesn't mean that they don't belong. Or that they don't have a place. Many of our friends and family members are more peripheral in our lives but we still like them, even love them. People who we enjoy seeing and spending time with when the time comes. Co-workers and colleagues who brighten our day when we see them. Neighbors we socialize with at block parties or a simultaneous moment at the mailbox. Ex-partners or spouses who you are still in contact with because you co-parent or still have mutual friends. The point of understanding how to achieve Soul Reciprocity is so that the people who you choose to have in your life in the closest and most intimate capacity are able to bring you the fulfillment that you need and want from someone in such a special position.

The Soul Tribe will not be comprised of everyone you know. It's not intended to be a requirement for the masses. However, having Soul Reciprocity with those closest to you will assist you in your daily interactions with the masses because you will have what you need emotionally already and won't find it necessary for everyone to provide you with pieces of what you need here and there. It will likely help you be more productive and even have more tolerance and respect for others you come across more casually in your life. You can let go of the crazy expectation levels you may have for some people. You will understand that everyone doesn't owe you the world. It won't make you as angry when some people don't show you the respect you show them. You may be nicer to the service people you encounter day to day. You may lighten up on the pressure you put on some friends or family members to be more in tune with you at the annual get together. You won't need to piecemeal your fulfillment from random folks who don't owe you some deep level of love or reciprocation because you will already have it in your life. And you can relax and enjoy people for who they are and love them *where* they are because you will have a better understanding and empathy for them.

God put a lot of amazing human beings on this earth. And if we're lucky, we come in contact with some of them every day of our lives. The point is to find balance and of course maintain incredible people in your broader community of family, social groups or working environment.

So don't turn your back on anyone that can add value or just bring a smile to your face. They are important to our overall sustainability as well.

I feel like I woke up one day and had a whole gang of friends. I wondered when that happened! I always felt like my girl circle was small because I had what I needed from those who were in it. I was known for saying that I wasn't looking for any new friends. Even if I moved to a new place or started a new activity. But low and behold, as I began to do my Soul Work and identifying my Soul Needs (and without even realizing it) I began to acquire a new Soul Tribe. I met people along the journey who added so much to my life. People who were at various stages of their own self-discovery. Women who were in the "Mind, Body, Spirit Transformation Bootcamp", women on the wellness retreats, associates who I opened up to more and realized how much we had in common, colleagues who were at various stages of transition in life, family members who had grown and evolved but because I had pigeonholed them into being who they were years ago, I never noticed. Even existing friends who I began to see in a whole new light. Understanding their trials and triumphs from a different perspective as the lens I saw the world through became clearer.

There may be more questions that come to you as you engage in the analysis of sorting your current circle. You will also become conscious of the fact that, although you may be ready for a change in the dynamics or proximity of where you hold certain people in your life, there are likely to be consequences associated with those changes and you need to be prepared for them. You may also realize that some of these people deserve a shot at becoming a member of your Soul Tribe. It may simply be that they are not yet where you are, but they may be just like you were: in a state of "unknowing." If you are able to share with them the journey you've been on and how they too can embark upon it, you may very well find a Soul Tribe member or two in your current circle that you didn't think was there.

This may be an especially important exercise for you and your spouse for example. But before rushing into a decision to discard or re-prioritize or reorganize the people in your life, especially a spousal relationship, you must make sure you've taken a look at the state of each relationship, why it's in the state it's in, and whether or not you are inclined to look deeper into salvaging it as a close relationship and if achieving Soul Reciprocity is possible. In order to avoid regretting the inevitable circumstances of any decision to purge someone from the inner circle, this process is necessary. But, as I stated previously, once you are clear the answers are obvious and the moves you make are relatively effortless.

We will discuss this process in more depth as we examine Soul Reciprocity in love and marriage, friendships and family relationships in Section 3.

NEXT STEPS

As you continue your journey of self-discovery, I invite you to complete the Soul Tribe Identifier Survey located in the Appendix H. This survey is designed to help you assess the relationships in your life and identify those individuals who truly resonate with your Soul Identity.

As you engage with the survey, take the time to reflect on your connections and the qualities that define your Soul Tribe. Consider how each relationship enriches your life and contributes to your sense of belonging and support.

After completing the survey, reflect on your results. Think about how you can nurture and strengthen your connections with your Soul Tribe, as well as any adjustments you may want to make in your relationships. Recognizing the importance of a supportive community is vital for your personal growth and well-being. Embrace the journey of discovering and cultivating your Soul Tribe!

SECTION 2 SUMMARY: THE PREPARATION

SOUL REFLECTIONS

Summary of Symbolism

The following terms represent the metaphors used to explore and discuss the concept of "Soul Reciprocity" in Section 2. Each metaphor represents an aspect of the journey toward understanding and fulfilling deeper soul connections, both with oneself and within a community. These terms will help illustrate the roles, actions, and dynamics involved in this process, offering a framework for identifying the different stages and participants in the quest for meaningful, reciprocal relationships. From the individual's role as a "bee" to the importance of creating a "meadow" for self-discovery, this guide serves as a lens through which we can better understand the pursuit of true Soul Reciprocity.

BEES – **Individuals** who seek soul fulfillment in some form

- Honeybees – **Person** who works to create reciprocity and a tribe
- Bee Mimics – **People** who pretend or operate like bees ("wanabees")
- Busy/Worker Bee – **Soul Work** required to achieve Soul Reciprocity with a Soul Tribe

MEADOW – **Place** where you discover your *Soul Identity*

- Plant – **Soul Identity** of the individuals who may need soul reciprocity
- Healthy Plants – **People** who have discovered their soul identity
- Unhealthy Plants – **People** who lack soul identity

NECTAR – **Your Soul Needs** fulfilled by you and others

POLLEN – **Others' Souls Needs** you fulfill or facilitate

HONEY – **Reward** of completing the Soul Work, or "*Reciprocity*"

- Honey Varieties – **Personality-Based** acts of reciprocity
- Shortcuts – **Common types** of mutuality that isn't Soul Reciprocity
- Shortfalls – **Problems** that prevent people from achieving Soul Reciprocity

BEE TRIBE – **Goal** to create a personal community (*Soul Tribe*) of Soul-Full individuals

Chapter 5 - The Bees: Understanding Your Role

Bees offer a powerful analogy for understanding Soul Reciprocity in human relationships. Just like bees have distinct roles in their hive, humans have roles in their relationships and communities, contributing based on their strengths and needs. Bees embody traits like hard work, loyalty, and cooperation, all of which are essential in relationships grounded in Soul Reciprocity.

In Soul-Full Relationships, the connection is instinctive, much like the natural bond between bees and flowers. These relationships are built on mutual nurturing, where each person naturally supports the other's well-being without overthinking it. Soul Reciprocity is the glue that holds these relationships together, making them effortless and fulfilling.

To achieve this level of connection, individuals must do Soul Work—self-reflection and discovery of their Soul Identity and Soul Needs. Without this work, it's difficult to experience or give Soul Reciprocity. Like bees working tirelessly for their hive, we must engage in this process to create healthy, balanced relationships.

Ultimately, Soul Reciprocity is about being in relationships where both parties understand, support, and nurture each other's souls. It's a destination reached through consistent Soul Work, leading to deeply fulfilling connections with others who are part of your Soul Tribe.

Chapter 6 - The Meadow: Discovering Your Identity

Crossroads in life present opportunities for growth, signaling moments to embrace discomfort and make necessary changes. Soul Work—introspection, receiving feedback, and making intentional changes—is essential for personal growth and building authentic, fulfilling relationships.

The meadow serves as a powerful metaphor for self-discovery and Soul Work. Just as bees play a vital role in pollinating flowers, human souls are interconnected and benefit from mutual support in their growth. The meadow also symbolizes a safe and nurturing space where individuals can ex-plore their Soul Identity and gain revelations about who you really are among the diverse souls (wildflowers) around them.

Discovering your Soul Identity requires honest self-examination, digging into your desires, core values, and the traits—both good and bad—that shape your life. True self-improvement is impos-sible without first understanding who you are and why you are the way you are. This level of self-awareness forms the foundation for Soul Reciprocity,

Chapter 7 - The Nectar and Pollen: Understanding Soul Needs

This chapter draws a parallel between the symbiotic relationship of bees and flowers with the concept of Soul Reciprocity in human relationships. Just as bees seek nectar to nourish themselves while pollinating flowers, humans nurture one another by meeting mutual Soul Needs, creating a balanced and reciprocal dynamic. The idea of reciprocity extends beyond basic survival needs like food and shelter to deeper Soul Needs such as truth, love, faith, and intimacy, which are essential for emotional and spiritual fulfillment.

Understanding and identifying these Soul Needs is key to cultivating relationships that are not "soul-less." When these needs go unmet, individuals may feel disconnected or unfulfilled in their relationships. This chapter delves into the importance of doing "Soul Work," which involves recognizing and honoring both personal and others' needs. In this way, Soul Needs become non-negotiable, reflecting our authentic selves.

Soul Needs are both universal and unique to each person. While certain needs like love, connection, and meaning are common to all, others are shaped by individuality—purpose, personality, and perspective. These diverse needs require mutual respect and empathy in relationships. The chapter also emphasizes the importance of recognizing others' emotional and spiritual needs, fostering an environment where reciprocity thrives, much like the relationship between bees and flowers. It explains how young children are some of the purest representations of Soul Needs.

Ultimately, doing Soul Work allows individuals to reconnect with their inner truths, guiding them toward meaningful connections that nurture and fulfill their soul's deepest desires.

Chapter 8 - The Honey: Producing Reciprocity

Reciprocity is a sweet and natural exchange, much like the relationship between bees and flowers, where both benefit and thrive. In human relationships, this reciprocity comes from understanding and responding to each other's needs in a supportive and compassionate way. In general, reciprocity involves empathy, support, communication, and consideration, all while maintaining a balance of giving and receiving.

Soul Reciprocity, however, goes beyond simple acts of exchange. It comes from a deeper connection and is more instinctive, creating lasting, fulfilling relationships. Unlike transactional interactions, it emerges from within and is driven by genuine care and mutual nurturing, leading to more enduring relationships.

Different types of reciprocity exist, such as physical, social, or emotional, but they often serve as shortcuts and do not foster the depth that Soul Reciprocity offers. Empathy is key, but alone it does not lead to a Soul-Full connection without mutual care and effort.

Several personal obstacles can hinder Soul Reciprocity, such as low self-esteem, bad habits, or an inability to forgive. These barriers keep people from experiencing meaningful connections. Overcoming these challenges through self-awareness and emotional growth is essential to fostering deeper, reciprocal relationships that nurture both individuals at a soul level.

Chapter 9 - The Bee Tribe: Finding Your Soul Tribe

After completing your Soul Work and understanding your Soul Needs, it's time to identify your Soul Tribe—the people who truly resonate with your authentic self and offer mutual support. These relationships, much like bees in a tribe, are based on reciprocity and shared values. Souls naturally attract those with similar energy, and as you gain clarity, you'll recognize who belongs in your close circle.

Not everyone in your life will meet the deep needs of a Soul Tribe member, but they may still have value. The goal isn't to cut everyone out but to ensure those closest to you bring emotional reciprocity. By building this core group, you'll have a strong foundation of support and fulfillment, allowing all your relationships to flourish.

SECTION 3:

THE APPLICATION

Lessons from Life

10

LOVE AND ROMANCE

THE BEE DANCE

"A soulmate is someone who has locks that fit our keys, and keys to fit our locks. When we feel safe enough to open the locks, our truest selves step out and we can be completely and honestly who we are."
~ Richard Bach

Over the course of the last ten years, I have made some profound discoveries about life and love. I really thought certain people would play the same role in my life forever. I thought my marriage was permanent for sure. I made my vows fully intending that they were a declaration of what was to be my life until death. I waited until my mid-30s to get married. I was that girl who, in my teens and 20s, believed very strongly that people shouldn't rush to be married and start a family. I believed it was impossible to make a forever decision about a life partner without living and experiencing as much of life as you can. I went to college and learned that boys liked me. I had been pretty sheltered throughout high school, so this was a bit of a shocking (but welcomed) discovery. I definitely had a good time living away from home, without all the strict rules and regulations and making up my own as and when I saw fit. Through the coming-of-age diatribes that come from college life, I learned a lot about myself, men, and relationships. Some lessons were exciting, but others were heartbreaking.

I can't just give you a magic formula for achieving balance in your romantic relationships without explaining *how* and *why* I developed these ideas. I've applied them in my own life, and they've worked for me. Sharing personal experiences is the only way to show that Soul Reciprocity isn't just a theoretical concept—it's something I've achieved after living without it. While sharing these private experiences is uncomfortable for me, it's necessary to provide real context. So, here it goes.

The Picture

At first glance, my life in Los Angeles seemed near perfect. I had a beautiful house behind gates, breathtaking views, luxury cars in the driveway, and a closet full of designer bags and shoes. My career as an entertainment attorney was thriving, and I was surrounded by a supportive family, incredible friends, and my husband of eight years, along with three beautiful stepchildren. I traveled often, hosted dinner parties, and made sure to celebrate the whole month of August with my fellow Leos. People would often tell me, "Girl, you are living your best life!" And while that was true in many ways, it didn't capture the deeper struggles that lay beneath the surface.

On the outside, I had it all. But the reality was different—my Soul Needs were going unmet. The connection between my husband and me had shifted, and I began to realize how emotionally absent we had become to each other. We shared a home, a life, but not the emotional intimacy or reciprocity that a true partnership demands. We had become two people living side by side, but with no deeper connection. For me, over time, our relationship had grown soul-less.

The Reality: Loss

For three years before moving to Los Angeles, my husband and I faced the emotional roller coaster of trying to conceive. Having married later in life—my husband already had three children while I had none—I felt an urgent desire to start a family. I had always envisioned becoming a mother after establishing my career and enjoying married life, but now in my late 30s, that dream seemed elusive.

My obsession with pregnancy soon consumed me. I read everything I could find, from medical articles to holistic remedies, seeking advice on Eastern and Western methods, even timing ovulation with testing kits. When I finally underwent fertility testing, I felt a glimmer of hope: my results showed I was healthy and had plenty of viable eggs. I was eager to share this news with my husband, but the next step was daunting.

Convincing him to undergo fertility testing was tough. I understood the stigma men face around fertility, but he agreed. Sadly, the results revealed that he faced significant challenges due to a medical procedure. With determination, he underwent surgery, and after a year of waiting, I finally became pregnant.

Instead of feeling closer to my husband, the strain from years of trying to conceive only widened the emotional gap between us. While I was consumed with the idea of starting a family, he remained distant, as if my need for emotional support and connection wasn't being heard. We were going through the motions, but the deeper connection that nourished our souls had long faded.

More Reality. More Loss.

On the day of our move to Los Angeles, instead of celebrating new beginnings, I was reeling from the loss of what could have been. The day started chaotically as we unpacked boxes in our new home. My two Shih Tzus, Ginger and Jazzy, were my comfort through this transition. Ginger, my first dog, was more than a pet; she was family.

Just as I began to settle in, tragedy struck. A neighbor knocked on my door, delivering devastating news. Ginger had run into the street and was hit by a car. She died instantly. The pain was unbearable and I was inconsolable.

Grim Reality and the Darkest of Days

As the day wore on, my body reacted to the emotional turmoil, and I began to miscarry naturally. The pain was excruciating, and at one point, I lost consciousness. I had never experienced anything like it. The physical process mirrored childbirth, and I felt like I was losing a part of myself. I couldn't process losing my loyal companion and the child I had so desperately wanted within hours of each other. I grieved not only the loss of Ginger and my pregnancy but also the dreams and connections I had envisioned.

In the aftermath, I leaned on my support system of friends and family, particularly my mom and one of my best friends, who came to be by my side. I decided to surrender my desire for a baby, redirecting my energy into work to maintain the lifestyle we had created. I thought, "Let go and let God," but the weight of my losses lingered, leaving me to navigate a new reality without my precious connections.

End of the Marriage: Lack of Soul Reciprocity

Overall, I thought my marriage was a good one. I had found a man who adored me. He understood my crazy life and career because he was in the same industry and had been born into a musical legacy. His entire life was centered around an industry that I was also in. That was important to me, because career-driven women can be misunderstood, and our professional lives can sometimes be intimidating to men. So many women with amazing jobs and success find themselves single because they say that a lot of men can't handle what comes with it. Add to that an industry like entertainment and a whole myriad of other complexities can arise. So, it was a blessing to have a spouse who understood and had that context.

We were great friends, enjoyed each other's company, and had so much in common that it made the day-to-day easy. Despite the great things, like so many relationships, there were challenges, most of which I didn't see as problematic in the beginning. It didn't bother me to be the breadwinner. I never sought out a relationship where I would be taken care of, and I have always been able to provide for myself. When he had trouble finding work as a musician, I was patient and understanding and "held things down" for our household and everyone in it. I didn't look at his shortcomings as weaknesses because he had many other strengths in areas I did not. I am a nurturer and a fixer. I see the best in people and am a devout cheerleader. I love hard and give all I have in every way. I'm loyal and a fighter, so I do whatever it takes to achieve the goals I set and to maintain happiness in relationships. Still, my optimism and drive weren't enough in my marriage.

Eventually, it became clear that my marriage was no longer a place of mutual soul connection. We were not tending to each other's emotional needs, and there was no reciprocity in our relationship. I had poured myself into creating a life, a family, and even into the idea of motherhood, hoping that it would bring us closer. In the midst of the craziest of times, my husband offered no solace. I had been waiting for him to show up in so many ways, to hold space for my struggles, but that support never came. Instead, I was left to navigate a lot alone. I realized then that my soul's needs—for understanding, empathy, and support—were being ignored in the very place they should have been nourished. But our souls were drifting further apart. We stopped seeing each other, hearing each other, and understanding the depths of each other's needs.

The lack of soul reciprocity—this deep exchange that binds two people together—was at the heart of our relationship's collapse. We had ignored our souls' calls for connection, for nurturing, for love in its truest form. In the end, my marriage dissolved not just because of the challenges we faced but because we had lost the ability to give and receive on a soul level.

I don't regret a day of my marriage and I likely would make the same decision if put back in time. I'm not resentful or angry. However, it became abundantly clear after a lot of self-reflection and "Soul Work" that it was not a relationship that I could continue, not because of any one "incident" or accumulation of problems, but because it was void of Soul Reciprocity. I had poured everything I had into that relationship, and I needed to be supported and encouraged in a similar manner.

Looking back, I realize that the things I went through between 2013 and 2015 would be the beginning of the end. It was the end of not taking proper care of me. It was the end of living with tunnel vision. The end of pretending I was invincible. It was the end of turning a blind eye. It was the end of sacrificing myself to my own detriment. It was the end of empowering others and forgetting myself. It was the end of lying to myself and allowing others to lie to me. It was the end of not expecting or demanding more. It was the end of painting pictures that were not accurate reflections of my life and instead, living a life of truth, authenticity, and purpose so that the picture is real and not a mirage.

Determining the end of a marriage or committed relationship is a deeply personal and subjective decision. Ultimately, deciding the end of a romantic relationship requires careful introspection, open communication, and honest self-reflection. It can be helpful to seek support from your trusted friends, family, religious leaders, or professionals, such as therapists or counselors, who can provide guidance and help you navigate this challenging decision-making process. Remember that prioritizing your well-being and those in your care is crucial when making such a significant decision.

Understanding the Dance

As I navigated the painful end of my marriage, I realized the lack of soul reciprocity wasn't just a personal struggle—it mirrored the way many relationships operate. Relationships, like a bee's dance, rely on a delicate rhythm of intention, mutual effort, and the commitment to nurture. In a bee colony, each bee plays a role in harmony with the others, moving with purpose to support the hive. Similarly, in relationships, both partners must invest energy, time, and care to keep the connection thriving. Just as a bee cannot sustain the hive alone, a relationship falters when one partner stops contributing to this shared dance.

Like the bee dance, relationships involve an ongoing exchange of energy, each partner moving in response to the other's cues. If one partner withholds, it disrupts the rhythm, leaving the other feeling disconnected. Relationships, much like the hive, thrive on the balance of giving and receiving. When one partner consistently withholds, the connection weakens, creating an imbalance that can ultimately bring the relationship to an end.

It Takes Two to Dance

In a bee colony, each bee contributes to a communal purpose, performing specific roles that support the hive's needs. Much like a bee returning from its foraging mission to share its findings through the dance, relationships depend on mutual involvement—a back-and-forth exchange that builds and sustains the partnership. While a bee might explore on its own, it ultimately relies on its return to the hive, where its contribution is shared and valued.

This continuous dance within the hive mirrors the reciprocity and connection that relationships need. Just as bees communicate and adapt to fulfill their roles, partners in a relationship must remain engaged, responding to each other's emotional cues. Relationships thrive on this interplay, where both individuals actively engage to foster understanding, harmony, and growth.

Unlike a competition where there's a victor, the bee dance embodies harmony—a fluid exchange that supports the collective good. In romantic relationships, too, the goal is not to outshine but to move in tune with each other, building connection, mutual support, and companionship. Soul reciprocity captures this essence, where partners join in a mutual exchange that nurtures both souls. Each partner's efforts feed into the relationship's growth, creating a foundation of empathy, compassion, and shared purpose.

Communication is the Guiding Dance

In the hive, communication is everything. Through subtle signals and the precise steps of their dance, bees share vital information to guide one another toward sustenance. Similarly, communication in a relationship is foundational. It allows partners to express themselves clearly, understand each other's needs, and create an environment where both feel seen and valued.

Like the bee dance, communication is an ongoing, mutual process. Effective communication in relationships promotes understanding and intimacy, helping partners navigate conflicts and find harmony. It's the rhythm that holds the relationship steady, guiding both partners toward reciprocity and fulfillment.

The Foundation of the Hive

Just as bees rely on a strong hive foundation to build their colony, relationships need a stable base to support growth. In a hive, environmental factors like weather or available resources can impact the bees' work, requiring them to adapt and adjust their roles. Similarly, relationships are shaped by external influences like social expectations, emotional backgrounds, and financial situations, which impact the connection between partners.

Adapting to these influences requires awareness, communication, and flexibility, much like bees responding to changes in their environment to protect the hive. By recognizing these factors, couples can navigate challenges and build resilience, creating a stable, thriving foundation.

The Sweet Spot of Connection

Within a hive, the "sweet spot" is the place where bees experience alignment and synergy in their roles, resulting in a productive and harmonious environment. This sweet spot, where each bee's actions contribute to the collective strength of the hive, resembles the high point in a relationship where connection, compatibility, and mutual support align.

Conversely, relationships can also experience a "dead spot"—a time of disconnection or stagnation, when the exchange of energy and effort slows. In these moments, partners may feel disconnected or out of sync, much like a bee without a clear path back to the hive. Recognizing and nurturing the sweet spots in a relationship can strengthen the bond, while addressing dead spots offers an opportunity for reflection, growth, and reconnection.

Trusting the Hive

In a bee colony, trust is implicit. Each bee relies on the others to fulfill their roles, knowing they work for the hive's collective good. In relationships, too, trust is essential. Trust allows partners to depend on each other, share responsibilities, and navigate challenges together. It fosters a sense of safety, mutual support, and emotional intimacy.

Building and maintaining trust requires consistency and reliability, much like the predictable patterns within the hive. When partners trust each other, they create a strong, secure foundation that allows the relationship to grow and flourish.

Identifying Your Soulmate

Finding a soulmate is like the bee's instinct to find its flower, a connection born of purpose and mutual benefit. Just as a bee is drawn to the flower that offers the sustenance it seeks, finding a soulmate involves discovering the person who complements our strengths, supports our growth, and shares our vision for the future. We should seek a love as true as a bee finding its flower, a love that moves in harmony like the bee dance, a silent rhythm of give and take, each step drawn by the soul toward the sweetness of shared purpose. Still, these relationships require adaptability, communication, and trust, sustaining a long-term commitment built on shared values.

In a soulmate, we find a partner with whom we choose to build a life. This chosen relationship, more than any other, is one where Soul Reciprocity becomes essential. With our soulmate, we engage in a partnership intended to last, where each partner fulfills a unique role in nurturing and strengthening the bond. The closeness of this connection, like that of the hive, relies on dedication, resilience, and a commitment to maintaining the balance and harmony that sustain the relationship over time.

One of the most important choices we make in our lives is to select our life partners. Our intentions are to create a forever decision. We take vows and make promises, and we intend to keep them, doing what it takes to preserve that relationship and make it work. With that said, we also know that the reality is that so many marriages don't make it. Divorce is far too common and often far too acceptable, but it's real. Although I have experienced it myself, I don't endorse it as a solution to all martial problems. I believe we have a duty to fight the good fight and to put our all into making it work. I believe the vows mean something, and that they shouldn't be given up or broken without deep contemplation and resolve.

I also believe that for those who are in a marriage or seeking to be in a committed relationship, this is the most important type of relationship to have Soul Reciprocity. This is arguably *the* closest of all chosen relationships in our lives. I say that because this is the one relationship we actually seek to be in for life. We are born into our family relationships. We choose our friendships, but we don't make a promise to our friends that the relationship is "until death do we part." So, marriages present a unique situation where we decide on a person to share our lives with on every level, and in doing so, we create the most intimate, impactful relationship that we will have. I believe that because of making such a monumental decision, we have a responsibility to take all steps possible to preserve it when we find that it is out of balance.

Failing Relationships

Soul Reciprocity is a mutual respect and response to "Soul Needs." My marriage failed because it was missing the most important foundational components. At the time, I didn't understand concepts of Soul Needs and Soul Reciprocity, so I wasn't able to describe what was wrong in those words. I did know I wasn't receiving what I was giving and that I felt alone, empty and unfulfilled.

There are a lot of reasons that romantic relationships fail. Typically, it comes down to one's negative experiences outweighing the positives, creating imbalance. Eventually, imbalance becomes intolerable. Other romantic relationships are doomed to fail because one or both people are:

- Unhappy, having unhealthy feelings or thoughts that create toxicity.
- Noncommittal, providing little to no sense of security.
- Self-Sabotaging, suffering low self-esteem so they reject or are unable to sustain true love.
- Superficial, focusing more on the appearance of the relationship.
- Servants, giving more than they get, ask for or even need.

By no means was my marriage my first failed romantic relationship. When I reflect back at others whom I loved and lost in my life, it's clear that those failures were also attributed to a lack of Soul Reciprocity. Unfortunately for me, I hadn't done the Soul Work necessary to understand my Soul Identity or Soul Needs. The result was that I missed early signs to avoid heartache and stayed in Soul-Less situations longer than I should have. What I now know for sure is that there are definitely signs when Soul Reciprocity is lacking in a romantic relationship. For example, you know Soul Reciprocity is missing from a romantic relationship when you:

1. **Feel Emotionally Exhausted.** You are drained or depleted by giving more support than your partner and not receiving the same in return.
2. **Feel Alone.** Love relationships take two- feeling alone is a sign that the other is not showing up in ways that they should.)
3. **Sense a Decline in Intimacy.** Emotional, physical and sexual intimacy are key components in romantic relationships. Lack of intimacy is a lack of reciprocal connection and affection necessary for Soul-Full relationships.

Then there are those situations when you may, in fact, have achieved (or thought you achieved) a Soul-Full relationship only to have it fail after time. The fact is Soul Reciprocity once achieved, can be lost if not properly maintained. We all have known or heard of couples who seemed to be the picture-perfect example of love. Power couples who appear to perfectly complement each other. High School sweethearts whose love seems to be unbreakable because it has stood the test of so much time. Online dating matches who were "put together" by scientific data, algorithms and personality assessments that should beat the odds of self-selection.

There are infinite examples of what appear to be aspirational couples whose breakups are a shock to all the onlookers and outsiders. But for those who are a part of those relationships that start out in a blissful state and later end, there are few surprises.

There are many ways that Soul Reciprocity can fail after being achieved in love. Some specific reasons are:

- **Misalignment of Expectations**: Over time, people who are aligned can become misaligned if their expectations of the other or the relationship are not met or shift from where they began. Different expectations about the relationship can lead to disappointment and misunderstandings which cause imbalance.
- **Communication Breakdown**: Disappointments, life traumas and other circumstances in life can cause people to withdraw, become angry or distant and change the way they communicate with their partner. Ineffective communication prevents partners from understanding and meeting each other's needs.
- **Waning Reciprocity**: Relationships are not 50/50 at all times. Sometimes they are 80/20 or some other ratio of give and take. Soul reciprocity can exist so long as in the aggregate, there is mutuality and alignment. However, when one partner feels they are giving more than they are receiving over time, it can create resentment and an uneven dynamic, causing Soul Reciprocity to become challenging to sustain.
- **Unresolved Conflicts**: Conflict is bound to happen in any relationship, no matter how loving. But persistent unresolved conflicts can undermine trust and affection, making reciprocity difficult for one party to sustain.

Successful Relationships

In the dance of bees, harmony, purpose, and instinct guide the way. When bees perform their dance, they aren't competing against one another; instead, they communicate with precision, leading each other to the life-sustaining nectar they seek. Similarly, successful relationships thrive not on competition, but on mutual support, clear communication, and shared goals. Like bees understanding their unique roles within the hive, partners in a relationship need self-awareness and emotional intelligence to navigate the needs of both individuals.

Just as the bee dance strengthens the hive and promotes survival, a fulfilling relationship fosters emotional growth, resilience, and a sense of inner peace. This connection can enhance both partners' lives in subtle, enduring ways—bringing a sense of joy, purpose, and unity that, much like the intricate movements of bees reveal itself as a beautiful, sustaining rhythm. The dance of love can be just as beautiful, a graceful exchange of energy and understanding, like the bee dance that guides and nurtures. In this shared rhythm, partners move together in harmony, creating something more than the sum of their individual parts. Just as bees work together for the good of the hive, a successful relationship is about finding a balance that allows each person to flourish while building a strong, lasting bond. Each step, each turn, becomes a way to grow closer, with shared purpose, joy, and mutual respect at its heart.

Some of the benefits of successful relationships are obvious and life-changing, as well as subtle. Here are examples of each:

Life-Changing Benefits

1. **Deepened Emotional Connection**: A stronger bond that leads to greater intimacy and a feeling of true partnership.
2. **Increased Relationship Satisfaction**: Overall happiness and satisfaction in the relationship improve, fostering long-term commitment and stability.
3. **Resilience During Challenges**: A united front during tough times, making it easier to navigate and overcome life's obstacles together.

Subtle Benefits
1. **Daily Joy and Comfort**: Small gestures, mutual understanding and alignment foster joy and increase comfortability between partners.
2. **Improved Communication**: A natural ease in communication exists which reduces misunderstandings and conflicts.
3. **Personal Growth**: Encouragement and support from a partner helps each individual grow and motivates you to strive to be the best version of yourself for you and your partner.

Lastly, the key to successfully finding a soul mate is knowing yourself, namely your strengths and weaknesses. In order to understand your potential or significant other in the dance of love, you must take the time to get to know them like you do yourself, recognizing and responding to their Soul Needs. Here are some tips to consider:

- Don't kid yourself about who you see them to really be.
- Be honest about who they are and where they are.
- Don't try to change them.
- Ask the difficult, real questions.
- Don't pick someone you can control in pursuit of getting what you want.
- Be open to breaking the patterns of your "type," especially if your type historically was created out of your own misperception of yourself, who you are and what you really need.

Knowing your partner in the dance of love is the key to building a strong, lasting connection. Understanding their emotional needs, triggers and values allows you to navigate challenges, communicate better and attend to their Soul Needs. Simply put, in tennis and in love, the more insight you have into the person on the other side the more likely you are to achieve success.

QUESTIONS

Assessing Soul Reciprocity in a romantic relationship requires a deep and honest look at the balance between giving and receiving love, support, and effort. Here are some introspective questions to help you evaluate reciprocity in your romantic relationship:

Evaluating Your Contributions:
1. How often do I go out of my way to show love and appreciation to my partner?
2. Am I attentive to my partner's needs, both emotional and practical?
3. Do I make an effort to support my partner's goals and dreams?
4. How do I express my love and care—through actions, words, or both?
5. Do I initiate positive experiences, like planning dates or doing something special for my partner?

Assessing the Balance:
1. Do I feel that I give as much as I receive in my relationship?
2. Are there areas where I feel I'm giving more than I'm receiving, or vice versa?
3. How do I feel about the balance of emotional support in our relationship?
4. Am I comfortable asking for what I need from my partner, or do I hesitate? Why?
5. How do I react when I feel my efforts aren't being reciprocated?

Understanding the Dynamics:
1. Do I offer support and affection to my partner without expecting anything in return?
2. Are there times when I feel taken for granted, and how do I address this?
3. Do I notice patterns in how we each contribute to the relationship? Is one of us more giving or more dependent?
4. Am I satisfied with how my partner reciprocates my efforts and love?
5. How do we handle situations where one of us feels the balance is off?

Reflecting on Growth:
1. How has the balance of give-and-take in our relationship changed over time?
2. What have I learned about my own needs and my partner's needs when it comes to reciprocity?
3. What can I do to improve the balance of giving and receiving in our relationship?
4. How do I measure the success of our relationship—by what I give, what I receive, or the mutual growth we experience together?
5. What steps can we take to ensure that our relationship is both nurturing and mutually fulfilling?

Exploring Emotional Impact:
1. Do I feel valued and appreciated for the love and support I provide to my partner?
2. How do I feel when my partner goes out of their way to support or care for me?
3. Am I able to communicate my needs and feelings openly with my partner?
4. Do I feel a sense of balance and fairness in our relationship?
5. How does our relationship contribute to my overall happiness and well-being?

Considering Future Actions:
1. What actions can I take to foster more reciprocity in our relationship?
2. How can I better express my appreciation for my partner's contributions?
3. Are there unresolved issues related to reciprocity that we need to address?
4. How can we create an environment where both of us feel equally supported and valued?
5. What do I need from my partner to feel more balanced and fulfilled in our relationship?

These questions can help you reflect on the dynamics of Soul Reciprocity in your romantic relationship, guiding you toward a more balanced and mutually supportive partnership, a Soul-Full relationship.

11

FRIENDS

HOW MANY OF US HAVE THEM?

"Friendship is composed of a single soul inhabiting two bodies."
~ Aristotle

It was the Soul Reciprocity within my friendships that cast a bright light on what I was missing in my marriage and some other close relationships. As I journeyed to understand my Soul Identity and Soul Needs, I devoted significant time to noticing how I *felt* around others. I realized there were certain people who stirred something visceral within me, even just at the thought of them. They were friends I couldn't wait to be with and found hard to part from when we were together. Meanwhile, there were others who left me questioning my own value or feeling drained.

Achieving Soul-Full friendships takes intention and effort from both people. It involves regular communication and check-ins, whether by calls, texts, or, when possible, in-person meet-ups. Even a quick message can show that you care and are thinking of your friend. Genuine interest and support are also essential to nurturing Soul Reciprocity in friendships. I take an active interest in my friends' lives. While many people talk mostly about themselves, rarely asking the other person questions, I make it a point to ask my friends about their days, listen to their concerns, celebrate their successes, and offer support during challenging times. When life gets busy and I realize I haven't connected in a while, I'm intentional about reaching out, acknowledging my absence and taking time to catch up.

With friendships, sometimes it takes an extra effort to make time for quality moments together. At this stage in my life, it's harder than ever to fit in everything I want to do. And with friends spread across the country, regular "face time" isn't always possible. Still, I know that spending meaningful time together whenever possible is invaluable. Whether it's sharing a hobby, a casual outing, or simply hanging out and talking, making time to connect is important in nurturing our bond.

We've all heard the phrase, "It's the little things that matter most." Regularly expressing appreciation for my friends' presence in my life is one of those little things I feel makes a big impact. Small gestures, words of thanks, and acts of kindness help strengthen our bond. I especially enjoy sending little gifts for no reason, mailing heartfelt notes, and texting out of the blue to remind them of my love and appreciation. One of my favorite ways to show this is through "love boxes"— gift boxes filled with carefully curated tokens chosen just for that friend. Each box typically includes something fun, whimsical, and heartfelt, inspired by their unique qualities. I want my friends to feel loved, thought of, and celebrated in a way that's personal to them.

In past relationships I thought were friendships, I often found myself giving freely without expecting anything in return. I took pride in being the friend who remembered birthdays with cards, sent flowers, offered support, sent encouraging texts, and invited others to special events as my guest. I never expected anything back. Recently, I realized that some people I considered friends don't actually meet my definition of friendship. They don't "friend" like I do. This has been a difficult truth to face, especially at this stage in my life. Despite previous "purges" of my friend circle, I kept some people around out of habit, obligation, or simply because they thought we were friends, and I went along with it. However, this journey of deeper self-understanding and evaluating my relationships through the lens of Soul Reciprocity has led me to another round of re-evaluation. This time, I'm making decisions from a different perspective, and some choices are surprisingly easy, while others are much harder. The difference between these choices, the ease versus the struggle, is best illustrated with examples.

"Friends" Who Aren't Friends

While definitions of friendship are easy to find, understanding what a friend truly is—and what we need from one—requires individual reflection. Distinguishing a true friend from an acquaintance can be challenging. Many of us have called certain people "friends" without fully considering our own Soul Needs and Soul Identity. But as we dig deeper into who we are, we may come to realize that certain people don't, or can't, meet those deeper needs or reflect the essence of who we are.

The first step in identifying a true Friend (capital F) is to see people for who they genuinely are, not who we hope they could be or the potential we see in them. A friend once reminded me, "You have to see people for who they are, not for who you think they can become."

The Taker

Some "friends" only receive and never give, basing the entire relationship on what you bring to the table. They wait for you to think of them, invite them, and prioritize their needs. These individuals have no reservations about asking—or even demanding—your time, resources, or connections. It's "Can I borrow some money?" or "Can you fix my emergency situation?" or "Can you get me tickets?" You find yourself feeling obligated, almost under pressure, to please them. You worry about disappointing them if you say no, often stressing yourself to meet their needs, sometimes above your own.

These "friends" are a unique type of "wanna-bee," like the bee fly, an insect that resembles a bee but doesn't share the bee's purpose or reciprocity. Bee flies, like honeybees, feed on flowers, making it easy to think they share our values. However, bee flies are trickier: they lay their eggs in other hives and take advantage of resources they didn't help create. Over time, the taker worms their way into your circles, your friendships, and your connections, only to reveal their true nature. Just as bee fly larvae are parasitic to many insects, including honeybees, takers often drain you without giving back.

They never reciprocate, and you might wonder if the friendship would hold up if you ever stopped "doing." The hard truth is that they take because they can, and they don't give because they don't have to. This reality forces us to face a tough question: are takers empowered because we don't demand Reciprocity from them?

The Wasp in Bee Clothing

A few years ago, I realized that I had included someone on my "friend" list who, in truth, has never been a friend to me. I'll call her "Bonita." Bonita and I share many friends, interests, and similar life philosophies, and we have fun together. However, the reality is, we aren't truly friends. We don't spend quality time together, nor do we know each other's dreams, fears, or Soul Needs. We don't confide in each other or even ask about each other's personal lives. Publicly, we've projected as friends, yet Bonita spends more time complaining about what we don't do together than creating moments to share—and, if I'm being honest, neither do I. Bonita can be jealous, petty, and self-absorbed. So, why was Bonita on my friend list to begin with? I think I thought there was potential for a real friendship, but there isn't.

Bonita is the perfect example of another type of wanna-bee: the wasp. While wasps are the honeybee's closest biological relatives, that's where their similarities largely end. Wasps aren't truly part of the bee family, and they don't work in hives like bees do. Yet, they provide some benefit to bees, preying on pests like caterpillars and aphids. Bonita, too, doesn't belong in my Soul Tribe or my hive. We may not share deep friendship, but we do share interests, overlapping friend groups, and similar philosophies. Bonita may not be part of my core tribe, but she can still have a place in my life.

The Energy Vampire

Some "friends" actually give too much. They shower you with love, affection, and adoration, smothering you with their devotion and constantly professing how much they value you. They make it clear that you're a top priority in their life and, in return, expect the same from you. These friends need and want you deeply, but their demands for your time and energy can quickly become overwhelming, creating a sense of pressure that makes their presence feel stifling.

This type of friend resembles the hoverfly, which, as the name suggests, hovers around flowers it wants nectar from. Like the hoverfly, these friends circle around you, reminding you of your importance to them and hoping for the same level of focus from you. Their hovering can reach a point where it's tempting to swat them away or step back from their constant buzzing.

The Diva

You know the one. The world revolves around them, and every conversation ends up about *them*. They never ask about *you*. They never check in with you but will readily criticize you for not calling, texting, or checking on them. They are the classic "I haven't heard from you in forever" type. If you didn't initiate contact, you might not hear from them at all.

Ironically, these people are often extremely charismatic and charming—the life of the party, the most popular, the funniest. Every time you're together, you have a great time. Yet somehow, the experience leaves you feeling a bit empty. At the end of the day, they are selfish and have limited capacity to give. It's not necessarily that they don't want to—they just can't. And often, we make the most excuses for them, justifying their inability to show up and sow into us, giving them a pass.

These friends see themselves as the queen bee of the hive, though it's really only in their minds. The queen bee in a hive has an essential role—mating with drones to lay eggs, producing pheromones to unite the hive, and creating a thriving colony. The "queen bee" friend twists this idea, though, seeing herself not as a unifier or leader but as the only one who matters.

The justification we provide for these friends stems from an unwillingness to see them for who they really are. In truth, they're limited in what they can give because they can't see beyond their own grandeur. Being self-absorbed means they can't make anyone else their priority, much less truly support others. A hive cannot survive with a queen who's focused only on herself, and true reciprocity cannot exist with someone who only sees things in one direction.

The Negative Nelly

Some people see every cup as half empty and feel the world is against them. For them, every problem or challenge is someone else's fault. They can't take accountability for their actions or recognize how they might be contributing to their own issues. No matter how many blessings they have, they're fixated on what they lack and on circumstances that don't go their way. This is the essence of a "Negative Nelly." I'm saddened by how many Nellys I know. Each time I'm with one, I realize they literally cannot let themselves experience joy. For them, the attention gained from negative drama feels like validation, and over time, they lose the ability to receive attention any other way.

A Negative Nelly will often begin each encounter with something like "You won't believe what happened," immediately steering the conversation into yet another negative situation. In the hive of friendship, the Negative Nelly is akin to the drone bee. Drone bees have one primary purpose: to mate with the queen and ensure the hive's survival. With a singular drive, the drone isn't involved in other hive activities and doesn't contribute much to the overall harmony. Similarly, the Negative Nelly is single-minded, fixated on their misfortunes, with no room for optimism or personal accountability. When times are tough, worker bees may drive drones out of the hive to conserve resources. Likewise, when something genuinely negative happens to you or a beloved member of the hive, there's little space to also carry the weight of a Nelly's unyielding negativity.

Chatty Cathy

I once considered someone in my life to be a friend until she proved otherwise. Let's call her Cathy. I knew Cathy for years—so long that I can't even remember how or under what circumstances we first met. Cathy could be attentive, helpful, and resourceful. We shared a lot of connections from different areas of our lives, and our mutual quirks helped us understand each other a bit more. Friendship with Cathy was easy; it wasn't very demanding, but it also wasn't very close. Even so, she looked out for me several times and went out of her way to help, just as I did for her. Because of these moments, I believed we were friends—until the day her betrayal came to light.

I was talking with someone I'd only recently met when it turned out she also knew Cathy. This person shared that Cathy had mentioned me in conversation a few times. Some things she said were harmless, even complimentary. But to my shock, Cathy had also shared personal, private details about my life—information this person could never have known unless Cathy disclosed it. Imagine getting to know someone, only to discover that they know deeply personal details about you that should never have left the confidence of a friend. Cathy's indiscretion was a violation of my privacy, and realizing this betrayal was painful. Yet removing her from my circle was surprisingly easy.

This type of friend isn't a "bee" at all. While the other "wanna bees" mentioned here might not be suited for the hive, each still belongs in the family of honey bees. Despite their shortcomings, I trusted each of them with some aspect of my soul. They may have disappointed me or failed to be a true friend in various ways, but none of them betrayed me the way Cathy did. Friends like Cathy are more like hive beetles, which are natural predators of honey bees. Hive beetle larvae burrow through the comb, destroying the intricate structure, honey, and pollen, sometimes causing the hive to collapse entirely. Betrayal has a similar destructive power. Just as hive beetles have no place in the hive, so do betrayers like Cathy have no place in your Soul Tribe.

When I set aside my rose-colored glasses and took a practical look at the people in my life, I began to see them as they truly are. This clarity helped me discern the qualities I need and want in my Soul Tribe—and just as importantly, what I don't. My focus shifted toward what I'd learned about my Soul Identity and Soul Needs, and everything changed.

Friend You Overlooked

On the other end of the spectrum are those I never consciously put on my "friends" list but who, without asking for any formal title, have proven themselves to be true friends. Through my soul-searching journey, I've had the pleasant surprise of discovering these beautiful souls along the way. You know the ones—the people you haven't actively kept in touch with but who somehow reach out at just the right time, checking in or simply saying hello. They're always there to encourage, lift you up, go the extra mile when others fall short, and never ask for anything in return. Quiet yet consistent, these friends are always considerate, gracious, and thoughtful. Their friendship is so pure and effortless that it weaves seamlessly into the fabric of your life.

And when you come to understand the type of person you need as a friend, you realize that these are exactly the ones you've been looking for all along.

These friends are like my worker bees. Worker bees go to great lengths to protect and provide for the hive; some vibrate their bodies in winter to keep the hive warm, while others may travel up to three miles in search of pollen. Some focus on nurturing the young, others on guarding the hive from intruders. Among thousands, it's easy to overlook certain worker bees, but each plays an essential role in the hive's survival. These friends may not stand out, but their loyalty and quiet support are vital, just like the worker bees' dedication to their hive.

Perfect Peace: The Soul Tribe

Some of my friends fill me with such good energy that I feel genuinely "full" after spending time with them. It's like a warm hug around my heart, the incredible feeling that comes from sharing a friendship rooted in Soul Reciprocity. There's a special warmth in my heart from the mutual love and respect we share. They nourish my soul, and I want them to feel that same depth of connection and joy in return. It's effortless and free of ego or competition. Every time I leave their presence—whether in person or virtually—I feel uplifted, better than I was before.

The difference between a friendship with Soul Reciprocity and one without is striking. Just as you may search for it in romantic relationships, you can't truly achieve Soul Reciprocity in friendships until you know your Soul Identity, understand your Soul Needs, and see people as they really are. Once you can do that, knowing who is worthy to be a member of your Soul Tribe becomes clear and effortless. It's like a natural selection, forming a hive with those who belong in your circle, the ones who are truly a part of your bee tribe.

Lessons Learned

Just because someone doesn't measure up to your new definition of a friend, doesn't necessarily mean they must be eliminated from your life or your hive. That is not the point of this exercise. Remember, the focus of this book is to show you how to experience the deepest level of fulfillment in the relationships you hold most valuable and the people who are closest to you. Soul Reciprocity isn't possible in every relationship you have, nor is it necessary. The Soul Tribe is a select group. The A List. So don't feel as though you have to eliminate every Taker, Chatty Cathy or Diva from your life. Some of them have other redeeming qualities, are necessary participants in your life journey and some are just simply a good time! Your challenge is to SEE them and decide for yourself what position they play in your life.

Failing Friendships

It's true that some friendships come and go, but there are those we think are meant to last forever. Sometimes Soul Reciprocity fails with friends we thought were permanent members of our Soul Tribe. That most commonly happens because of:

- **Lack of Commitment:** Friendships generally have less formal commitment compared to familial and romantic relationships, making it easier for them to dissolve when challenges arise. Despite the fact some of our friendships may feel like family (or even closer), the fact is there really is no "forever" connection that exists unless the parties want it to. So, if someone is not committed to the work involved in maintaining Soul Reciprocity, it may not be as difficult for the other to walk away.
- **Evolving Interests and time constraints**: Friends might drift apart due to changes in interests, hobbies, or life paths, leading to a natural decline in reciprocity. Likewise, busy schedules and differing priorities can make it difficult for friends to maintain regular contact and support, unlike family or romantic partners who often prioritize time together. These issues can create feelings of inequality and resentment that undermine Soul Reciprocity.
- **Changing Social Circles**: Changes in social circles, such as moving to a new location or developing new friendships, can weaken existing friendships and even cause competition and jealousy. Perceptions of changes in social status, competition over achievements or jealousy over new relationships can cause a strain and sever bonds that previously existed.

The key is to take the blinders off and allow yourself to SEE what kind of friend you are dealing with and identify their capacity for Soul Reciprocity so that you can determine if that person belongs (or should remain) in your Soul Tribe- or if they should be repositioned. You know Soul Reciprocity is missing from friendships when:

1. **Communication is one-sided**. One person consistently initiates contact, plans activities, and drives the conversation, while the other rarely reciprocates with the same level of effort or enthusiasm.
2. **There is a lack of emotional support.** During tough times, one friend is always there for the other, but when roles are reversed, the support is not equally given or is noticeably absent.
3. **You are feeling drained**. One friend feels emotionally exhausted or taken advantage of because they are always giving, listening, or helping without receiving similar support in return.

Successful Friendships

I began this chapter by sharing with you the incredible feeling that you get when you have a Soul Tribe of friends with whom you share Soul Reciprocity. Members of your tribe come into your life because your souls recognize each other. Your soul identities are aligned, and you share the mutual desire to meet the other's Soul Needs. I am so grateful for my bee tribe filled with workers, drones, queens who all contribute significantly to my life in different ways. The honeybees who nourish and nurture me and the beautiful meadow we co-exist and thrive within.

Life-Changing Benefits

Obviously, there are benefits to having a Soul Tribe of true friends. Some of the benefits can create positive shifts in the course of your life. Here are a few:

1. **Reliable Support Network**: Soul Reciprocity between friends creates a dependable group of "Soul Tribers" who provide emotional, practical, and social support.

2. **Increased Mental Health and Wellness**: Improved mental and emotional health due to strong, supportive friendships.
3. **Longevity and True Happiness**: Real, authentic friendships are the essence of life and greater happiness. Studies even show that the happiness that results from strong friendships extends one's lifespan.

Subtle Benefits

Achieving Soul Reciprocity in friendships can also create subtle shifts in your everyday life that, although not as noticeable as life changing benefits, are nonetheless impactful and contribute to your overall sense of fulfillment.

1. **Frequent Laughter and Joy**: Having Soul Reciprocity creates more moments of joy and laughter, making life more enjoyable.
2. **Reduced Stress**: Having people to freely share your feelings and receive support from helps to manage and reduce stress. There is security in knowing you have a tribe that has your back and you can rely on.
3. **Continual Growth**: Friends inspire and motivate each other to try new things and grow. Friendships rooted in Soul Reciprocity are the ultimate personal growth incubation system.

To achieve and maintain success and Soul-Full connections in friendships, you must tend to one another's Soul Needs. Communicating effectively is one way to do so. Here are some examples of things that you can "say" in your own quest to Soul Reciprocity:

- "I miss hearing your voice and seeing your face. Let's put a date on the calendar to catch up soon."
- "I'm here for you. Tell me three things that I can take off your plate?"
- "I am grateful for our friendship, who you are and all you do."
- "No matter the distance or time that may separate us, know that I'm always here for you."

QUESTIONS

Reflecting on reciprocity in friendships involves examining the balance between giving and receiving emotional, social, and practical support. Here are some questions to help assess this balance:

Evaluating Your Contributions:
1. How often do I go out of my way to support or help my friends?
2. Do I listen to my friends' concerns and offer advice or comfort when they need it?
3. When was the last time I initiated contact or made plans with a friend to show I care?
4. Am I willing to make sacrifices or adjust my schedule to be there for my friends?
5. Do I regularly check in on my friends, even when I don't need anything from them?

Assessing the Balance:
1. Do I feel that I give as much as I receive in my friendships?
2. Are there friends who consistently support me more than I support them? How do I feel about that?
3. Do I notice an imbalance in certain friendships? How does that affect my feelings toward those relationships?
4. Am I comfortable asking my friends for help, or do I hesitate? Why?
5. How do I feel when a friend doesn't reciprocate my efforts or support?

Understanding the Dynamics:
1. Do I offer help or support to my friends without expecting anything in return?
2. Are there friends who take more than they give? How do I manage these relationships?
3. Do I have friends who consistently show up for me, and how do I acknowledge and reciprocate their efforts?
4. Am I selective about which friends I help based on what they can do for me, or do I help out of genuine care?

5. How do I handle feelings of resentment or disappointment when I feel a lack of reciprocity?

Reflecting on Growth:
1. How have my friendships changed over time in terms of reciprocity?
2. What have I learned about my own patterns of giving and receiving in friendships?
3. What actions can I take to create more balanced and mutually supportive friendships?
4. How do I measure the health of my friendships—by what I gain, what I give, or the mutual joy and support we share?
5. What steps can I take to ensure that my friendships are both nurturing and mutually beneficial?

Exploring Emotional Impact:
1. Do I feel valued and appreciated by my friends for the support I provide?
2. How do I feel when a friend goes out of their way to help or support me?
3. Am I able to express my needs and feelings openly in my friendships?
4. Do I feel a sense of balance and fairness in my closest friendships?
5. How do my friendships contribute to my overall happiness and well-being?

These questions can help you reflect on the nature of Soul Reciprocity in your friendships, allowing you to nurture relationships that are balanced, supportive, and fulfilling.

12

FAMILY

THE FIRST TRIBE

"Souls tend to go back to who feels like home"
~ N.R. Hart

You might wonder why we need a chapter on Soul Reciprocity within family relationships, especially since we often believe family bonds are unbreakable. Yet, not everyone grows up in an ideal nurturing environment, making it difficult to achieve true reciprocal connections with all family members. While some relationships naturally achieve deep soulful bonds, others may be strained or even nonexistent.

The reality is, unlike friends or partners, we can't choose our family, so Soul reciprocity with family members can be the most challenging to achieve. While some family ties are strong and loving, others can be fraught with complications or are simply indifferent. Overall, achieving Soul Reciprocity within a family can be the most rewarding experience, but it's not always possible. Although we can choose to distance ourselves from some family members with whom we have no Soul Reciprocity, the fact is that there are certain family members with whom we may need or desire to achieve it. We might find ourselves naturally distanced from certain family members due to differences in values, goals, or personality. Yet, there can be an undeniable pull—whether due to shared history, familial roles, or a deep-seated desire for closeness—that leads us to seek Soul Reciprocity with family members despite these challenges. This process often requires patience, understanding, and a willingness to address unresolved issues, but the rewards of genuine connection and harmony within the family can make the journey deeply worthwhile.

The Foundation

Family relationships shape us profoundly from birth, forming our first and most influential social circle. These early interactions lay the foundation for how we understand love and connection, which are influenced by the behaviors, communication styles, and emotions we witness and experience. These foundational encounters shape not only our future relationships but also our perception of the world and those around us. Through our observations, we begin to learn what love looks like: seeing the expressions on family members' faces, reading their body language, and observing their interactions with us and each other. We understand what love sounds like by listening to the way they speak to us and others. And we come to know what love feels like by experiencing the energy they bring to our presence and the environment of our home.

When these relationships are loving, affirming, and Soul-Full, we start to see family as a source of positive, fulfilling connections. If we "see" family members attending to each other's Soul Needs through gentle touches, hugs, hand-holding, encouraging pats, or warm smiles, we subconsciously associate love with these gestures. If we "hear" laughter, lighthearted conversations, positive tones, and affirming words, we internalize this as the loving language of family. And if we "feel" calm, peaceful, joyful vibes and a sense of safety and inclusion, we associate these sensations with the harmony and fulfillment of family love.

Even how conflict is handled within a family can significantly impact how we approach disagreements later in life. Observing family members talking through problems constructively and reaching resolutions teaches us to view conflict as a manageable, even healthy part of relationships. When parental figures discourage rivalry, prevent physical aggression, and avoid verbal abuse, children learn to see family as a safe haven, a place where individuals protect rather than harm one another. A child raised in this environment becomes attuned to and seeks future relationships, particularly family connections, grounded in Soul Reciprocity.

However, when family dynamics are marked by negativity, neglect, abuse, conflict, or an otherwise stressful, Soul-Less environment, we may come to associate family with distrust, fear, disloyalty, and disconnection. Too many of us bear early experiences within family settings that left negative impressions, fostered harmful habits, or, tragically, were traumatizing. In such settings, children may witness or even experience toxic interactions, sad or angry expressions, a lack of intimacy, and an absence of affectionate gestures. They may hear constant arguments, hurtful words, or disruptive noise—or experience an eerie silence borne from neglect, disinterest, or physical absence. Most impactful of all is what children "feel" when surrounded by family. Experiencing constant negativity, a lack of connection and attention, or the lingering toxicity after conflicts or abusive episodes can have lasting emotional impacts, making it more difficult to establish Soul Reciprocity within family and other relationships throughout children's lives.

Whatever the circumstances—good or bad—one undeniable truth is that during our formative years, we do not control who we spend the most time with. Consider how profoundly our childhoods are shaped by the people we don't consciously choose to include in our lives! Our perspectives on achieving Soul Reciprocity (or not) within family relationships are formed through this limited lens, creating a shaky foundation for the relationships we build later on.

As adults, these weak foundations often crumble, leaving us scrambling to undo the damage and learn new relationship-building skills. We find ourselves needing to learn how to resolve conflict healthily, show affection, express feelings, and maintain healthy relationships. Some of us recognize that our bad habits stem from learned behaviors within the family circles we were raised in. Others may attribute their low relationship IQs to broader societal norms. Regardless, whether we end up in therapy or casually discussing our experiences with peers, much time is spent revisiting our childhoods and the people who influenced them in order to address our adult relationship issues. Dysfunctional environments in our youth become the focus of our adult work to "unlearn," reprogram, and acquire new skills that will help us heal and fix our problems. This "work" is Soul Work, and it is essential for discovering Soul Reciprocity and identifying your Soul Tribe.

As I've discussed, Soul Work requires us to examine both the good and the bad that arise from our past experiences, learned behaviors, traumas, and perspectives. As we sort through these elements, we confront our own realities and uncover our Soul Identity, which allows us to understand the sources of our pain and identify those who have harmed us or no longer serve our growth. Soul Work also involves tapping into the sources of our joy and positive experiences, reflecting on the people and situations that have uplifted us, the lessons learned, and the outcomes of choices well made (which relates to understanding our Soul Needs). Through my own Soul Work, I discovered that I was fortunate to have examples of Soul Reciprocity within my family. These examples provided hope for cultivating Soul-Full relationships, even when they were lacking. Moreover, I gained valuable lessons from familial connections that were devoid of Soul Reciprocity.

My Familial Soul Tribe

If you were to ask me if I have Soul Reciprocity with anyone in my family, fortunately, my answer is yes. At the top of the list is the relationship I have with my mother. She was the first example of Soul Reciprocity that I ever had – even before I gave it a name. Our souls are forever connected because we know each other's' Soul Needs and we know how to meet them. She's a constant in my life that I don't take for granted. In fact, a key factor in my unshakable loyalty and adoration of her is the effort I know she has always put into loving me.

Mommy

My mother was just 18 when I was born and fought for me in countless ways. She sacrificed everything to protect and support me, as doting as she was a firm disciplinarian. Though she had limited means, she did everything she could to make sure I had opportunities to explore my interests and grow my gifts, no matter what it cost her.

The relationship I share with my mother is the most natural, perfect example of Soul Reciprocity. She is the undisputed queen of my hive. We talk regularly—practically every day. She even works with me as my executive assistant and case manager, the key to keeping both my law practice and my life in order. It's incredible to think that after spending my childhood and rebellious teen years trying to keep her out of my business, she would one day be running my business!

My mother is also my biggest cheerleader and has no problem showing it. She celebrates the places I travel, the clients I work with, and even the photos I post on social media. You can always find her warm, encouraging comments on my timeline. She's thoughtful and nurturing, constantly giving of herself through her time, work, attention, and even her gifts. The gifts she gives are always the most wonderful because she pours her soul into them. She often sends me beautiful cards, many featuring sunrise or sunset photos she's taken herself.

A few years ago, she sent me a handmade thank-you card after I helped her through recovery from surgery. The card had a picture she'd taken from her condo balcony on the Florida waterfront. I always knew I was a nature lover, but as I saw her taking and sharing these "views from my balcony" pictures, I realized my appreciation for nature's beauty was something I inherited from her.

To show her gratitude, she used a particular photo she'd taken a few months earlier—a stunning image of the clouds over her balcony. She had sent it to me at the time, excited for me to look closely at the cloud formations. And sure enough, there was a perfect, light pink, heart-shaped opening in the middle of the clouds right in front of her view.

Side note: Mom and I both believe that God uses nature to send us messages of love, affirmations, and reminders of His presence. Rainbows remind us of His promises. And that heart in the sky that day was like a love note from the heavens. So, it was this "God-sent" heart in the clouds photo that my mother chose for the cover of my handmade thank-you card. Inside, she wrote her heartfelt sentiments of gratitude.

What made this simple gift so special? Beyond my deep appreciation, there are profound lessons in my mom's gesture as the giver and in the way I received it as the receiver. The biggest lesson is that *love is a verb*. True, soul-filled love lives in the little things. As a giver, putting thoughtful care into a gift means not only doing something for the recipient but also considering who they are and what will resonate most with them. And as the receiver, heartfelt appreciation for the time and effort is important, but there is a deeper gratitude that arises when you recognize that a part of the giver's soul was poured into the moment curated just for you.

Though Mom had endless options, she chose to create something from a shared memory that would touch my soul. And, because of the reciprocal relationship we share, she knew I would recognize every ounce of thought she put into it. There are a million more reasons why she's amazing and the queen of my hive, but the bottom line is that from the day I was born, she has loved me in ways no one else could. Through my best and my worst, my wins and losses, and every embarrassing or even disrespectful mistake I've made, she has shown empathy and grace and never wavered. No matter what challenge we've faced, my love for her has been unwavering. Over time, our relationship has evolved into one rooted in authentic love, nurturing, and nourishing—Soul Reciprocity in its purest form.

Family Tribe Members

Like many of you, I have a myriad of people who have influenced my definition of family- some of whom were examples of what Soul Reciprocity is NOT and some who taught me what Soul Reciprocity is. Examples of functional and dysfunctional.

I've been blessed to have Soul Reciprocity in multiple familial relationships. Some are biological family members and quite frankly, some not. Sometimes our most significant family connections are formed with people we least expect, including relatives we never knew we had, were estranged from, or didn't get along with until later in life. Then there are "non-biologicals" with whom you form a familial bond. I am grateful for Soul-Full connections with multiple "types" of family members and for Soul-Less ones as well, because they have both taught me some of the most important lessons about Soul Reciprocity.

Cousin

My cousin Sonya is the sister I had before I knew I had biological sisters. She trained me for the bonds I would later form with others, and to this day, we are in perfect harmony. There is literally no other human I feel more naturally connected to at a soul level than her. It's as if I've known her for several lifetimes. I know her heart, her mind, her motivation. That which I may not have known, I've understood. I've always felt unequivocally that she experiences the same connection that I do. She is as beautiful inside as she is externally. She is loyal as the day is long and principled without compromise. Though a year younger (almost to the day), I have always looked up to her and admired her sense of self and confidence- it seems she has always been aware of her Soul Identity and Soul Needs. She is a doting daughter, a supportive sister, a faithful soulmate and the absolute most self-sacrificing, loving mother who always puts her sons' needs before hers without question or regret. A true Soul Work Warrior, she has evolved into many versions of herself, each one even better than the last, but each one as authentic as the prior.

Sonya and I have lost contact a few times over the years. Sometimes for quite long stretches. But it has never changed the relationship dynamics. Good, bad or indifferent, we always know we will receive the truth from one another. We can't b.s. one another. Ever. But because of the trust we have, there's also no need to. We honor each other's' truths. Our connection is one of effortless love, respect, and understanding—a bond that will last forever.

Siblings

I didn't meet my sisters and brother until my early 40s. After my parents' divorce when I was two, I had no memory of my biological father. Though I'd always heard rumors of siblings from his second marriage, I assumed I'd never know them, as I had no connection to my father's side. That changed when my cousin sat me down and said, "I met your sisters—and I have photos."

This revelation came from an unexpected family reunion, where relatives disconnected through absent fathers were meeting for the first time. As I saw the faces of my sisters—faces I'd never known but somehow felt familiar—I was overwhelmed. There was joy in discovering sisters, relief in getting answers, but also sadness for the lost time and anger at our father's role in keeping us apart. It was a powerful moment that touched on my deep need for connection and my Soul Identity.

Shortly after, I learned there were two more sisters and a brother. We arranged a gathering to meet, and it was an emotional experience, staring into the eyes of siblings I shared blood with but no shared history. While some relationships grew into meaningful connections, others never reached that depth. This was a lesson in Soul Reciprocity—family doesn't automatically meet your Soul Needs, and not every relationship will lead to that deeper soul connection.

Through this process, I found siblings who became part of my Soul Tribe, offering the kind of reciprocity and support I needed. At the same time, I accepted that not all family bonds would fulfill my soul's desires. The experience taught me that Soul Reciprocity is rare, even within family, and that recognizing and nurturing those who truly meet your Soul Needs is what matters most.

Stepchildren

When I married, the idea of stepchildren worried me. Having been a stepchild myself, I knew the complexities involved. Friends had shared stories of bitter exes and children caught in their parents' conflicts. I feared I would face similar challenges and wanted to avoid the drama.

Ironically, after my divorce, I realized that during my marriage I formed a lasting bond with my ex-husband's eldest son, Brandon. He had little contact with his father growing up due to strained relations with his mother. Knowing the pain of parental absence, I was determined to ensure he never felt that void. When we first met, he was 14, and though the meeting was awkward, it marked the beginning of a deep connection. I became a constant support for Brandon, helping him navigate his complex family dynamics, all while recognizing the emotional scars he carried.

Family relationships, especially those we don't choose, can be difficult to manage. Hurt people often hurt others, perpetuating a cycle of pain. But through Soul Reciprocity, we can foster deeper connections that meet our Soul Needs.

After my marriage ended, I let my ex tell the children about the divorce. When Brandon found out, he called me, asking, "What am I supposed to do now?" At 28, he still sought reassurance, and I made it clear I wasn't going anywhere if he didn't want me to. This moment affirmed our bond, showing that our relationship went beyond my marriage to his father.

Today, Brandon calls me "Mom," not as a replacement for his biological mother, but as a reflection of the connection we've built. While we may not have been born into each other's family Soul Tribe, Brandon is undeniably part of mine, and I know I am part of his.

Biological Father

It's just as important to learn from negative experiences as it is from positive ones. In fact, we often learn more from the negative, as we strive to avoid those outcomes at all costs. My non-existent relationship with my biological father is a clear example of what Soul Reciprocity is NOT. As I mentioned previously, my mother divorced my father when I was two years old. After the divorce, I lived with my mother, and to my knowledge, my father never returned. Despite my hopes for a relationship, one never materialized. Because of promises he never kept and efforts he never made, I wouldn't recognize him if he walked into a room and introduced himself with ID in hand.

There is clearly no reciprocity—or any relationship at all—when one person walks out of your life and makes no effort to show up thereafter. Unless, of course, a social media request at age 53 constitutes "showing up," but I would venture to say it does NOT. Absence cannot create a soul connection, and a tribe cannot be formed with people who are not present. It would be an understatement to say that I have been deeply affected by my biological father's abandonment. The scars have manifested throughout my life as feelings of unworthiness, mistrust, and continual fears of abandonment. Although I've done a lot of Soul Work to address these issues, those scars may never fully heal. However, through my quest to find Soul-Full relationships, I've gained the skills to avoid Soul-Less Connections, like the one I never had with my father, at all costs.

Stepfather

In stark contrast to my biological father, my stepfather, whom I refer to as "FD," was present in my life. He's a brilliant and educated man who broke numerous stereotypes, earning multiple degrees, including a Master's in Computer Science in the 1960s when many schools were just beginning to integrate. He has worked for Fortune 500 companies like Xerox, served as a commodities broker in the 1970s, served time in the military, and has been both a professor and an entrepreneur.

FD entered my life when I was very young, unfortunately coinciding with the onset of my "daddy issues" stemming from my biological father's absence. As a result, I was not a willing recipient of a father figure; after all, I had previously had my mother all to myself, making his role a challenging one. Parent-child relationships are inherently complex, and stepparent-child relationships are even more so. Taking on the responsibility of co-parenting a child you didn't "create" requires a vow of selflessness, a sacrifice in its purest form. You make an awesome promise to your partner to assume the role of parent voluntarily, even if the child resists or rejects it. Having taken on this role myself in adulthood, I understand the level of martyrdom involved. There were times after becoming a stepparent when I asked him how he managed it. While I don't know if I ever received a direct answer, what I do know is that he was a man who fell in love with a woman who had a child. Rather than shy away from the added responsibility, he leaned in, made me a priority, and impacted my life as if he were my biological father.

Despite the many peaks and valleys in our relationship, he affectionately gave me the nickname "FD" (Favorite Daughter), and I reciprocated with the same nickname for him (Favorite Dad).

FD introduced me to tennis and recognized my natural talent, devoting his time to teach me the game and coaching me through my junior career, which culminated in top rankings and even some historic achievements. Although he had a bit of a "Tiger Dad" approach with tough love, he taught me critical life lessons and exposed me to experiences I would have never encountered otherwise. Most importantly, he was consistent. He seemed to understand my Soul Needs before I did and nurtured them. Despite my strongest periods of resistance, he remains a strong presence in my life and the love of my mother's life.

FD and my mom share a love that has outlasted many naysayers and puts their partnerships to shame. From their daily walks to sharing every meal together at the table and enjoying "date nights" at restaurants featuring live music, their relationship is a testament to enduring love. This is what Soul Reciprocity looks like: two committed people with mutual desire for each other's happiness, working through life's challenges together, ignoring the court of public opinion, and pouring into each other's lives with a shared vision.

After decades together, having overcome adversities and raised me along the way, they remain inseparable, spending nearly every minute of every day together. FD is undeniably the father I never had, and I credit him with significantly contributing to the woman I am. I'm forever grateful to have learned from FD what sacrifice, commitment, and unconditional love in families look like. Even when I did not reciprocate, he never abandoned me. Instead, he remains an example of the love and loyalty that define a Soul-Full family tribe.

Aunt

Many people have what we call "play aunts" or "play uncles"—individuals who come into our lives and form soul connections that feel as familial as blood relations. "Auntie Karen" was the personal assistant to my ex-father-in-law for over 30 years. As elegant as she is pragmatic, she is a principled woman whose life reads like an adventure novel. In her role, she bore the immense responsibility of managing the personal and professional affairs of a celebrity, juggling an impossible number of obligations while dealing with a wide spectrum of personality types.

From the moment we met, our soul connection was uncanny. When we were introduced, we immediately immersed ourselves in conversation. Within just 15 minutes, she began to tear up and declared, "Oh, Heather! I'm so happy to have you here! You have no idea the blessing you are about to be to this family." Our souls recognized each other at first sight. It took me a while to digest her words, but as their truth unfolded, it became clear that she saw the authentic me before I could even reveal myself.

Our auntie-niece bond has always been special. We exchange love gifts just because, provide advice and counsel to one another, cry together, and pray together. When she received her cancer diagnosis and would be alone for her pre-op consultation, I understood her Soul Needs and flew to town, arriving at the hospital with my suitcase in tow. When she walked in, shock and awe on her face, I reassured her that she does too much for too many to be alone during such a difficult time. The reciprocal nature of our relationship has always felt effortless.

Auntie Karen is a protector of many, and she has been my protector even when I didn't fully realize it. The way she sacrificed and embraced her "employer" and his family as her own made me want to call her my family member, too. Our relationship was a cornerstone during my marriage, and my divorce did not necessitate an end to it. To this day, Auntie Karen remains a constant in my life—a reliable confidante with whom I have shared a true experiential journey of Soul Reciprocity.

Uncle

Uncle Jimmy taught me early lessons in reciprocity and sacrifice. He had developmental disabilities and required 24-hour care and oversight. Bound to a wheelchair, he wore protective headgear in case he had a seizure and fell. As my grandparents aged, caring for Jimmy became too much for them to manage, leading to his move into a nursing home. When my mother and her siblings were young, they rallied together like worker bees, nourishing and nurturing him. He required physical therapy and assistance with eating, bathing, and all other basic routines. The family came together in true Soul Tribe fashion to meet his physical, emotional, and spiritual needs.

From the time I was born until Uncle Jimmy's untimely passing, I was also involved in his life. We would visit my grandparents' house on Sundays, have dinner, and spend time with Jimmy. He loved to watch old movies of himself and the family from my grandparents' archives. Grandpa would cue up the movie projector and set the reels so Jimmy could enjoy the films. In my tweens, I would often get annoyed at having to watch those black-and-white movies repeatedly. But Jimmy would squeal with delight when he saw himself on the screen in his cowboy Halloween costume or with one of his childhood pets. His excitement was infectious, and we were all drawn in, naming the familiar faces and listening to Grandma and Grandpa repeat the family stories.

Jimmy was a vessel through which our souls connected. Through his eyes, we experienced the simple joys of life and were reminded of the strength of family bonds grounded in Soul Reciprocity. Although his verbal communication skills were limited, my bond with him was deep, nonetheless. When we were with him, we saw the world through a narrower lens, revealing a beautiful meadow where the little things mattered, and joy resided in places you'd least expect—if you just paid attention. Despite the collective efforts required to care for Jimmy, he gave back so much more through his big smiles, hearty laughs, playful tosses of the ball, and moments of reminiscing together.

Grandmother

My Grandma Kolbo taught me the value of discipline and structure. She was a formidable woman of great faith and principles—opinionated and vocal, running her household with the precision and efficiency of a military officer. To some, she may have seemed stern and unemotional, but I understood her deeper story and could see her soul. With my Grandpa Kolbo, they built a large family together, ultimately raising seven children.

I would often laugh as Grandma recounted tales of my mom, aunts and uncles-the sibling rivalries, and the intricate system she established to keep her home running smoothly. Kitchen cleanups operated like assembly lines, chores were rotated, and a schedule was set for assisting Uncle Jimmy. Grandma was a true spitfire, often expressing her frustrations about navigating family dynamics, yet you knew it was her life's purpose and she was living authentically and obediently within it.

I believe she struggled with the balance between her love for her children, her strict Catholic beliefs, and the prejudices she had encountered throughout her life. Despite her challenges, her family represented many non-traditional lifestyles for the time.

Somehow, over the years, we forged a bond that became one of the most special in my life. Our relationship was marked by honest communication; she never hesitated to voice her anger but was equally quick to express her pride in me. In many ways, she was my protector, equipping me with the tools to become a principled woman with an independent spirit.

Through her transparency and unapologetic nature, she taught me resilience and independence. While she wasn't the "warm and fuzzy" type, Soul Reciprocity doesn't have to be in order to be real. Her love was evident in how she protected and always guided me (and I feel her spirit still does). Grandmothers like her may not fit the traditional mold of nurturing, they are queen bees nonetheless and can profoundly influence our lives and the lives of their entire colony. Whether they become part of our Soul Tribe depends on the bonds we build by leaning in and showing up for them as well, transcending mere familial ties and evolving into reciprocally nourishing relationships that shape our identities.

Failing Relationships

While it may be assumed that Soul Reciprocity between family members is automatic by the very nature of the biological connection, Soul Reciprocity may never exist between family members. Or, even if it does at one point in time, there may be another instance, when it might fail. The non-existence or dissipation of Soul Reciprocity in a familial relationship could be the result of:

- **Sibling Rivalry**: Competition and jealousy among siblings can strain relationships and make reciprocal emotional support difficult.
- **Obligations and Expectations**: Family members often have specific roles and obligations imposed by cultural or societal norms, which can lead to unrealistic expectations and resentment if not met. Overbearing or excessively parents on adult children, intrusive siblings, dependent children are all dynamics that can cause Soul Reciprocity to fail in a familial relationship.
- **Lack of Choice**: Unlike romantic relationships, which are chosen, you typically can't choose your family members, making it harder to establish reciprocity if fundamental incompatibilities exist. And if neither party has done Soul Work and otherwise fails to put in the effort necessary to connect with the other, Soul Reciprocity will be impossible to establish or sustain.

You know Soul Reciprocity is missing from a familial relationship when:

1. **There is a lack of emotional support**. One family member feels consistently unsupported emotionally during difficult times, not feeling validated or perhaps understood.
2. **You experience persistent resentment and conflict**. This is a sign of lack of mutual respect, understanding and willingness to compromise.
3. **The interactions are obligatory**. Relationships are driven by a sense of obligation rather than genuine affection and interest can result in surface-level interactions, lacking in genuine Soul Reciprocity and emotional depth.

Successful Relationships

I have amazing human beings that make up my family tribe. Yet, achieving and keeping Soul-Full relationships with them is admittedly a more challenging exercise for me at this point in my life. Not because of any lack of desire to do so, but because of time and proximity limitations. I've moved several times in my life, and I don't even live in the same state as any of my "closest" family members. So, it takes a concerted effort to stay connected to relatives who you don't see or speak to on a regular basis. When the opportunity does present itself (or when I create the opportunity), I make it count by expressing my love and appreciation both with my words and actions. Some examples are:

- **Participating in Family Traditions**. In any way I can, I try to engage in family traditions and activities. Doing so fosters a sense of shared history and belonging. Celebrating holidays, attending family gatherings (even if that means popping in by video call), and participating in cultural or religious traditions help strengthen family bonds. I have joined "Zoom" baby showers, FaceTimed at Christmas and shown up to cross country graduations, birthday parties, etc. And I love sending cards and personalizing them with notes that express love and appreciation even though time and space may separate us physically.
- **Supporting Family Across Generations**. A key to Soul Reciprocity in families and something I'm intentional about doing is providing and seeking support across different generations. This can involve caring for elderly relatives, mentoring younger family members, or working together to solve intergenerational issues, which fosters a sense of continuity and mutual respect. When my grandmother was alive, I spoke to her regularly, even keeping up with our Sunday calls when I left for college and beyond. Today, I advise a young cousin regarding his animated series, attend sports competitions, graduations and other key life events of young nieces and nephews. I also rely on the support I receive from my mother who works with me and keeps my world in order!
- **Resolving Conflicts Constructively**. In any close relationship, there's going to be conflict and differences of opinion from time to

time. Addressing and resolving family conflicts with patience and understanding is critical and something I'm very mindful of. I'm known for calling a family meeting or initiating open discussions to work through disagreements to ensuring that the family unit remains strong and cohesive. It's not always comfortable, and sometimes emotions will escalate, but I do my best to diffuse as much drama as possible and keep conflict resolution conversations measured and focused on the goal of sorting through the disconnections, disagreements or hurt feelings so we can restore peace and interconnectedness.

Like most people, I have experienced a variety of familial relationships—some good, some not so good, and some non-existent. I've learned that the notion that family relationships should be effortless and strong simply because of shared lineage often conflicts with reality. The truth is, our environments shape us, and over time, we begin to see the world and those in it through a different lens of discernment. We become capable of distinguishing what feels authentic from what does not.

Through deep personal reflection and my Soul Work, I've gained a clearer understanding of who I am and what I need at the soul level. With this knowledge, I am better equipped to manage the complexities of my biological connections. This self-awareness enables me to discern who genuinely fulfills my Soul Needs and helps me confidently identify my most supportive family members—those with whom I am most compatible—and ultimately understand who is (and who is not) a part of my Soul Tribe.

These are some of the benefits of doing Soul Work focused on family relationships:

Life-Changing Benefits

1. **Stronger Family Bond**: Soul Reciprocity creates a cohesive and united family that provides a reliable support system to one another.
2. **Harmony Between Generations**: Familial Soul reciprocity creates connected relationships across generations, fosters mutual respect and shared wisdom which will change family dynamics and benefit generations to come.

3. **Emotional Security**: A deep sense of belonging and emotional security is formed because you know family members are always there for you.

Subtle Benefits
1. **Peaceful Home Environment**: A calm and supportive home atmosphere that reduces stress and makes you feel safe.
2. **Positive Examples**: Family members who achieve Soul Reciprocity demonstrate what healthy relationships look like and are an example for younger family members.
3. **Shared Joys and Traditions**: Soul Reciprocity makes it possible to enjoy family traditions and shared activities which strengthens family bonds.

QUESTIONS

Evaluating Soul Reciprocity in family relationships involves considering the balance of support, love, and responsibilities among family members. Here are some questions to help you assess reciprocity in your family relationships:

Evaluating Your Contributions:
1. How often do I offer help or support to my family members without being asked?
2. Am I attentive to the needs of my family, both emotional and practical?
3. Do I make an effort to stay connected and maintain a strong relationship with my family members?
4. How do I show appreciation and care for my family?
5. Am I willing to make sacrifices for the well-being of my family members?

Assessing the Balance:
1. Do I feel that I give as much as I receive in my family relationships?

2. Are there family members who consistently give more or less than others? How does this affect our dynamics?
3. How do I feel about the balance of responsibilities and support within my family?
4. Am I comfortable asking for help or support from my family, or do I hesitate? Why?
5. How do I react when I feel that my contributions aren't being reciprocated?

Understanding the Dynamics:
1. Do I offer support to my family members without expecting anything in return?
2. Are there times when I feel taken for granted within my family? How do I address this?
3. Do I notice any patterns in how different family members contribute to the household or emotional support?
4. Am I satisfied with how my family reciprocates my efforts and support?
5. How do we handle situations where one family member feels the balance is off?

Reflecting on Growth:
1. How has the balance of give-and-take in my family relationships changed over time?
2. What have I learned about my own needs and my family's needs when it comes to reciprocity?
3. What actions can I take to improve the balance of giving and receiving in my family relationships?
4. How do I measure the health of my family relationships—by what I give, what I receive, or the mutual growth we experience together?
5. What steps can my family take to ensure that our relationships are both nurturing and mutually fulfilling?

Exploring Emotional Impact:
1. Do I feel valued and appreciated by my family for the support I provide?

2. How do I feel when a family member goes out of their way to support or care for me?
  3. Am I able to communicate my needs and feelings openly with my family?
  4. Do I feel a sense of balance and fairness in my family relationships?
  5. How do my family relationships contribute to my overall happiness and well-being?

Considering Family Dynamics:
  1. Are there unresolved issues related to reciprocity within my family that need to be addressed?
  2. How do I manage expectations and boundaries when it comes to giving and receiving within my family?
  3. Am I contributing to a positive and supportive family environment?
  4. What actions can I take to encourage more open communication and mutual support in my family?
  5. How can I ensure that my family relationships are both supportive and healthy, for both me and my family members?

These questions can help you reflect on the dynamics of reciprocity in your family relationships, allowing you to foster more balanced, supportive, and fulfilling connections with your family members.

13

BUSINESS

THE TRADE OF RECIPROCITY

"A little reciprocity goes a long way."
~Malcolm Forbes

The capitalistic business culture in America often revolves around maximizing personal gain while giving as little in return as possible. This approach can sometimes feel "Soul-Less", where truth is negotiable, love is irrelevant, and faith in others is often self-serving. In such a climate, true reciprocity is rare, and instead, business interactions focus on leverage—what advantage one can use to extract more from the other party. However, in my journey to understand Soul Reciprocity, I discovered that I had been unconsciously applying its principles in business long before I fully realized how to incorporate them into my personal life. As an attorney, I naturally focused on building authentic, reciprocal relationships with my clients, often tapping into their deeper Soul Identities to serve them effectively as individuals, not just as business entities. By doing so, I gain understanding of their Soul Needs and service their careers with that in mind. I take time to learn my clients' Soul Identity, embark on the Soul Work necessary to understand their Soul Needs, and, from there, I help them build a Soul Tribe of strategic partners. By nurturing this understanding, I ensure we approach every deal, every challenge, with their unique vision of success in mind.

While there are many types of business relationships—each requiring me to engage in different ways—those that are founded on principals of Soul Reciprocity have consistently been the most fulfilling. These relationships transcend transactional exchanges, fostering mutual respect, collaboration, and authentic connection. And when you think about it, the people we work with are the people we often spend the majority of our time with, so it makes sense that achieving reciprocity here can lead to some of the most rewarding connections in life. To achieve Soul Reciprocity in professional/work relationships with colleagues, business partners, and clients, I focus on these practices:

With Colleagues:
- **Open Communication and Transparency**. It's important to me to foster an environment where open, honest communication is encouraged. I want my colleagues to share information and provide me with constructive feedback. And it's just as important that I listen actively to their perspectives so that I gain their respect and trust.
- **Mutual Support and Collaboration**. I am big on making it clear that I support my colleagues' professional development and projects. The lawyers and other professional staff I work with are younger than me and growing in their careers. I genuinely want them to gain something positive from having worked with me, so I offer help when needed and collaborate with them on their individual projects and endeavors as well as my businesses.
- **Recognition and Appreciation**. Everyone loves a celebration, especially when it's for them. I tend to be the Grand Marshall of any show in support of people I care about. I regularly acknowledge and appreciate my colleagues' efforts and contributions. We celebrate successes together and I express gratitude for their support and hard work. After all, they don't have to be there or care or have chosen me to work with. So, I don't take anything they do for granted.

With Business Partners:
- **Build Trust Through Reliability**. You can never have trust and mutual respect in any relationship where the other person can't rely on you. I am conscious of this with any business partnership and

work hard to ensure that I am reliable and consistent in my actions. That can be as simple as meeting deadlines, fulfilling commitments, and being dependable in my business dealings.

- **Have Shared Goals and Alignment**. Partnerships exist because people see each other as assets to one another and benefits to working together in their business endeavors. However, we may still have individual goals in mind for the enterprise that differ from the rest. In any business partnership I've ever had, I have consistently worked towards aligning my goals and objectives with those of my partners. I'm most driven to foster a sense of shared purpose and mutual benefit in my collaborations to ensure we don't lose sight of the big picture and get off track from the original vision. I call it "hitting the reset button". It's the best way to keep an environment of connectedness.

- **Open Dialogue and Feedback**. All relationships need this. And those with Soul Reciprocity require it. I make it a priority to maintain open lines of communication with my business partners. There is no true partnership if you exist on your own islands. I make sure that we regularly discuss progress, address concerns, and seek each other's feedback to improve the partnership and ultimately to reach our business goals.

With Clients:

- **Understand Their Needs**. Just as you can't know what *you* need if you don't know who you are, the same holds true for serving the needs of your clients. You can't fully understand what they need if you don't understand them. And in my opinion, there is no such thing as a "one size fits all" approach when it comes to my clients. I take the time and put in the effort to understand their individual needs, goals, and challenges. This ensures that I can provide them each with a tailored solution that genuinely addresses their specific situation.

- **Exceptional Service and Follow-up**. Satisfaction is my primary goal when dealing with clients. I am not happy unless they are. Even when dealing with difficult subjects and seemingly no-win situations, there is still a level of service that I can provide to ensure the best experience possible for my clients. I strive to deliver exceptional service consistently and follow up to ensure satisfaction and to check in to see if they have any further needs. And because nobody is perfect (not even me) I make sure that I address any issues or dissatisfaction head on and promptly. I go the extra mile to correct any issues and move forward to exceed their expectations. That's the only way to meet a client's Soul Needs.

- **Build Long-term Relationships**. Having a "one off" experience with a client is never my goal. Instead, I focus on building long-term relationships with them. I pride myself on the number of clients with whom I've worked for decades or since the inception of their careers. Whether my representation is ongoing or whether they intermittently call upon me when something comes up, there is something special about a relationship with a client that endures. I find that this is a result of engaging with them regularly, keeping them informed, and showing genuine interest in their success and well-being. Because I take the time to understand them and their needs at the soul level, they feel connected in a way that feels more familial than strictly business.

In Spirit

How does Soul Reciprocity connect to business or professional life? I'll explain some personal experience first for context, and then I'll explore some scientific research on the "Reciprocity Ring," a method successfully employed by companies like GM, IBM, and UPS.

I have experienced several profound revelations in my professional life which have given me perspective. I've owned an entertainment law firm for over two decades, and from the start, I've been blessed with a steady flow of work, expanding the firm's services and growing alongside a loyal base of clients. Many of these clients have been with me for years, and our relationships have grown beyond just business—some have become like members of my hive, a tightly-knit group that has shared triumphs and setbacks together.

Over the years, I've developed deep, trusting relationships with my clients, which often go beyond handling legal matters to encompass broader business consulting and even life planning. But, as with anything, there have been challenges along the way. I'll start with an example of what "not" having Soul Reciprocity in business relationships looks like.

What Happens When There's No Soul Reciprocity

There are many reasons why Soul Reciprocity may come and then go, or never form at all in business relationships. A colleague may withhold critical information for their advantage, a business partner may not contribute their part, a client may not pay their bill. Whatever the cause, absence of Soul Reciprocity in key business relationships can be devastating. Especially if it once existed.

One client I represented for over a decade had an incredibly successful career. I handled their first major recording deal, which included beneficial terms that were unheard of at the time. As they grew, we had to undo some deals that no longer served them and negotiated new, groundbreaking ones that reflected their evolution. But as the entertainment industry changed—with shifts in corporate structures, staffing, and an ongoing imbalance between corporations and creatives—my client became disillusioned. Despite their success, they felt betrayed by broken promises from others in the business, leading to frustration and bitterness.

Unfortunately, during this period of increasing tension, I was also going through significant personal life transitions that affected my communication and attentiveness. I was transparent with my client about my challenges and apologized, but my inability to meet their high expectations, coupled with their frustrations with others, led to a breakdown in our relationship. Conversations grew tense and unproductive. No advice could be heard, no progress could be made and despite my efforts, the client did not believe their Soul Needs were being met. We had lost the honey between us, the mutual trust and faith that had once made our relationship so strong.

In the end, we parted ways in one of the most painful professional breakups I've ever experienced. Despite understanding that their frustrations were not solely because of me, I recognized that our relationship could not survive without the elements of Soul Reciprocity—trust, faith, and understanding—being intact. I lost that client from my hive.

More common examples of what Soul Reciprocity is NOT in business relate to situations where one person's contributions are overlooked, unacknowledged or unappreciated. We have all experienced situations where this has occurred. For me, I feel a culmination of all three at once when it comes to being compensated for my services. As a business owner, my entire staff depends on me for their livelihoods. I rely on the revenues generated by our clients to pay them (and myself). When we go the extra mile to provide advice and counsel, solve problems and deliver results, we expect those efforts to be acknowledged via the compensation we receive. However, there are times when clients delay or fail to pay for services rendered. Other times, clients try to negotiate reductions in fees or otherwise try to avoid paying the full amounts due.

Although this is a frustration that business owners of all types experience from time to time, in the world of Soul Reciprocity this is more than anticipated losses to be written off in the course of ordinary business, rather, it is a violation of fundamental trust and signals that the client doesn't value the agreement with me nor the work provided. It's disrespectful. It's also a sign that a client isn't vested in the long-term relationship. And perhaps most importantly, non-payment is a lack of reciprocation which diminishes the emotional connection I have, creates mistrust and inevitably disincentivizes me from providing all of the "extras" that come with a relationship rooted in Soul Reciprocity.

The Power of Soul Reciprocity: Relationships That Thrive

Fortunately, most of my professional relationships are the opposite of this story. Many are familial, and some clients even call me "Momma Bear" or "Sister." These relationships feel more like dinner table conversations with family than formal business meetings. One client, whom I've served for nearly 20 years, has become a dear friend and "brother". I was at his wedding, and I've watched him grow into one of my favorite humans—professionally, personally, and spiritually. He and his wife gave me one of the greatest honors of my life by naming me the godmother of their only daughter. This is Soul Reciprocity in its truest form: a professional relationship that has deepened into something personal and profound—an all-around Soul-Full connection.

How Soul Reciprocity Takes Root in Business

How do relationships like these evolve in such a professional and often high-stakes environment, especially one as an attorney-client dynamic? And how are boundaries maintained while fostering such deep, meaningful connections?

I had an epiphany while reflecting on these questions. During a year marked by global upheaval—pandemic, civil rights activism, political division—my law practice experienced a growth surge. The entertainment industry, while affected by the broader turmoil, thrived in certain areas. I hired more staff and even brought in an operations management team to help streamline processes.

The operations team quickly pointed out that I spent an unusual amount of time on the phone with each client. They suggested that I set stricter time limits on calls and delegate more to other attorneys. While I understood their logic, I had to respectfully disagree.

I explained that I invest this time because I don't see my job as solving the immediate problem or negotiating the current contract. I want to truly understand my clients—who they are, what drives them, their long-term goals, and their challenges. I don't just focus on what they need today; I'm committed to being an asset for the long haul as their needs evolve and their careers grow. This approach, I believe, makes me a more effective attorney, advisor, and dealmaker.

In articulating this, I realized that what I've been doing all along is applying the principles of Soul Reciprocity in my business. I take time to learn my clients' Soul Identity, embark on the Soul Work necessary to understand their Soul Needs, and, from there, I help them build a Soul Tribe of strategic partners. By nurturing this understanding, I ensure we approach every deal, every challenge, with their unique vision of success in mind.

Having said that, Soul Reciprocity in business is centered around mutual success, shared professional values and pursuing common goals. It is not about crossing boundaries of professionalism or getting too personal. Yes, you want to connect more deeply with colleagues, business partners and clients—however, the connection is tied to trust and respect within the professional context and obviously not personal intimacy. As such, boundaries must be clear, expectations articulated, business decisions made with objectivity, conflict resolution handled with professionalism, and the long term vision of success kept in alignment.

How You Can Begin the Journey to Soul Reciprocity

Soul Reciprocity in business isn't just about long conversations or building personal relationships—it's about truly seeing the other person. It's about recognizing their needs, values, and aspirations and working in alignment with those deeper elements. It's about fostering mutual growth and trust, even when the stakes are high or the work gets tough.

To begin your own journey into Soul Reciprocity, start by committing to understanding the people you work with on a deeper level. Go beyond the transaction at hand and invest in your business associate's long-term success and well-being. Engage with them as individuals, not just clients, partners, or colleagues. Think about your work environment as your hive and you and your business associates as the worker bees who work harmoniously and with each other's best interests in mind for the survival and achievement of your collective goals. And in doing the above, you'll find that the professional relationships you cultivate become some of the most successful, rewarding and enduring connections in your life.

In Theory

University of Michigan sociologist Wayne Baker and his wife Cheryl developed a method called the Reciprocity Ring, where a group of people gather for the purpose of members asking and offering help for something important for them in their personal or professional lives. The Reciprocity Ring is a powerful tool for fostering a cooperative environment in business, where individuals are encouraged to share their resources and reciprocate favors, leading to mutual benefits and stronger professional relationships.

Here is one method of executing a Reciprocity Ring:

- Form groups of up to 24 people per group
- Each group has a facilitator
- Groups do either one or two rounds of requests and offers

- Once the requests are made, the group collectively tries to fulfill each one. Participants may offer their own resources, networks, or knowledge to help meet the requests.
- Set a time limit of no more than three hours

A thought provoking fact drawn from research on the Reciprocity Ring: We tend to underestimate the number of people who will give. The Reciprocity Ring can create a business environment where the natural impulse to help can be cultivated and supported (Tomasulo 2013). It is particularly useful in business settings as it promotes a culture of collaboration, engagement, mutual support, and resource sharing.

Best-selling author of *"Give and Take: A Revolutionary Approach to Success,"* Adam Grant, says people are either takers, matchers or givers. "Takers" is a term Grant uses to describe people who are self-interested and do not share resources or ideas. Matchers aim to trade evenly. A "giver" contributes to others without expecting anything in return and is a rare breed (Grant 2014).

Takers are clearly not the type of people you want in your Soul Tribe, whether personal or work related. They are the antithesis of persons with whom you can achieve Soul Reciprocity. Matchers, though reciprocal by nature, may not be willing to go the extra mile that you'd hope you could rely upon from a tribe member. Even a Giver may not be the best "type" to achieve Soul-Full balance in business. They may be unable to receive reciprocity, making the relationship one way nonetheless. Or they may lose sight of their own objectives and goals and find themselves unfulfilled. Any one of the foregoing kinds of people, without the benefits of corrective Soul Work, may in fact be a weak link and contribute to the failure of a work relationship. So what are the signs to look for?

You will know Soul Reciprocity is missing from work relationships when there is:

- **Lack of mutual support and respect**. When one colleague consistently helps and supports others with their tasks or challenges but receives little to no assistance in return. Or, when clients fail to (or fail to timely) compensate their contracted professionals

indicating a lack of respect for the time and effort of services rendered.
- **Exclusion from decision-making**. If a certain team member or business partner is regularly excluded from important discussions and decisions, it signals a lack of respect for their input and a failure to recognize their value within the team.
- **Poor communication**. When there is a lack of open, honest, and effective communication, it can result in misunderstandings, mistrust, and a failure to collaborate effectively. You can't expect Soul Reciprocity in a work relationship if one party isn't capable of clearly expressing their visions, goals, needs, expectations or challenges- all essential for Soul-Full experiences.
-

Failing Work Relationships

In professional relationships, Soul Reciprocity can fail (or fail to form) as a result of:

- **Workplace Politics and Professional Boundaries**: The work ecosystem can be a maze of policies and protocols. Navigating workplace politics and alliances can strain relationships and reduce trust, making reciprocal support more challenging. Likewise, inherent professional boundaries can discourage personal disclosure and thus limit the depth of personal connection, making it harder to establish genuine reciprocity and the deep connections necessary for fostering mutual understanding and emotional support involved in Soul Reciprocity.
- **Competition and Ambition**: The need to win can cause work relationships to fail. Professional competition and personal ambition can create conflicts of interest and undermine mutual support. This is a key reason Soul Reciprocity may never even occur between some people in the workplace or may struggle to maintain it.
- **Work-Life Balance Issues**: Developing Soul-Full relationships, even in business, require a commitment of time and effort. Personal life demands and a quest for balance can limit the time and energy available to invest in work relationships. Colleagues may also have

different goals, work styles and priorities which leads to misalignment of expectations and support of one another which can create imbalance and interfere with Soul Reciprocity.
- **Lack of Appreciation:** Everyone needs to feel valued, and business is no exception. Failing to acknowledge someone's contributions to a collective effort deflating and unmotivating. Ignoring an accomplishment, not rewarding success or paying an invoice late (or not at all) show lack of respect and will undermine the relationship and lead to its ultimate failure.

Successful Work Relationships

All business relationships don't have to last for decades or result in "God-motherhood" to be successful. However, achieving Soul Reciprocity in business relationships is measured by a different metric of success than traditional work relationships. Typically, we consider a "win" in business to mean individual achievement, financial gain or reaching a certain status. But a working relationship with Soul Reciprocity is built on understanding the Soul Identity and needs of one another which fosters a deep trust and commitment to the shared vision. Both parties are aligned in their intentions and their success is interconnected. Whether with a colleague, partner or client, achieving Soul Reciprocity in the workplace can positively affect your life.

Life-Changing Benefits

1. **Career Advancement**: With Soul Reciprocity, there is room for everyone to win. Strong, reciprocal relationships can lead to new opportunities, promotions, and career growth that benefits everyone involved.
2. **Business Success**: The whole hive can thrive. Enhanced collaboration and trust lead to more successful business ventures and partnerships.
3. **Professional Fulfillment**: Satisfaction guaranteed. A supportive and respectful work environment with people who get you and are of like mind and spirit increases job satisfaction and overall fulfillment.

Subtle Benefits
1. **Positive Work Environment**: A more pleasant and motivating workplace and a comfortability between colleagues, partners or with clients, leading to better overall performance and/or results.
2. **Efficient Problem-Solving**: Two (or more) minds are better than one. Trust and open communication facilitates quicker and more effective problem resolution.
3. **Networking and Resources**: Stronger together. With Soul Reciprocity in business relationships dynamics change. People are willing to provide access to a wider network of contacts and resources, benefiting professional growth and business operations.

To achieve and maintain Soul-Full connections in work or business relationships, you must take certain actions and communicate effectively. Here are some examples of things that you can "do" and "say" in your own quest to Soul Reciprocity:

1. What to do?
- Get to know the people you work with on a deeper level. Identify their Soul Needs.
- Be dependable in meeting deadlines and fulfilling commitments to build trust.
- Collaborate and provide support on projects, sharing knowledge and resources.
- Provide recognition by acknowledging and showing appreciation for the efforts and contributions of colleagues, partners, and clients.

2. What to say?
- "I value your partnership and the expertise you bring to the table."
- "How can we collaborate more effectively to reach our goals?"
- "Thank you for your dedication to the team. I know you could work anywhere and I don't take for granted that you've chosen here."
- "I understand what your needs are and I will work to ensure that we exceed your expectations with the work we do on your behalf."

QUESTIONS

Reflecting on reciprocity in professional relationships involves evaluating the balance between giving and receiving support. Here are some questions that can help you assess this balance:

Evaluating Your Contributions:
1. How often do I offer help to my colleagues or business partners without expecting anything in return?
2. Do I actively share my knowledge, resources, or network with others?
3. When was the last time I initiated support for someone in my professional circle?
4. Do I make myself available when others need assistance, even if it's not convenient for me?
5. Am I known as someone who contributes to the success of others?

Assessing the Balance:
1. Do I feel that I give as much as I receive in my professional relationships?
2. Are there individuals or situations where I feel I'm giving more than I'm receiving?
3. How do I react when I notice an imbalance in give-and-take? Do I address it or let it persist?
4. Am I comfortable asking for help when I need it, or do I hesitate? Why?
5. Do I find myself expecting reciprocation from others when I offer help, and how do I feel if it doesn't happen?

Understanding the Dynamics:
1. Do I choose to help others based on who they are, what they can do for me, or purely out of goodwill?
2. 2. Are there people in my professional life who consistently support me? How do I acknowledge and reciprocate their efforts?
3. 3. Do I engage in relationships that are mutually beneficial, or do some feel one-sided?

4. How do I handle situations where I feel taken advantage of or unappreciated?
5. In what ways can I improve the reciprocity in my relationships to ensure they are fair and balanced?

Reflecting on Growth:
1. How have my professional relationships evolved over time in terms of reciprocity?
2. What have I learned about my own tendencies to give or receive in professional settings?
3. What actions can I take to foster more reciprocal relationships moving forward?
4. How do I measure the success of my relationships—by what I gain, what I give, or the mutual growth that occurs?
5. What steps can I take to ensure that I am both contributing to and benefiting from my professional network?

These questions can help you gain clarity on the nature of Soul Reciprocity in your professional relationships, guiding you toward more balanced and fulfilling interactions.

14

GENESIS

TIME TO FLY!

"When you love and accept yourself, when you know who really cares about you and when you learn from your own mistakes, then you stop caring about what people who don't know you think."
~ Beyoncé

The essence of Soul Reciprocity is simple but profound: it's an optimal state in relationships where each party understands who they are, recognizes their needs, and remains aligned at their core. It's more than just shared beliefs; it's an authentic connection that allows both individuals to experience peace, balance, and fulfillment. When you achieve Soul Reciprocity, it's not just a fleeting moment; it's the result of deep Soul Work and the mutual understanding that comes from it. It's the foundation of a Soul Tribe, a collective of people who stand by you through all facets of life.

Let's be clear—Soul Reciprocity either exists between two people, or it doesn't. It's not something that appears magically; it's a product of growth and inner work. It's possible to have it at one point and lose it if that growth halts or diverges, but when it's real, it doesn't easily waver. And if you've had it before, you can get it again.

For me, discovering Soul Reciprocity has been life-changing. The greatest shift? Freedom. I am free from anxiety, from wondering if certain relationships serve me, from the pressure to please everyone, and most importantly, free to prioritize "me". This clarity allows me to move through life without fear, without compromising my values, and without doubting my worth. I finally understand what I need from others and what I'm willing to give—and, just as importantly, I'm free to make the tough decisions to remove anything that no longer serves me. That's why I say that Soul Reciprocity also involves the relationship you have with yourself.

Soul Reciprocity in Relationships

Each of us deserves fulfillment in our foundational relationships—be it family, friends, love, or business. Those closest to us should reflect our highest values, align with our principles, and share in the journey toward Soul Reciprocity. It's not perfection, but rather a harmonious balance, where give and take naturally flow. When you experience this, you know without a doubt that you belong, that you're wanted, needed, and appreciated. You can finally close the "eyes on the back of your head" that were always watching for betrayal or disappointment.

I didn't write this book to preach anything that I haven't practiced. I also didn't spend all this time explaining the importance of looking at relationships from a soul perspective, the goals of Soul Work, the necessity for understanding your Soul Identity and Soul Needs just to tell you that Soul Reciprocity and finding a Soul Tribe isn't attainable. That would be the worst ending ever. I am thrilled to report that by espousing these ideals, believing in these concepts and implementing the process in my life, I can say I've arrived! I have done the Soul Work, discovered my Soul Identity, understand my Soul Needs, and now I have an incredible Soul Tribe—people who feed my soul as I do theirs. These Soul-Full connections form the foundation of my personal and professional life.

Friendships

Let me tell you, my girl gang is "fierce." They are everything from entertainment lawyers to stylists, from marketers to caregivers. These women inspire me daily, and the love and support we share is unmatched. They focus on family and being their best selves. They allow me to be me and vice versa. We're each other's biggest cheerleaders, without competition or judgment. We support one another with grace and understanding, no matter how much time passes between interactions. We show up and show out and have grace when we can't. I'm so blessed to have such an inspiring and uplifting group of Soul-Full friends.

Family Bonds

In my family, I've found pillars of strength—true boulders. My mother is the embodiment of Soul Reciprocity, and together, we are the honey in each other's hive. The depth of our connection is indescribable, a love that simply "is". I only wish I had understood it sooner, but now that I do, I'm committed to giving back every ounce of love she has poured into me.

I'm blessed with other family members who model what Soul Reciprocity looks like. From my grandparents to my sisters, they've taught me the meaning of unconditional love, support, and connection. They're my hive, and I am honored to be part of theirs.

Work and Business

Even in business, I've found connections that transcend mere transactions. I work with staff members who are family, both literally and figuratively. We share a mutual respect and dedication that makes work feel like a joint passion project, not a job. I have clients who oot for my success as much as I do for theirs. Associates have become close friends, and even adversaries who have become allies because of the mutual respect and reciprocal environment we've cultivated.

Romantic Love

When I began writing this book, I wasn't sure if I would ever experience Soul Reciprocity in a romantic relationship. I knew what it should look like—I just hadn't felt it in my own life. But that all changed when "he" walked back into my life.

Cornell Forrest Norwood, Sr., a man I met in my early 20s, a man I dated twice before, and a man I hadn't seen in almost 15 years. We first met at Prince's Glam Slam club in Minneapolis in the '90s, and although life took us in different directions, we never truly let go of each other.

Years later, after marriages, careers, and transitions, fate brought us back together. We call this chapter of our story "3.0" or "3. Forever." What we have now is unlike anything we had before. It's a connection that only two souls who have done the work can experience—a love built on mutual understanding, authenticity, acceptance, and support. We are worker bees in each other's hives, teammates in the truest sense. Yet and still, I am his Queen.

We both searched high and low for love, only to realize that we had it all along, in each other. Our journey wasn't easy, but it was worth it. We are living proof that when two people do the work, find their Soul Identities, and align with their Soul Needs , their soul connection will be undeniable and Soul Reciprocity is not only possible—it's inevitable.

Bee Analogy: A Blueprint for Human Behavior

In this book, I've talked a lot about bees. Various species, behaviors, and their importance to our ecosystem. I have also provided analogies between bee and human behavior. To me, the parallels are obvious and provide context for understanding human behavior. Bees offer an ideal metaphor for understanding how human relationships should function when rooted in Soul Reciprocity. The way a hive operates provides key insights into how we can cultivate and maintain harmonious, Soul-Full relationships.

1. **Shared Purpose**: In a hive, every bee has a role—whether it's a worker bee gathering nectar, a drone fertilizing the queen, or the queen laying eggs. Each member is focused on a common goal: the survival and thriving of the hive. In human relationships, a shared purpose is essential. When people are aligned in their goals, values, and intentions, the relationship thrives like a well-tended hive.
2. **Non-Competition**: In a bee colony, no one competes for attention or resources. They each play their role without the need to one-up each other. Human relationships often falter due to competition and ego clashes. But in Soul-Full relationships, competition is replaced by collaboration. Each person understands that their success is tied to the success of the collective, and they support each other wholeheartedly.
3. **Continuous Nourishment**: Bees don't just gather nectar; they pollinate flowers, ensuring the growth of new life. Similarly, in human relationships, it's important to constantly nourish each

other's Soul Needs. This could be through acts of love, words of affirmation, or simply being present. It's about giving as much as you receive, and sometimes even more, to ensure that the relationship remains strong and vibrant.
4. **Protection of the Hive**: Bees work tirelessly to protect their hive from threats, just as we must protect our relationships from external influences or internal challenges that can cause harm. This includes maintaining boundaries, being proactive in addressing conflict, and preserving the integrity of the connection by staying loyal and trustworthy.
5. **Harmony in Diversity**: A beehive is made up of different types of bees, each with distinct functions and roles. Likewise, in human relationships, each person brings something unique to the table. Soul-Full relationships don't require sameness but rather celebrate differences that complement and enhance the whole. By acknowledging and respecting individual Soul Needs, we create a harmonious balance where diversity is an asset, not a barrier.

Honoring Soul Needs to Achieve Success

In Soul Reciprocity, identifying and honoring the unique "Soul Needs" of each individual is essential for fostering successful, Soul-Full relationships. Just as bees in a hive work collaboratively to ensure the hive thrives, human relationships must operate with a similar sense of reciprocity, cooperation, and shared purpose. When everyone's Soul Needs are acknowledged, respected, and nourished, the collective strength and harmony of the relationship soar to new heights. To recap, here's how it works:

Soul Needs are the essential emotional, psychological, and spiritual requirements that make us feel fulfilled, loved, and supported. These are unique to every individual, but they fall into some core categories such as:

1. **Belonging and Connection**: The deep need to feel part of something greater than oneself. This might be a family, friendship circle, romantic relationship, or work partnership.

2. **Trust and Safety**: Knowing that the other person in the relationship has your back. This is about creating a safe space where vulnerability can exist without fear of judgment or betrayal.
3. **Growth and Purpose**: A need for personal and collective evolution. Healthy relationships encourage mutual growth and development, rather than competition or stagnation.
4. **Respect and Validation**: Acknowledging the intrinsic value of the other person. This means understanding, accepting, and celebrating one another's differences and individual contributions.
5. **Love and Care**: A mutual exchange of affection and care that is consistent, unwavering, and not transactional. It's about showing up for each other even when it's inconvenient.

In Soul-Full relationships, these needs must be actively understood and met by all parties. Just like bees in a hive, every individual has a role, and the relationship depends on mutual respect for each other's needs and contributions. When Soul Needs are recognized, there's no one-sided effort or resentment. Instead, reciprocity creates a flow of energy that propels both individuals—and the relationship—toward success.

Nourishing Soul Needs: The Key to Flying

In order to "fly" and achieve success in any relationship—whether it's love, friendship, family, or business—there must be a conscious effort to understand and nourish the Soul Needs of all involved. The following steps help cultivate and nurture this environment:

1. **Clear Communication**: Just as bees use dance to communicate, people must be clear about what they need from others. Open and honest communication is key to ensuring that each person's Soul Needs are understood and respected.
2. **Reciprocal Effort**: For a relationship to truly thrive, there must be a balance in giving and receiving. This doesn't mean every action is equally matched in the moment, but over time, the

emotional and spiritual exchange should feel equitable. Each person should feel valued and supported.
3. **Grace and Patience**: Relationships, like hives, don't thrive overnight. They require time, grace, and patience to build. Be like the bees—steadily contributing to the relationship, weathering storms, and trusting in the process.
4. **Adaptation**: Bees adapt to changing conditions in their environment, whether it's adjusting to weather changes or finding new sources of nectar. In Soul-Full relationships, people must also be adaptable. There will be moments of change, growth, or challenge, and success depends on being flexible and adjusting to those dynamics.

The Journey to Soul Reciprocity

The path to Soul Reciprocity isn't always straightforward, but like a bee's unwavering flight from flower to flower, it is intentional and purposeful. There will be obstacles, detours, and moments when progress seems slow, but each step forward nourishes the relationship and strengthens its foundation.

When everyone in the relationship understands and respects the Soul Needs of others—just as the bees work collectively to maintain the hive—it creates an environment where success is inevitable. Soul-Full relationships, much like a flourishing hive, produce sweetness in the form of love, trust, and joy. This is where you truly begin to fly, free and empowered by the balance and reciprocity you've cultivated.

I'm not selling a fairytale here. Soul Reciprocity isn't about perfection. It's about balance, mutual respect, and working together to achieve a life of peace and fulfillment. When you find your Soul Tribe—whether in love, friendship, family, or business—you can finally breathe. You can be yourself unapologetically, because the people around you "get" you. They don't need explanations, and they have grace when you make mistakes. And when you reach this place, you do the same for them. You give freely, love openly, and trust without reservation. The energy you radiate is healing and uplifting. You experience life with a heightened sense of awareness, where colors are brighter, sounds are sweeter, and everything feels more alive.

Flying Together

When Soul Reciprocity is achieved, there is a sense of freedom, connection, and peace. Just as bees soar through the air after a hard day's work, knowing their hive is secure, we too can soar when our relationships are aligned with our core beliefs, values, and Soul Needs. When we fly together, we win in all aspects of life—love, friendships, family, and business. So, find your Soul Tribe, honor each other's needs, and watch how you soar together.

Your quest will lead you across many terrains. There will be crossroads and detours, and you will have to navigate many signs. Ultimately, when you arrive to this place called Soul Reciprocity, it will feel like home, and you'll never want to leave.

SECTION 3 SUMMARY: THE APPLICATION

SOUL REFLECTIONS

Chapter 10 - Love and Romance: The Be Dance

Over the past decade, I gained profound insights into life, love, and the power of Soul Reciprocity—the key ingredient that's essential for true connection. In marriage, I thought I had forever, yet as time passed, I realized my Soul Needs for emotional intimacy and support were unmet, especially during times of challenge and struggle. Beneath the surface, there was a lack of true reciprocity, exposing the gap between outward appearances and genuine soul nourishment.

Love, like the bee's intricate dance, requires a balanced give-and-take where both partners respond to each other's needs and move together toward shared fulfillment. When one partner stops participating, the harmony is broken and the dance is Soul-Less, leaving the other feeling isolated and unfulfilled. Looking back on my experience, I saw that while I had invested deeply, our relationship lacked the synchronized rhythm that Soul Reciprocity requires.

True success in love is like a bee dance—where bees lead each other to life-sustaining nectar. Fulfilling relationships rely on both partners each partner's actions support and strengthen the other.

Winning in love is not about personal gain but about fostering a partnership rooted in mutual growth, respect, and resilience—a bond that, like the dance of bees, sustains and nurtures each soul involved.

Chapter 11 - Friends: How Many of Us Have Them?

Soul Reciprocity applies to friendships, family, and work, not just romantic relationships. Building Soul-Full friendships requires consistent communication, genuine interest, and thoughtful gestures from both sides. Simple actions like check-ins, support during hard times, and shared joy strengthen bonds with friends.

Recently, I had to reevaluate my relationships and recognize that some people I considered friends didn't meet my definition of friendship. This realization led me to reassess who truly belongs in my life. There are "Takers," who seek only what you offer, and others like "Mrs. One-Way" and "Negative Nellys," who either don't reciprocate or drain your energy. Yet, there are also those true "worker bees" who consistently show up, offering genuine love and support. These people belong in your Soul Tribe.

Soul Reciprocity in friendships is life-changing, offering reliable support, increased well-being, and true happiness. It also brings more joy, reduces stress, and fosters personal growth. To maintain these connections, regular, heartfelt communication is key, allowing both parties to tend to each other's Soul Needs. But you don't have to eliminate every Taker, Chatty Cathy or Diva from your life. Some of them have other redeeming qualities, are necessary participants in your life journey and some are just simply a good time! Your challenge is to see your friends for who they are and determine how to reposition them accordingly.

Chapter 12 - Family: Hey Sister, Soul Sister

The chapter on family relationships explores the unique challenges and rewards of seeking Soul-Full connections within family ties. While family is often assumed to provide a natural foundation for support and love, the reality is more complex. Unlike friendships or romantic partnerships, we don't choose our family members, which can make achieving deep reciprocity with them more difficult—especially when relationships are strained by sibling rivalry, unmet expectations, or fundamental incompatibilities.

Family relationships profoundly shape our perceptions of love and connection, often forming the earliest examples of both positive and negative dynamics. When familial bonds are Soul-Full, they offer a sense of emotional security and foster strong, enduring relationships. However, when they lack reciprocity, they can leave lasting emotional wounds that shape future connections.

Through personal stories and reflections, this chapter highlights my journey of Soul Work—uncovering and understanding my Soul Identity to heal from past family dynamics and find reciprocity with family members. Ultimately, the chapter shows that cultivating Soul Reciprocity with family, though sometimes challenging, can be one of life's most rewarding pursuits, providing emotional security, generational harmony, and a supportive family tribe.

Chapter 13 - Business: The Trade of Reciprocity

In American business culture, relationships often focus on personal gain, leaving genuine reciprocity a rare occurrence. However, my quest to Soul Reciprocity taught me the power of applying its principles in my business. In fact, unbeknownst to me, I had been applying foundational elements within relationships with my clients for years! Just as bees work harmoniously within their hive for collective benefit, business relationships flourish when grounded in mutual respect, shared goals, and authentic connection.

With colleagues, open communication, mutual support, and recognition create a collaborative, trusting environment. In partnerships, reliability and alignment build a shared vision, ensuring all parties move forward together. With clients, taking the time to understand their unique needs transforms transactional exchanges into lasting, loyal connections. This approach turns professional relationships into a hive where everyone's contributions are valued, fostering resilience and growth.

Soul Reciprocity in business strengthens the work Soul Tribe, offering benefits like career advancement, business success, and a positive work environment. Like the intricate bee dance that leads others in the colony to shared sustenance, reciprocal business relationships create a rhythm of mutual support and shared achievement, allowing each person to thrive while working toward common goals.

Chapter 14 - Genesis: Time to Fly!

In the final chapter, "Genesis: Time to Fly!," the journey culminates in a powerful metaphor that likens the soul's journey to the purposeful flight of a bee. Just as a bee moves with unwavering intent from flower to flower, gathering nectar and nourishing its hive, we too must approach our relationships—be it love, friendship, family, or business—with intentionality and purpose. This chapter challenges readers to take flight with clarity and commitment, emphasizing that successful, Soul-Full relationships demand a conscious understanding and nurturing of the Soul Needs of all involved.

Soul Needs are the essential emotional, psychological, and spiritual elements that help us feel fulfilled, valued, and supported. Through the bee's journey and the hive's cohesive operation, we gain insight into the importance of reciprocity and collaboration in maintaining harmonious connections. The hive symbolizes the collective power of honoring each individual's unique Soul Needs, working together in unity, and fostering a supportive community.

"Genesis: Time to Fly!" is both a conclusion and a call to action, urging readers to apply the principles of Soul Reciprocity in every relationship they cultivate. It's an invitation to move forward with purpose, to nourish oneself and others, and to participate in relationships that are both fulfilling and mutually supportive—relationships that, like the hive, thrive when everyone's needs are understood and valued. This final chapter leaves readers inspired to fly boldly, with the insight and wisdom of Soul Reciprocity guiding their journey.

APPENDIX

A

RELATIONSHIPS QUESTIONNAIRE

Relationship Reflection

1. Are you in any relationships that feel:
    - Empty
    - One-sided
    - Unfulfilling
    - Stressful
    - Overbearing
    - Lacking depth or substance
    - Lacking communication
    - Disconnected
    - Obligatory
    - Manipulative
    - Forced

Reflect:
Which relationship(s) make you feel this way, and why do you think that is? How does this impact your well-being?

2. Are you in any relationships that feel:
    - Whole and complete
    - Mutual and balanced
    - Fulfilling and enriching
    - Stress-free
    - Effortless and natural
    - Meaningful and substantive
    - Safe for open expression and communication
    - Deeply connected
    - Free of hidden expectations or obligations
    - Authentic and genuine
    - Voluntary and desired

Reflect:
Which relationship(s) give you these feelings, and what contributes to this sense of ease and fulfillment?

Evaluating the Quality of Your Relationships:

1. **Defining Relationships:**
   How do you personally define the term "relationship"?

2. **Significance:**
   Do you believe some relationships hold more significance than others? Why or why not?

3. **Assessing Value:**
   What kind of value do you seek in your closest relationships—whether friendships, romantic partnerships, family connections, or work collaborations?

4. **Expectations:**
   What expectations do you hold for the people in your "inner circle"?

5. **Your Contribution:**
   What value do you think you bring to your most important relationships—be they friendships, romantic, family, or professional?

6. **Soul Perspective:**
   Have you ever considered your relationships from a soul-level perspective? Take time to evaluate relationships in different areas of your life and journal your insights.

7. **Origins:**
   Reflect on the people in your life: How did they come to be

there? Consider the pathways of circumstance, experience, or deeper soul connections.

8. **Circumstances and Experiences:**
   List the people in your life who are there because of specific circumstances or shared experiences. How did you form those connections?

9. **Soul-Level Connections:**
   Do you believe anyone in your life is there because of a "Soul Experience"? If so, who? Reflect on the nature of the experience or situation where you met.

10. **Quality Comparison:**
    Is there a noticeable difference in the quality of relationships based on how they came into your life (circumstances, experiences, soul experiences)? What are these differences, and how do they shape the relationship?

B

SOUL QUESTIONNAIRE

1. **Defining the Soul:**
How do you personally define your soul?

2. **Soul Alignment:**
Do you feel aligned with your soul and its needs? How do you recognize when you are in tune or out of sync?

3. **Trusting Your Intuition:**
Do you follow your gut instincts or inner voice when making decisions? If yes, in what situations? If no, what holds you back from trusting your instincts?

4. **Soul-Led Connections:**
Are you open to the idea that your soul can guide you toward more fulfilling and meaningful connections with others? How might this change the way you approach relationships?

5. **Soul Perspective in Relationships:**
Have you ever analyzed your deeper relationships through the lens of your soul? What insights have you gained?

6. **Identifying Soul Connections:**
Do you believe any of your current relationships are based on a soul-level connection? Which ones? What characteristics or experiences make these relationships feel rooted in the soul?

7. **Soul Connections vs. Others:**
How do relationships built on Soul Connections differ from those that are not? Consider the dynamics with your family, friends, significant others, or co-workers.

8. **Soul Work and Growth:**
   Are you willing to engage in self-work to better understand your soul's identity and its needs? How might this process lead to deeper fulfillment in your closest relationships?

C

RECIPROCITY QUESTIONNAIRE

- Have you ever given someone something nice without any expectation of getting something in return, not even a "thank you"? What was it? Why did you do it?

- How many times have you given someone a gift or put together a surprise only to feel as though it is not received in the way you intended?

- Do you ever find yourself in a never-ending cycle of giving with no expectation of receiving? How do you really feel about that?

- Have you ever felt overwhelmed by the pressure of someone else's expectations of you? What was the situation? How did it make you feel? What did you do about it?

- Have you ever thought that you had given a lot to someone (time, energy, thought, material things) only to find out that they feel you don't give as much as they give you? So the other person feels the relationship is imbalanced because you fall short? How did that make you feel?

- Have you experienced positive reciprocity? Describe the experience and how it was balanced.

- Have you experienced negative reciprocity? Describe the experience and how it was imbalanced.

- Do you have the ability to reciprocate? Does it ever feel burdensome to do so? Does it ever feel that way in your closest and most important relationships? Why do you think you struggle with reciprocation?

- Have you ever felt uncomfortable when someone has shown you reciprocity? In what circumstance? Why do you think you felt uncomfortable being on the receiving end in that/those situations?

- Do you make sacrifices for the ones you love? Write down some examples. Do you feel burdened by the sacrifices or do you willingly and happily make them?

- Think of some of your most fulfilling relationships in each category: romantic, friendships, family and business. What makes them fulfilling? Can you think of examples of reciprocity that creates balance in those relationships?

D

SOUL RECIPROCITY QUESTION-NAIRE

Exploring Soul Reciprocity:

1. **Defining Soul Reciprocity:**
   With your current understanding, what does the concept of "Soul Reciprocity" mean to you?

2. **Identifying Soul Reciprocity in Relationships:**
   Do you believe you have any relationships that embody Soul Reciprocity? Who are these relationships with, and what specific qualities or experiences exemplify this in your connection?

3. **Attraction to Soul Reciprocity:**
   What aspects of relationships built on Soul Reciprocity appeal to you the most? Do you feel it's possible to cultivate Soul Reciprocity in more of your relationships? Why or why not?

4. **Meeting Your Soul Needs:**
   Do you know what your soul needs in your closest relationships? Do you express these needs to those around you, and are they being met? If not, what do you think is preventing this from happening?

Barriers to Soul Reciprocity:

1. **Feelings of Unworthiness:**
   Have you ever felt unworthy of friendship, love, or genuine connection? What led to those feelings, and have you taken any steps to address or change them? If so, what actions have you taken? If not, what has prevented you from doing so?

2. **Habitual Relationships:**
   Are there relationships in your life that continue out of habit rather than a deep, meaningful connection? If so, do these relationships fulfill you? Why or why not?

3. **Struggles with Showing Up:**
   Have you ever found yourself unable to fully engage or show up in a relationship, making it difficult to nurture or participate actively? What were the circumstances, and how did this impact you emotionally and within the relationship?

4. **Fear and Avoidance:**
   Do you ever find yourself avoiding deeper connections out of fear—fear of rejection, vulnerability, or failure? How has this avoidance impacted your relationships, and what do you think it would take for you to overcome these fears?

E

SOUL INDENTITY QUESTIONNAIRE

To discover our Soul Identity, we must ask and answer certain questions for ourselves. In this process, there can be no concern for others' opinions, no right or wrong answers, no judgments, no morality, no biblical or spiritual principles, no overthinking, and no regard for public opinion. Just real questions with honest answers. Below are some of the questions I asked myself during my own journey. Try asking and answering them for yourself.

For me, the best place to engage in these exercises is in a journal. If you've never journaled before, this is a great way to start! Use the questions below and throughout the Appendix as prompts for your journaling. Take your time—perhaps focus on one question per day or week. For questions that reference "others," consider answering from the perspective of different people in your life, such as significant others, family members, friends, and business associates.

FROM THE OUTSIDE LOOKING IN (THE SURFACE)
First, consider the 30,000-foot view of your life.

- What does your life look like to YOU when you look down at it from above?
- What do you think others see when they look at your life from the outside?
- Do the two observations match?
- Do you like what you see when you observe yourself from the outside looking in?
- Do you think others like what they see when they observe you from the outside looking in?

A PEEK BELOW THE SURFACE:

Self-Awareness and Reflection
- What words would you use to describe your personality?

- How do you define yourself? Are these definitions shaped by others' perceptions or your own?
- Who are you beyond the career, domestic or social roles you play in your daily life?
- Do you regularly take time to self-reflect?
- Is self-reflection comfortable or uncomfortable for you? Why?

Accountability and Conflict

- How do you typically handle conflict in your relationships?
- Do you take accountability for your role in difficult situations with others?
- Do you tend to blame others when you face challenges in relationships or interactions?
- When faced with unresolved relationship issues, do you accept the situation and move on, or do you seek deeper understanding and resolution—both within yourself and with the other person?

Emotional Awareness

- How well do you manage your emotions? Do you express them openly, or do you suppress them?
- How do you react to emotional triggers? Are you reactive or reflective when confronted with strong feelings?

Criticism and Judgment

- How well do you handle criticism from others?
- How often do you criticize others, and for what reasons?
- How accepting are you of others' decisions and lifestyle choices? Do you find yourself judging others in ways that lead to frustration?
- How do you feel when people closest to you don't accept your decisions and lifestyle choices?

Communication and Needs

- Do you freely communicate your wants and needs with others, or do you hesitate to do so? Why?
- If you do communicate your needs, what types of things do you typically ask for? (material items, direct assistance, quality time, advice?)

Considering Others' Needs
- Do you regularly ask others what they want and need from you? Why or why not?
- If yes, what kinds of things do you typically inquire about? (material items, direct assistance, quality time, advice?)

Connections with Others
- How do you show up in your relationships—with family, friends, romantic partners, and colleagues?
- Do you find it difficult to connect with others on a deep level? If so, why?

Core Beliefs and Values
- What core beliefs shape your actions and decisions?
- How do your personal values align with the life you're living right now?

Internal Struggles and Self-Sabotage
- What internal battles do you face regularly?
- Are there any self-destructive behaviors you engage in that you feel powerless to change?

Fear and Vulnerability
- What scares you the most about being vulnerable with others?
- How often do you let fear hold you back from pursuing what you want?

Following Through on Support
- When someone tells you what they need, are you eager to provide support, or do you feel burdened by their requests?
- Do you ask simply to be polite, or do you sincerely intend to act on their requests if they accept your offer?

DEEP DIVE INTO YOUR SOUL IDENTITY

Reflecting on Your Childhood and Self-Image
- When you were a child, how did you imagine yourself as an adult? Who did you want to be when you grew up?
- How does your childhood vision of your future self compare to the person you've become?
- Does your outward, public persona match how you feel about yourself inwardly? If not, how do they differ, and why?

Exploring Your Identity and Relationships
- Write a brief bio of yourself as a person, focusing on who you are beyond your professional life.
- What kind of friend, family member, significant other, and business associate are you?
- What brings you joy?
- What causes you pain?

Understanding Your Fears, Successes, and Failures
- What are your biggest fears?
- What are your greatest successes? Your biggest failures?
- What emotional baggage do you carry from your youth?
- What baggage do you carry from past relationships—romantic, friendships, family, or business-related?

Purpose and Vision
- What is your purpose or your "WHY"?
- Does your life today reflect the vision you had for it 1 year ago, 5 years ago, or 10 years ago? How does it compare to the dreams you had as a child? Is it better, worse or just different? In what ways?
- What do you want your life to look like in 1 year? In 5 years? In 10 years?

Facing Fears and Accepting Yourself

- Do you have fears about your future?
- Do you fear being alone? If so, why? If not, why not?
- What do you like about yourself?
- What do you dislike about yourself?
- What aspects of yourself do you want to change?
- What things do you think you should change, but are unwilling to?
- What traits can you accept about yourself?

Taking Ownership and Facing Truths

- What falsehoods do you tell yourself to feel better about your situation?
- What wrongs have you failed to right?
- What ownership can you take for the reality you are currently living in?
- What self-improvements have you failed to make, even though no one has stopped you but yourself?

F

SOUL NEEDS IDENTIFIER SURVEY

Each of us carries unique needs that stem from the deepest part of who we are—our soul. While some Soul Needs are universal, rooted in fundamental principles like love, security, and belonging, others are deeply personal and shaped by our purpose, personality, and life experiences. These needs are not something we can cultivate or change—they are inherent to our being, reflecting how we use our talents, express our emotions, and navigate our relationships.

Soul Needs are what make us feel alive, fulfilled, and true to ourselves. They show up in various ways: through the activities that energize us, the environments where we feel most authentic, and the relationships that nourish us. When our Soul Needs are met, we thrive and seek to nourish others. When they are neglected, we may feel drained, unfulfilled, or disconnected.

This questionnaire is designed to help you explore your unique Soul Needs. By reflecting on your purpose, talents, emotional needs, and relationships, you'll gain a clearer understanding of what makes your soul feel nourished and how to align your life with these truths. Take your time with these questions, allowing yourself to be honest and open as you dive deeper into discovering what your soul truly craves.

1. Purpose
- What activities make you lose track of time?
- When do you feel most alive or energized?
- What problems or causes deeply resonate with you?
- What do you believe is your purpose in life?
- When do you feel the most fulfilled and aligned with your purpose?
- What activities or tasks give you a sense of deep meaning and satisfaction?
- Are there any recurring themes or passions that have persisted throughout your life that point to your purpose?

- How do you currently use your time to pursue or express your purpose?
- What would your ideal day look like if it were spent living in full alignment with your purpose?

2. Talent & Gifts
- What are your natural talents or gifts? (These could be anything from creativity, leadership, problem-solving, empathy, communication, etc.)
- How often do you get to use your natural talents in your daily life or work?
- When you use your talents, how do you feel? (Energized? Satisfied? Drained?)
- Do you feel you are fully utilizing your talents, or is there room to explore them further?
- Are there talents or gifts you haven't tapped into yet that you feel compelled to develop?

3. Personality
- How would you describe your personality? (Introverted, extroverted, analytical, spontaneous, empathetic, driven, etc.)
- How does your personality influence your needs in relationships, work, and personal life?
- Do you feel your current lifestyle and environment align with your personality? If not, what changes could help you feel more aligned?
- How do you typically react in times of stress or challenge, and what does that reveal about your core needs?
- What environment or situation makes you feel the most like yourself?

4. Emotional Needs
- What emotional needs do you find most important in relationships? (love, security, respect, understanding, trust, etc.)
- How do you feel when your emotional needs are unmet? What are the signs?

- Do you openly communicate your emotional needs to those closest to you?
- How do you balance meeting your emotional needs with the needs of others in your life?
- What can others do to make you feel most supported emotionally?

5. Spiritual Connection
- How do you connect with something larger than yourself, whether it be through spirituality, religion, nature, or another practice?
- How important is spiritual fulfillment in your life?
- When do you feel most connected to your higher self or a greater force?
- What practices or routines bring you peace, clarity, and a sense of purpose in your spiritual journey?
- Are there spiritual or soulful rituals you'd like to incorporate more regularly into your life?

6. Time & Energy
- How do you prioritize your time? What do you feel gets most of your time and attention daily?
- Are there activities or obligations that drain your energy rather than fulfilling you? What are they?
- What activities make you lose track of time because you enjoy them so much?
- Do you feel you manage your time in a way that allows you to pursue your passions and nourish your soul?
- How could you better align your schedule with your soul's desires?

7. Relationships
- What do you need from your relationships to feel fulfilled? (Honesty, loyalty, mutual growth, shared values, etc.)
- Do you feel you are receiving what you need from the important relationships in your life? If not, what's missing?
- How do you support the Soul Tribe of the people closest to you?
- Are there any boundaries or limits you need to set in your relationships to better honor your soul's needs?

- What kind of people or relationships energize you and bring out the best in you?

8. Personal Growth
- How important is personal growth to you? What does growth look like for you personally?
- In what areas of your life do you feel the need to evolve or grow?
- How often do you engage in activities or practices that challenge you to grow and expand your mind or heart?
- What limiting beliefs or obstacles are holding you back from meeting your soul's true potential?
- How can you prioritize your growth in the coming months or years to align with your soul's needs?

9. Creativity & Expression
- How do you express yourself creatively?
- Do you feel you have enough outlets to express your thoughts, emotions, or ideas?
- What form of creative expression makes you feel most alive or free?
- Is there something creative you've been wanting to explore but haven't yet?
- How could embracing your creativity more fully meet your soul's needs?

10. Freedom & Autonomy
- How much freedom do you need in your life to feel fulfilled?
- Are there areas where you feel restricted or constrained? What are they?
- What changes could you make to experience more freedom in your work, relationships, or personal time?
- What kind of environment allows you to feel independent and authentic in your decision-making?
- How do you balance your need for autonomy with your responsibilities or commitments to others?

SOUL NEEDS IDENTIFIER SURVEY

G

RECIPROCITY TEST: DISCOVERING YOUR TYPE OF RECIPROCITY

Answer the following questions to determine how you typically express reciprocity in your relationships. Each question will help you identify whether you are practicing a form of "Physical", "Mental", "Social", or "Emotional" reciprocity. After completing the test, reflect on whether you're truly producing "Soul Reciprocity", or if you are falling into common shortfalls.

Part 1: Identifying Your Reciprocity Type

1. When someone does something for you, how do you typically respond?
    a) I try to do something of equal value in return. (*Physical Reciprocity*)
    b) I believe they'll get what they deserve later, good or bad. (*Mental Reciprocity*)
    c) I evaluate whether continuing this relationship benefits both of us. (*Social Reciprocity*)
    d) I feel more connected to those who've gone through similar experiences as me. (*Emotional Reciprocity*)

2. How do you choose your closest friends or partners?
    a) I surround myself with people who do things for me when I do things for them. (*Physical Reciprocity*)
    b) I'm drawn to people who share my belief that what goes around comes around. (*Mental Reciprocity*)
    c) I prefer relationships that offer mutual advantage and help us both grow. (*Social Reciprocity*)

d) I feel closest to those who've been through similar emotional journeys. (*Emotional Reciprocity*)

3. When someone expresses pain or hardship, how do you respond?
   a) I try to fix the problem practically or offer help. (*Physical Reciprocity*)
   b) I feel it's part of life's natural consequences—good or bad. (*Mental Reciprocity*)
   c) I look for a way we can both benefit from a solution. (*Social Reciprocity*)
   d) I empathize deeply and connect with their emotions. (*Emotional Reciprocity*)

Part 2: Soul Reciprocity vs. Shortfalls

Now that you've identified your type of reciprocity, let's explore whether you're engaging in Soul Reciprocity or encountering common "shortfalls". Soul Reciprocity requires a deep awareness of others' feelings and experiences, taking empathy a step further by nourishing and nurturing others from the soul. Below are common "shortfalls" that prevent people from reaching Soul Reciprocity:

1. **Low Self-Esteem**:
   Do you second-guess your ability to give or receive love and care? Do you hold back from showing kindness because you don't feel worthy of it yourself?

2. **Bad Habits**:
   Are there patterns in your behavior that prevent you from fully engaging with others (e.g., avoidance, procrastination, or withdrawal)?

3. **Second-Guessing**:
   Do you often question whether you've done enough or wonder if others truly deserve your efforts?

4. **Apathy**:
   Have you become indifferent toward others' needs, possibly due to emotional burnout or fatigue?

5. **Unforgiveness**:
   Are you holding onto past hurts, which prevents you from fully showing up in relationships and offering reciprocal care?

6. **Lack of Capacity**:
   Do you feel emotionally or mentally drained, making it difficult to give your energy to others?

7. **Fear**:
   Do you fear vulnerability or rejection, and does that stop you from extending care or love to others?

Part 3: Reflection and Growth

Where are you practicing reciprocity, and where are you falling short?

Take a moment to reflect on your answers. Are you practicing "Physical", "Mental", "Social", or "Emotional" reciprocity? And are you truly moving toward "Soul Reciprocity", or do you fall into the shortfalls listed above?

Moving toward Soul Reciprocity:

Consider how you can take your empathy and care to the next level by deeply nurturing the souls of those around you. Use the awareness of their emotional, mental, and spiritual needs to offer not just equal exchanges, but transformative care that enriches both of your lives.

H

SOUL TRIBE IDENTIFIER SURVEY

As you embark on your Soul Work, you will ask yourself many difficult questions during the Soul Identity phase. This process will lead you to a deep understanding of who you truly are—the good, the bad, and the ugly. As your self-awareness grows, you'll naturally start to reassess the people around you, viewing them through a new lens. You'll need to ask yourself some tough questions about them too.

Begin to envision your Soul Tribe, the circle of people with whom you can experience true Soul Reciprocity. Who will qualify to be part of that tribe? Who won't?

Use the survey below to help identify the characteristics and qualities that each of your Soul Tribe members should possess.

Soul Tribe Survey

1. Defining Your Soul Tribe
- How do you define a Soul Tribe?
- How do you distinguish who is in your Soul Tribe versus your general circle of friends and associates?

2. Size and Composition
- How large do you think a Soul Tribe should be? Why?
- Who›s in your tribe? (Categorize by significant others, family, friends, business associates/partners/co-workers.)
- How did your tribe members become part of your tribe?

3. Communication & Interaction
- How often are you in contact with your tribe members?
- How do you usually interact with them? (In person? Phone? Email? Only on special occasions?)

- Do you and your tribe members randomly check in on each other just to see how things are going?

4. Feelings & Emotional Support
- How do you feel when you're around your tribe members?
- Do your tribe members express how they feel about you? What do they say?
- How do you feel when you think about your tribe members?

5. Conversations & Topics
- What topics do you generally discuss with your tribe members?
- Are your conversations typically surface-level, or do you delve into deeper issues in each other's lives?
- Do your tribe members ask about your other important relationships? (Significant other, children, parents, siblings, friends?) Do you ask about theirs?

6. Problem-Solving & Support
- Do your tribe members help you solve problems? Do you help them?
- If either of you needs something, do you ask each other?
- When you or your tribe members are in need, is the other there to provide support?
- Are you able to anticipate the needs of your tribe members? Do they anticipate yours?

7. Connection & Special Occasions
- Do you spend special days, holidays, or birthdays together? If not, do you connect in other ways during these occasions?
- Do you ever do unexpected things to express gratitude or show how important your tribe members are in your life? (Notes, cards, gifts, phone calls, or texts?) Do they do the same for you?

8. Reflection on Relationships
- What do you love and respect most about your tribe members?

- What have your tribe members told you they love or respect most about you?
- Are there things you least respect or like about your tribe members? What do you think they may feel the same about you?

9. Contribution & Growth
- What do your tribe members contribute to your life? What do you contribute to theirs?
- Have you ever felt like you've outgrown anyone in your tribe?
- What makes you feel this way about them? What do you think they feel about you?

10. Changes & Additions
- If you were to remove someone from your tribe, how would you feel? (Relieved? Guilty? Sad?)
- Are there people not currently in your tribe whom you believe should be? Who are they, and why do you think they would be good members? Would they want to be in your tribe?

Who Is Your Bee?

Who are your bees in the following relationships and what type are they:

Love	_____
Friends	_____
Family	_____
Business	_____

BIBLIOGRAPHY

BIBLIOGRAPHY

Booth, Jessica. 2023. *9 Enneagram Personality Types: Strengths, Weaknesses and More.* October 17. Accessed July 2022. https://www.forbes.com/health/mind/enneagram-types.

BuzzAboutBees.net. n.d. "What Do Bees Symbolize?" Buzz About Bees. Accessed February 12, 2020. https://www.buzzaboutbees.net/what-do-bees-symbolize.html.

Cherry, Kendra. 2021. *IQ vs. EQ: How Are They Different?*. December 7. Accessed November 2022. https://www.verywellmind.com/iq-or-eq-which-one-is-more-important-2795287.

Childs, Brevard S. 1985. *Old Testament Theology in a Canonical Context.* Fortress.

n.d. *Compelling Truth.* Accessed January 15, 2023. compellingtruth.org.

Encyclopedia.com. n.d. *Soul: Jewish Concept.* Accessed February 23, 2023. https://www.encyclopedia.com/environment/encyclopedias-almanacs-transcripts-and-maps/soul-jewish-concept.

Grant, Adam. 2014. *Give and Take: Why Helping Others Drives Our Success.* March 25. https://adamgrant.net/book/give-and-take.

Griffiths, Richard. 2011. *Ego and Soul.* Accessed October 2022. https://sqi.co/ego-and-soul.

—. 2012. *How to Experience Spiritual Intelligence.* Accessed October 2022. https://sqi.co/how-to-experience-spiritual-intelligence.

—. 2012. *The Spiritual Intelligence Paradigm.* Accessed October 2022. https://sqi.co/the-spiritual-intelligence-paradigm.

Grudem, Wayne. 2018. *Zondervan Academic.* May 15. Accessed January 2023. https://zondervanacademic.com/blog/what-is-the-soul.

Haught, John F. n.d. *The Cosmic Adventure: Science, Religion and the Quest for Purpose.* Accessed November 2022. https://

www.religion-online.org/book-chapter/chapter-2-scientific-materialism.

IsraelU. 2021. *What Is the Hebrew Word for Soul.* Accessed December 2022. https://youtu.be/7HTLiBz-R2c.

Jeanne Segal, Ph.D., Melinda Smith, M.A., Lawrence Robinson and Jennifer Shubin. n.d. *Improving Emotional Intelligence (EQ).* Accessed November 2022. https://www.helpguide.org/articles/mental-health/emotional-intelligence-eq.htm.

Lechner, Tamara. 2016. *Understanding Mind, Intellect, and Ego.* January 7. Accessed October 2022. https://chopra.com/articles/understanding-mind-intellect-and-ego.

Merriam-Webster. n.d. *Relationship.* Accessed November 14, 2021. Merriam-Webster.com/dictionary/relationship.

Oxford Learners Dictionaries. n.d. *Relationship.* Accessed November 14, 2021. https://www.oxfordlearnersdictionaries.com/us/definition/american_english/relationship.

2013. *Reciprocity.* September. Accessed October 2022. https://www.studocu.com/id/document/universitas-islam-sultan-agung/economy/catatan-reciprocity/46901039.

Rumie.org. n.d. *Recognize the Feelings & Needs of Others.* https://learn.rumie.org/jR/bytes/recognize-the-feelings-needs-of-others/.

Sahebalzamani M, Farahani H, Abasi R, Talebi M. 2013. "The relationship between spiritual intelligence with psychological well-being and purpose in life of nurses." *Iran J Nurs Midwifery Res* 18 (1): 38-41.

Santana, Sally. 2003. *What does your soul mean to you and how do you feed it?* October 25. Accessed October 2022. https://products.kitsapsun.com/archive/2003/10-25/292825_what_does_your_soul_mean_to_you.html.

Tomasulo, Dr. Dan J. 2013. "What is the Reciprocity Ring?" *Psychology Today*, August 29: https://www.psychologytoday.com/us/blog/the-healing-crowd/201308/what-is-the-reciprocity-ring.

www.ingramcontent.com/pod-product-compliance
Lightning Source LLC
Chambersburg PA
CBHW060454030426
42337CB00015B/1589